RAISING THE BANNER

OFFICIAL BIOGRAPHY OF GER LOUGHNANE

with

John Scally

BLACKWATER PRESS

Editor
Aidan Culhane

Design/Layout
Paula Byrne

Cover Design
Paula Byrne

© – John Scally 2001

Produced in Ireland by
Blackwater Press
c/o Folens Publishers
Hibernian Industrial Estate,
Greenhills Road,
Tallaght, Dublin 24.

DEDICATION

This book is dedicated to all those players who wore the saffron and blue with pride down through the years, who gave their best for Clare with no reward in terms of medals, but who passed on the hurling torch that lit the flame that burned so brightly in Croke Park on 3 September 1995 and afterwards.

ACKNOWLEDGEMENTS

The Late Donal Foley of the *Irish Times* who gave very solid advice to a young reporter on the lines that 'going around making a name for yourself is all very fine but the best thing you can leave behind in this world is children.' Whatever about leaving things behind, the best thing you can have in this world is a good family. The last thing Mary, Barry and Conor want to see is their names in a book yet their contribution is greater than the combined efforts of all the marvellous people mentioned in this story.

CONTENTS

FOREWORD

The overriding impression that remains above all else is the fun we had. From the first day we came together in September 1994, not a session or a meeting went by without a laugh or joke, usually from Tony Considine. A sense of mischief and adventure seemed to permeate all our encounters. True, there were gruelling training sessions, confrontational matches and bitter controversies but even when the storm was at its zenith a little light relief was never far away. At times the unity of purpose of the entire group was so great that fear became extinct and the exhilaration of facing a challenge was so great that we felt totally indestructible. Any time we were in that mode, we just couldn't be beaten. Added to this was the satisfaction of bringing so much joy to others. This is one of the greatest gifts of all. How many times have I heard phrases like 'you'll never know what it meant to our family' or 'I thought I'd never see that day' or 'I'm so glad my father was alive for it.' Isn't it marvellous that sport can provide such moments of solace and fulfilment for the stresses and chaos of everyday life.

When John Scally finally persuaded me to assist him with this book, I insisted on two conditions:

(a)   There would be no long-winded accounts of matches in the book as these were already well documented and:

(b)   There would be no holding back.

I wanted people to get a fly-on-the-wall insight into the dynamics that drive a successful team, the characters of the magnificent men who delivered the Holy Grail for Clare, the methods employed, the controversies and their origins, as well as the psychological factors that made this team such a formidable force.

Of course it provides the opportunity to revisit the controversies of that era in a more clinical way, backed up by more evidence than was available at the time, some of it documented. People will now have a clearer picture of the rights and wrongs of these.

Very few teams in a sport could have endured so many bitter and frustrating defeats, such a dismal record in major games, such poor organisation and yet survive as these did. Without an All-Ireland title for 81 years, without even a provincial title for 63 years, Clare entered the 1995 Championship on the back of three defeats in finals in the previous two years. Yet they triumphed. This is the story of how it was achieved.

Ger Loughnane
October 2001

INTRODUCTION

It was the morning after Valentine's Day. I was feeling distinctly nervous. I had a right to be.

There was a definite acceleration of my heartbeat and a tremor in my voice as I rang a total stranger, the most (in)famous name in Gaelic games, and asked if I could write his biography. The conversation went better than I expected but not as well as I had hoped. It wasn't a yes but at least it wasn't a definite no. 'If you ever hear I've retired from the Clare team give me a call.'

He did a few months later. I rang within days. I knew immediately he wasn't ready to attack the bestsellers list the way he had attacked the established hurling order – but again he didn't say no. There followed another series of phone calls and many, many letters. At one stage I was beginning to feel like Saint Paul.

2000 gave away to 2001 and still no decision. The day after Valentine's Day came again. It seemed like an opportune time to make another phone call. At last progress of sorts, 'Ring me on the 20th of March and I'll give you a definite decision.' The night before I didn't sleep very much. As I picked up the phone – again a knot in the stomach. Another step closer to an ulcer. I braced myself for the worst. 'I think we should do it.' We had lift-off.

This was the story I really wanted to write. Few sports people have managed to come up with characters and plots that can satisfy the demands of great fiction. Ger Loughnane is an honourable exception to the trend. The clichés about managers crumble in his presence. For this reason I wanted, as far as it was practicable, to let him tell his story in his own words. What are the secrets that made his Clare team the talk of the country? What did it take to lead his team into hurling's promised land after 81 years in the wilderness?

His career had more twists than a bad bog road but above all this is a spiritual story: of a man, his team and his county.

No hurling team had ever captivated me like Clare. Maybe it was because the Clare colours are remarkably similar to those of my native Roscommon, so when the Banner County exploded on the scene in 1995 I felt they were winning for counties like mine, for fans that had been reared on a diet of defeat.

No hurling match has ever given me more pleasure than the '95 All-Ireland. A memory like that can only make the good times better.

Some day. Some fans. Some team.

Some manager.

A man apart.

1

Don't Look Back in Anger

I look at photos of myself after the '97 All-Ireland and I think that I look absolutely terrible. I appear thin and drawn. That All-Ireland, especially because it was against Tipperary, took an enormous psychological and emotional toll on me. It took a massive effort to keep driving the team. We had beaten them in the Munster final. To come back and defeat them a second time was going to be very difficult.

Everybody in Clare was afraid of their lives that we were going to lose to Tipperary. Earlier that year, Babs Keating had written an article about the back-door system and had used an example to illustrate it: supposing Clare beat Tipp in the Munster final then Tipperary could beat them in the All-Ireland 'when it really mattered'. For months that comment was really playing on my mind.

Then there had been a lot of controversy over Anthony Daly's 'No longer the whipping boys of Munster' speech after the Munster final. Then came the controversy about me allegedly accusing Wexford of 'roughhouse tactics'. It was the first time I had encountered real controversy.

Coping with all that and at the same time managing the team was very draining. The All-Ireland itself was such a knife-edge affair and I was pulling every trick in the book to win it all of which leaves you drained. I have never been more focused going into a game and it took me days to recover from it.

The day after the game on the way to the airport, Anthony Daly, sitting beside me remarked, 'I suppose this is the end for you now.'

'Definitely', was my instant reply.

I n the great scheme of things, hurling may seem a peripheral pursuit. But to those within, hurling *is* the great scheme of things. As the architect of the Banner County's golden age, Ger Loughnane might have felt justified in stepping down, but after '97 the team were looking fresh and brimming with vigour. That physical wellbeing would enable them to retain their sharpness so that there was no danger of their famed hunger drowning in a slow tide of apathy. He allowed himself to be persuaded to stay on.

> Not long after Jamesie, Brian Lohan, Anthony Daly and Seanie McMahon and a few others came down to me and they asked me to stay on for another year as they were looking forward to the new year already. '97 hadn't taken as much out of them as '95 had.

By 1999, Loughnane's commitment to winning, though undiluted, was less raw in its expression. But his fellow managers did not enjoy any additional peace of mind, for Loughnane continued to improve Clare's chances in major games by angling so insistently for the tactical and psychological advantage. He maintained his unashamedly romantic vision of what his team could accomplish on the pitch. He insisted that they could not settle for simply winning matches, but must try to fill every performance with flair, verve and originality. The fat lady was preparing to sing though.

> When Kilkenny beat us in the All-Ireland semi-final in '99. I said to myself in the dressing-room, 'We will not climb this mountain again. We're not going to be in here again.' I had no desire to be there again. That was even worse.

> The really wonderful thing was that it wasn't a question of leaving with any regret or having to leave. It was a question of going because it was time to go. I don't think you should look back with regret on your career in sport when you're an amateur. What really is on my mind as I think back on my playing career is what could have been. We could have won a Munster title and an All-Ireland title. We had a tremendous set-up. The big problem was that when we came to the big day we always seemed to lower our performance. We played brilliantly in League games, but we played badly in the Munster Championship. The truth was that the '95 team always upped their performances on the big games. They played much better on the big day in Croke Park than they did in League games. The satisfaction of having helped to bring about this transformation was the greatest reward of all.

TIME TO SAY GOODBYE

The thought of Clare experiencing a rapid descent from the dizzy heights of 1995–1997 preyed heavily on Loughnane's mind. In 1999, he wanted to leave the management in safe hands. Seán Stack was controversially dropped from the backroom team and Louis Mulqueen and Cyril Lyons were brought in.

> *The main reason I stayed on was to put in a really good system with the right personnel that would serve Clare well down the years. I didn't want it all collapsing when I went and for people to be saying, 'Bring back Loughnane.'*

Many managers' career statistics have been grossly distorted by an addiction to hurling that caused them to go on managing far past their prime. Loughnane was not going to fall into that trap.

> *I'd say the one thing I've always been is realistic. I was realistic enough to know when my own hurling career was over, at both inter-county and club level. I was battling for my own survival, and when you're battling for survival, it's time to go.*

Given the pressure, the controversy and the sheer intensity, how much of it did he actually enjoy?

> *There was no part I didn't enjoy up to '99. I know myself I shouldn't have stayed on in 2000, but Cyril said he wouldn't go forward as manager unless I stayed with him for a year. I stayed on largely for that reason, and maybe that wasn't a good reason to stay. Nonetheless I turned up for every training session and put in the same effort as the previous years, but I just didn't have the same bite in me as before. Maybe that's a good thing in a way because you are getting out of it knowing you should be getting out of it. So many people are forced out at a time not of their choosing. I got out when it was time to get out.*

An amateur with a professional approach, Loughnane had piloted the Clare ship through many stormy waters. He had decided it was time to go, but what memories he left behind.

> *That's why going to watch Clare since I retired has been such an eye-opener for me. I never really appreciated the affection the Clare people had for these players. It's unreal. That doesn't happen over nothing. People know what's going on. It doesn't matter what the media say. People see for themselves. For all of us to come together at the same time was just a fluke. All of us made each other stronger. All of our combined qualities produced the mix that made Clare the great team it was.*

For the moment, Ger Loughnane has no involvement in hurling.

> *I'm one of these people that when I'm in something I give it a 100 per cent, and when I'm out, I just leave it. I don't miss it one bit! In 2000, I had been involved for such a long time that the thing had gone a bit dreary – a bit dead. When we were beaten by Tipperary in the Championship, instead of being disappointed, I was just relieved. The day you feel relieved to be beaten is the time to give it up. It was time to take a break from it.*

He laughs when he's asked if he's been snowed under with requests to coach various teams since his retirement.

> *Funny enough, there haven't been that many. I think most people understood that I'd been in it for a long time and that I needed a break. Only time will tell if I can get the appetite back again and the only way I would get involved with hurling at any level: juvenile, senior, club, county is if the appetite came back.*

'A Strange Kind of Glory.' A totally drained Loughnane meets the media after the '97 All-Ireland victory

Loughnane's legacy is that Clare are no longer the poor men vainly trying to sup at the rich man's table. The established order of hurling was openly challenged. His was a contribution that would lead many astute judges to put him at the top of the list of the greatest hurling managers in history. Unequivocal declarations that he must be the best are pointless, since they can be neither conclusively validated nor refuted. For the multitude who are acquainted with him only at a distance, his immortality is based on astonishing achievements. His place in the lore of the sport is made additionally secure by the award of the manager of the millennium. His achievement has no equivalent in the past, and is never likely to find even an echo in the future.

Of course he has his flaws, but Loughnane was the hero of one of the most captivating stories in the lore of hurling – a tale of such delicious joy and freedom that no Clare person wanted it to stop. What lingers in the imagination is not merely the towering scale of his accomplishments but the unique sense of drama he brought to hurling. Loughnane is a very different man to Christy Ring, but they are linked by obsession, inspiration and self-belief and it may take the toss of a coin to decide who rates as the most electrifying presence hurling has seen. People who regard Ring as a kind of divinity are bound to find that comparison ridiculously wild. But has there ever been a more talked about, albeit much of it unflattering, figure in hurling than Ger Loughnane? His grip on the public imagination extended way beyond the cognoscenti of the clash of the ash.

How will a man apparently consumed by an almost demonic compulsion to compete find anything in life to replace the adrenaline charge that hurling provided? A small weight is placed upon the heart by the thought of the sport without a man who thrilled and infuriated so many. Hurling will remain a wonder, whoever has quit its stage, but the loss of such a presence cannot be negligible. The life of the nation will be duller without him.

2

The Saffron and Blue

When I think back to some of the officials on the county board, it's not a question of why did Clare not win anything, but how could Clare possibly have won anything? They had a vice-like grip on everything and a total lack of respect for the players. I had seen many examples of this kind of attitude in my playing career, but I was shocked to discover that these old attitudes still prevailed towards the end of the twentieth century.

This was brought home to me by one county board officer before the All-Ireland in '95. We were obviously going to be staying in a hotel in Dublin on the night of the All-Ireland. About a fortnight before the final, I met two officers of the county board, one being Pat Fitzgerald the county secretary, to discuss the arrangements. We were standing on Abbey Street in Ennis, with people passing by. I said, 'Now that we're going up to the All-Ireland. The crucial thing at this stage is to book the hotel. The least thing every player should get is a room of his own'. Pat was completely genuine and as all the players were bachelors he was concerned about the 'extra-curricular activities' that might go on in these rooms and of the Clare county board being seeing as condoning them. His attitude was on ethical grounds and I totally respected that. The other official said, 'Oh, them c**ts will be riding like f**k all night.' That was his attitude to Clare players going out to play in an All-Ireland final, for the very first time.

Both sides reflected the two different kinds of approach: Pat, the new, that respected the players; the other man, the old, that treated players with contempt. I thought to myself 'we've got to take things out of the hands of people with that mindset.'

S ome officials on the Clare county board never forgave Ger Loughnane for not living down to their expectations.

The Clare that Loughnane grew up in was a very stratified society. Irish people often delude themselves that, unlike the British, they do not have a class system. That is not true, because we have something much more subtle. In rural Ireland, there was a very definite social hierarchy in every parish which kept everybody in their preordained niche. The only way to break free from your appointed status was to move out.

Once the English domination went in the 1920s a new order was needed to keep people in their place. That only crumbled in the late 1960s when free education was introduced. Young people started to go to university and to mix with people from other counties and to see they were as good as anybody else. The revolution started from down below. Our parents' generation were afraid of authority. Nowadays, younger people do not have the hang-ups that other generations had.

Hurling was between the big three, the rich farming lands of Tipperary, Cork and Kilkenny. The view was that when it really came down to it you could never beat those, and so what you did was try and become kingpins in your small pool. This created all kinds of feuds in the county and very little commitment to the county team. Players wanted to get the jersey, but they had no real commitment to it. That was a huge impediment to Clare. When they had good teams, internal feuds often prevented them making the breakthrough. They blamed referees, drinking, pitches and anything else they could think of. The reality, though, was it was the fault of the divisions within the team that brought about their destruction. Once you understood that, you can understand how to remedy it.

It all came down to self-belief. Our All-Ireland winning team were not overawed by anyone or anything. In fact, far from being overawed, they were all anxious to prove themselves and to show exactly what they could do. We had so many of those, I suppose you could call them leaders: Anthony Daly, Brian Lohan, Davy Fitzgerald, Seánie McMahon, Ollie Baker, Jamesie O'Connor. You could go on and on. Far from shirking the challenge, they were going to embrace it. The bigger the challenge the better they were going to perform and that was actually the crucial difference between the team I played on and the team I managed. The change that took place in the Clare team was a reflection of a lot of changes that had taken place in society.

In Clare hurling, the hierarchy was very clearly defined. When I was a player, the county board blocked everything that would have been a step to progress. They considered the team not even secondary, but tertiary. They were the most important, there was no doubt about that. They weren't sure what was the second most important thing, but the players were way down the line. That was the mentality that was there for years and years. It wasn't just the case in Clare. It was the same in a lot of counties and is still the same in some counties.

After a Clare match, the hotel would be full to the rafters with county board officers of all types. They were willing to provide meals for players but never for their wives or girlfriends. Most players wouldn't go in for a meal for that reason, though the wives of the officials were always brought in for meals. Players would have expenses but rarely would they get the full amount. The county board always found some pretext to dock them. When I was playing, there was no such thing as swapping jerseys. When the practice did become commonplace, there was uproar from the county board. It didn't matter whether you won a game or not. The officers came in and checked off each jersey on their list to ensure nobody slipped one away. When you've just lost a big game, this is not the sort of thing you want to see happening. They also made a big deal out of socks. If you lost your socks you had to replace them yourself. It was at that ridiculous level.

Worst of all was that the county board only appointed selectors they could dominate, intimidate and keep control of. The selectors were usually as afraid of the county board as the players were. The county board wanted to control and dominate everything. If they did it in a way that was best for the county team, I wouldn't have minded but it was their pettiness that destroyed morale on the Clare team. They were just watching their own careers and everybody else suffered because of that.

Following his retirement as a player, Loughnane attempted to step into management. He was not greeted with open arms. In 1989, he sought the position of manager of the Clare minor team but was not appointed. Instead the Clare county board opted for a selection committee. Loughnane's long-term ambition, though, was to take over the reins of the senior team, particularly after one particular match.

THE NEW AVENGERS

Munster finals had, for a long time, tortured the Banner county. Clare people had specialised in applying balms to wounded spirits, to make more bearable the pain of humiliating defeats like the 1993 Munster final. Of course there were reasons for that defeat. But failure that day was no less painful a memory for being readily explained.

Apart from the magnitude of Clare's defeat, the 1993 Munster final is best remembered for an incident when Nicky English was alleged to have insulted the Clare fans. Fact or fiction?

I marked Nicky English a few times. I thought he was a really fantastic player.

Sometimes though, Nicky's too honest and too open. There is no deviousness about him. What happened in '93 was something I used subsequently to motivate Clare.

I went to see Clare beat Limerick in the League in April 2001 as an ordinary fan, with my son, Barry. On the way in, he asked, 'do you remember the last Clare match we went to together?' It was the '93 Munster final. Barry was only 11, but he remembered it clearly. It shows how much the trouncing we got that day was on the mind of every Clare person. It wasn't just a trouncing. It was a total and utter embarrassment.

Tipperary had effectively beaten us after 10 minutes. I decided to stay on until the end of the game. English scored a point and he went out and had the 'high fives' with Pat Fox and had this big smile across his face. It wasn't that English was laughing at Clare, but it encapsulated what was wrong with Clare. They were nothing. These guys didn't matter.

Why do I still remember where I was sitting in the stand that day? Why would Barry still remember that day? Why would all Clare supporters remember that day? Everyone remembers the trouncing by Tipp, but what left an indelible memory was Nicky English's grinning gumshield. I can still see it – eight years later. It was unfair to say it was English. It was total annihilation, but what symbolised it was English's grin and that was the thing that really hurt. Every Clare person felt that 'snub' keenly. English didn't mean it that way. That defeat had to be avenged. That was what drove us all on.

THE SCHOOL OF HARD KNOCKS

In 1991, Len Gaynor was appointed as Clare manager. The following year, Loughnane was appointed as one of his selectors. As he was manager of the under-21 team that season, and because there was an overlap of players like Anthony Daly and Brian Lohan, he was a natural choice to assist Gaynor. It was to prove to be at once a formative and a bruising experience for Loughnane, and would shape his subsequent relationship with the county board. In 1992, his under-21 team qualified for the Munster final against Waterford. Waterford were powered by Tony Browne, Fergal Hartley, Johnny Brenner and Paul Flynn and in a superb final emerged victorious 0–17 to 1–12. They went on to beat Offaly in a replay in the All-Ireland final.

There was such a furore over Clare losing the under-21 final that people never wanted me in charge of a Clare team of any kind again. Clare imagined they had a super under-21 team because they had been in the minor final in '89 and were beaten by Offaly. People assumed that there was an automatic co-relation between minor and under-21, but that doesn't always happen. The reality was that we had a very average team and very few of them went on to make it at senior level. I had introduced this new system in training of moving the ball really fast, which I later used with the senior team, and had explained to the county board that it would take three years of this type of training to make proper players out of those lads.

We beat Limerick and Tipperary playing beautiful hurling, but were beaten by a superb Waterford team. What really annoyed me about the county board's attitude was they were only interested in winning. The fact that we were producing great hurling didn't matter. They didn't care if we kicked the ball as long as we won. What did it matter if we won an under-21 title or not as long as these players were developing and could make it on to the senior team?

That experience did teach me a valuable lesson. Up to that Munster final, I always felt that the best place to observe what was happening on the pitch was to stand in the one place and keep a close eye on proceedings, but after that match I decided that the best thing was for me to move around and force more life into the players.

Loughnane was sacked as coach of the under-21 team and senior selector in the one night.

The county board meeting came a night or two after the Munster under-21 final. They went absolutely ballistic! I was totally to blame for losing the under-21 final. While some of the criticism was sincerely motivated, the main thrust came from a small clique who wanted to put their own man in charge because they saw their opportunity for the following year. A lot of people at the meeting had their own agendas. They wanted more players from their clubs on the team or people from their backroom teams on the management team. The real sickener was that 17 of our panel were still eligible to play under-21 the following year, and they had a great future if they were 'minded' properly. The next year, under a different manager, the Clare under-21s were trounced by Limerick. Seánie McMahon was left on the sideline for that game, while players with a

fraction of his talent were playing. That whole episode left me with a
complete distrust of the Clare county board.

Typically, Loughnane did not take his dismissal lying down.

I went to the next meeting of the county board and stood right up in front
of the lot of them and faced them all down. I especially stared at the ones
who were chiefly responsible for my dismissal. I said, 'At your last
meeting you were all complaining about me. Stand up now and I'll
answer any question ye have to ask me.' Nobody stood up.

IT COULD HAPPEN TO A BISHOP

Although Loughnane was bloodied from his experiences as a selector,
the upside was that he had once again forged an alliance with his former
mentor in St Flannans, a man destined to become Clare's most prominent
cleric.

Willie Walsh was a selector with me. It was a personality more than
anything else that made him such a force. He is a totally genuine person.
He is devoid of a nasty streak or ruthlessness, so he'd never be a
manager!

There is one evening I especially recall spending with him. He came into
training and said nothing. Afterwards, we went over to the Sherwood
where many a discussion about hurling battles took place. He sat down
in front of me. I noticed his head was down and that he seemed very
upset. I asked him what was wrong. He replied, 'I've just been appointed
bishop.' I replied, 'That's mighty.'

'But it's such a huge responsibility.'

'You're exactly the right man for the job. I'll tell you straight out you
were the best candidate they could have got no matter who else was
available.'

He appreciated that. Len Gaynor came over. When he heard the news, he
was equally delighted and supportive. It's like everything else. You need
the approval of those around you. Everything that has happened since
confirms that we couldn't possibly have got a better bishop.

A VERY CLARE COUP

In 1993, Loughnane came back into the fold, but only on the condition
that he would become manager the next time the post became vacant.

After Clare were trounced in the Munster final, Len Gaynor came to me
and asked if I would I return as selector. I said immediately, 'No way'.

He went off and tried to get other selectors, but he found it very hard to get them. He visited my home one night and he asked, 'Will you come back?' I said, 'I'll come back on one condition. When you pull out as manager of Clare I will succeed you.' He asked, 'How will we arrange that?'

Brendan Vaughan was chairman of the county board, so Len went to Brendan and put the case to him, explaining the problem of getting selectors. Brendan talked to me and again raised the problem of getting it through. I told him, 'Brendan, the only way you'll get it through is if you launch it on them and have a decision made straight away.'

When Brendan raised it with them a few speakers spoke against, including the present chairman, Fr Michael McNamara, though I never held it against him. They were trying to play for time, but selectors were crucial for Len so it got through. The last person many of them wanted was me. Ultimately it got through because of the shrewd tactics that Vaughan used. He wouldn't tolerate having the decision postponed. To many officers on the county board I couldn't do much damage for the moment, and they were confident they would clip my wings for me.

Len was happy to go along with the arrangement that I would replace him. In fairness, Len did everything possible. Whatever he's involved in, he'll give it his best. He did tremendous work here. He's the most genuine person you could meet. In my last year with him, he let me do a lot of the coaching of the Clare team. I think he might have felt that he lost a small bit of contact with the modern way of training. We got on tremendously well together. I think he did a great service to Clare while he was here. I don't think he'd ever have won with Clare, but he definitely did an awful lot to bridge the gap between the total chaos of the previous era and the great organisation that came later on.

Loughnane's admiration and friendship for Gaynor would later cast a shadow across one of his greatest days.

Before the final whistle was blown in the '97 All-Ireland, after Davy Fitzgerald saved from John Leahy, Len came over and shook hands with me and said, 'Ye have it now.' It took some of the good out of winning the All-Ireland for me because I was with him in Clare and I knew the pain losing was going to cause him, and what the consequences were going to be. He was going to get the blame for Tipp's defeat. I really liked him and fully appreciated what he had done for Clare. While the game was on, I'd have done anything for us to win, but when the final whistle blew I remember thinking to myself, 'It's great to win and beat Tipp but I wish somebody else was in charge.' He had given everything of himself in his time with Clare and had an incredible passion for Clare to win.

*The three wise men. Loughnane scrutinises Clare's progress with
Fr Willie Walsh (in his pre-bishop days) and Len Gaynor.*

1993 had been a year of ignominy for Clare hurling because of the scale
of the defeat to Tipperary. 1994 was payback time. Loughnane was
shocked by the person who made that point most forcefully.

*It was something that was born out of a tragedy. Playing for Clare in the
'93 Munster final was a man called John Moroney. His cousin, John
Russell was playing as well. Later that year, John Moroney was killed
just outside Croom, coming back to Ennis from work. He was one of
those quiet, really respected players and his one ambition was to play for
Clare against Tipperary the following year to avenge the defeat. He had
made this statement to everybody, and Anthony Daly, who was very
friendly with John, and the other players were very conscious of that. The
next year I was a selector and it was a huge motivation force for all of us
to beat Tipp and avenge the defeat.*

*Coming up to the Championship in '94, the Clare minors were playing
in Limerick so Len decided we'd go to watch them and have a team
meeting afterwards to discuss our plans for the Championship. We met
in the Two Mile Inn, near Limerick. Seánie McMahon had just come on
to the panel that year. At the time, I would have seen Seánie as one of
those quiet lads, who plays away and never says anything, but who
wouldn't be half aggressive enough for inter-county hurling. The
meeting was nearly over and Seánie got up. Well, you could hear a pin
drop. Here was a young lad of 20 years of age and he gave a speech of
such viciousness that it left everybody absolutely stunned! The gist of it*

was: look at what those Tipp f**kers have done to Clare, and by Jesus this year we're going to put them down. When he was finished I said to Len, 'Stop it now.' There was no need to say another word.

We beat Tipp. They were missing a lot of players like English and Leahy. It wasn't the real thing but it was still great. The real thing was to come later on!

Clare were trounced by Limerick in the Munster final. The scale of the defeat came as no surprise to Loughnane.

I knew we were going to be eaten alive that day. On the morning of the game, all our players were as unsure and as nervous as could be. I wanted to say something but I didn't because I didn't want to impose on Len's domain. The pace of the training coming up to the Munster final wasn't fast enough. One night, I was in the dugout watching the training and was horrified. Everything seemed to be moving in slow motion. I jumped up in the dugout and hit my head off the roof and lifted the galvanised off it. Martin Flanagan, the caretaker in Cusack Park, asked, 'What's wrong with you?' I barked back, 'Can't you see the f**king training that's going on here. We'll be destroyed in the Munster final.' He said, 'Ah, take it easy.' He often spoke to me about it afterwards. Sure enough, Limerick devoured us in the Munster final.

When Len Gaynor retired, Loughnane got the job by default. There was no ringing endorsement from the powers that be.

When Len stepped down in '94, the job was there. A lot of people tried to persuade him to stay on, largely because they didn't want me! Before the county board met, I went on Clare FM with Alan Cantwell and declared that I was Clare manager because of what had happened the year before. He asked me, 'What can you do for Clare that Len Gaynor hasn't done?' I turned it back on him and I said, 'When Len Gaynor was here, he did everything he possibly could for Clare to win and that's what I'll be doing as well.'

The county board met and they were really lukewarm. I sat at the back of the room. Michael Daly, from Feakle, said Ger Loughnane had to be manager of the Clare team because the thing has been agreed, and wished me well, but he was the only one who spoke apart from myself. There was no enthusiasm and no round of applause when I finished. It was a coup. Of all my difficulties as Clare manager, the biggest one I had was getting appointed in the first place.

THREE MENTORS AND A COUNTY SECRETARY

Loughnane and his backroom team assembled a collection of players, all single, whose status as a dream team had more to do with potential than achievement. In a county where hurling has been a painful passion, he wanted the doors of victory to be opened to his team. As a former player, Loughnane is imbued with the ethos of Gaelic games, an ethos rooted in a sense of community that enables so many to give so much for so little in material terms.

The last time Clare had won the Munster final, Eamon de Valera had just been elected Taoiseach for the first time. Clare fans had had nothing but false dawns and shattered expectations, but they waited and hoped, sang and dreamed. That anticipation, togetherness, fervour and love of the county team, even in bad times, was awesome. Even when the county team treated the fans to some dreadful performances, they never wavered in their commitment. Loughnane and his mentors felt they were entitled to success. They came with a guarantee that they would never ease up on themselves. Loughnane brought the lessons of his playing career to bear on the task.

Our manager, Fr Harry Bohan, was a charismatic figure. When you went to a meeting with him you felt energised by what he said and felt that you wanted to be part of it. Even players who had been lackadaisical about training got enthusiastic about it once Harry got involved. Everybody was on his side. Initially he trained the team, but that wasn't his forte so he got in Justin McCarthy to coach the hurling skills and Colm Flynn to do the physical coaching.

With the three of them, the whole scene was transformed. Harry brought a professionalism that was never there before and everyone responded. He was the first person to eliminate the differences that had been there between parishes. What club you came from didn't matter. All that mattered was ability. He brought in players from intermediate and junior clubs, from all parts of the county. He also looked for certain qualities from the people he brought in. He wanted no player who was going to act the maggot.

For his time, Justin McCarthy was a good coach. He was an outsider, had won an All-Ireland with Cork, was very articulate and thorough in his approach. I found him really good but a lot of players didn't take to him. There was conflict between himself and Colm as to how much physical training would be done. The mix wasn't right between the backroom personnel and this led to many conflicts.

Justin was very professional. He would always be first to training. He always presented himself very well. There wouldn't even be a hair out of place. Even though he had a great knowledge of hurling, he lacked the ability to get inside players's heads. He wasn't able to make that vital link which would enable us to get out of the old ways of thinking. He did great work but sometimes you've got to drive the horse over the fence. Bringing him up to the fence and asking him to jump often isn't enough. If he's forced over the first fence, he'll jump all the other fences. We didn't have anyone to force us over the fence.

Harry was badly treated by the county board. There was a massive conflict between what he wanted and what the county board officers, who were stuck in a time-warp would allow. They weren't prepared to come forward with things like meals after training, proper facilities, proper gear and proper travelling expenses. There was a constant battle between Harry and the Clare county board.

We didn't have the harmony that we needed. We had a coach who was out of sync with the trainer, and both were pulling out of the manager. The manager was also being dragged by the county board. Harry should have said: Colm, you do this. Justin you do that. It was a great lesson for me. It's much better to prevent problems arising. It's better to create a situation where everybody gravitates towards you and asks, 'What'll we do next?'

As he set out to change the course of hurling history, Loughnane could be reassured by the knowledge that he had useful men in his corner to complement the belligerent practicality of his own nature. He brought in Mike McNamara to assist him on the physical side, and Tony Considine who with his friendly, warm personality created an atmosphere of working together. The two were as distinct as Apollo and Dionysus, but throve in the demanding atmosphere of big matches.

We started training for the '95 Munster Championship the previous September. We trained all the way through the League. Luxurious conditions were not conducive to good winter training, so we trained in Crusheen. Mike McNamara was excellent for putting the players through that hard physical slog. The players will never forget their introduction to Mike's training methods and personality. On his very first night standing on the pitch in Crusheen he said, 'Okay ladies. Let's go for a jog!' He was humorous as well. Some of the things he'd say would be so over the top that you could only laugh! He had no doubts in his mind about what was needed and the players responded to that. In '94, Clare had been pushed around and they had to be built up. Mike was a very solid bloke. He was crucial to our success. Whatever you'd suggest he'd go along with.

Loughnane liked to have strong people around him. It was clear to those players that Tony and Mike's views should be taken seriously. The triumvirate didn't always see things the same way, but the interplay of opinions stimulated everybody's creativity.

In 1995, we went up to train in Croke Park before the All-Ireland semifinal to get used to the feel of the pitch. The Munster under-21 final was on the same night in Thurles where Clare were playing Tipperary. Clare had never won the Munster under-21 title and this was their best chance ever of winning it. We had all the under-21 players on the senior panel up in Croke Park and not in Thurles. That was more of the tunnel vision. Who was going to care in ten years time who won the Munster under-21 final in 1995? Everyone was going to care if the Clare team went on to win the senior All-Ireland that year.

Lucky enough, Mike McNamara was managing the Clare under-21 team that year and he was absolutely brilliant. I've got to hand it to him. When I said I wanted all the senior panelists, there was just no hesitation. The senior team was going to take precedence. Mike could have said, 'Listen, I'm manager of the under-21 side, we're in the Munster final. I've got to have those players. Clare have never won the under-21 Munster title. This is our year.' Collectively all of our backroom team felt that we'd got one chance of winning an All-Ireland and we were going to give it everything.

The Famous Five: Tony Considine, Anthony Daly, Pat O'Donnell,
Loughnane and Mike McNamara bask in the glory
of their first All-Ireland triumph.

All the management team expected everyone on the team to be treated equally. That was not to say that they did not cater for specific talents. Each had enormous respect for what the likes of Jamesie O'Connor could do with the ball and was reluctant to try anything that might inhibit his creative process. Everyone liked Tony Considine because he was guileless, unassuming and had a generous heart as well as intelligence and level-headedness. He has a quality about him, a blending of strength and good nature that lead to both respect and affection. Listening to Loughnane talk about him, it is clear that their relationship brims with mutual respect.

> I met Tony Considine at the Munster under-21 hurling final in '94. I didn't know him beforehand. Mike Mac was in charge of the under-21s at the time. I chatted to Tony for a long time after the match and I found that his ideas were very much like my own. We met on and off afterwards. I found we got on really well together and were really in tune as to what was needed in Clare. Tony is really successful in his own job. He is a very intelligent man and knew the game inside out. He had been with Mike Mac when Clare won the junior hurling All-Ireland in 1993. I thought to myself here's a new man who had none of the hang-ups and who was not perceived as unsuccessful. Mike had taken Clare to the All-Ireland minor final in 1989, only to be beaten by Offaly. They were different faces.

There was one more link in the chain that Loughnane needed if the team's promise was to be fulfilled, a protecting harbour in the raging storm. If you travel the hurling world, the people who impress you the most are not necessarily those in the spotlight. It is often the reverse.

> When I had those in place, I sought Colm Flynn as my physio. I knew Colm from when I was playing for Clare myself and met him for lunch one day. It was difficult to persuade him to come back. He was with Galway at that stage. He was reluctant because the Clare county board had treated him very badly. He was used to the old way in Clare hurling where everything was secondary to the board officers, but I told him it was going to be very different this time. Players would be the number one from here on in. We'll be in total charge.

> He came back in March of '95. It was the best thing that ever happened. I always liked to surround myself with strong, intelligent characters. He was one of those. He was very perceptive. He'd been with Galway hurlers when they made the breakthrough, and in '86 and '87. He's a fantastic physio. People come to all over Ireland for him. I've never seen him wrong in his diagnosis of an injury. He's a kind of psychologist. When I'd be giving players a hard time in training and they'd get injured,

they'd go into him and complain about me. They got everything off their chest. He could soothe their limbs and minds.

In the '95 All-Ireland, a ball came across the field to the Sparrow and he seemed certain to score. Then the sheer brilliance of Brian Whelahan was illustrated, as the Sparrow flicked the ball, Whelahan hooked him from what seemed a mile away. Whelahan's wrists are like lightning. They're unbelievable. The ball went wide. I turned around to Colm and said, 'We'll never get that goal.' He looked back at me and said, 'Ger, we'll get it.' in a calm, soothing voice. We did. That typifies him, a soothing voice, calming everybody down. To have a man like that is invaluable. Outside Clare few people would know him and that's the way he'd like it. He was a fantastic grounding influence on the team.

In the week leading up to the Munster final in '95, there was a debate about whether Seánie McMahon should play after his shoulder injury. Opinion in our group was divided. Their job was to advise me. My job was to make the decision. I decided that we'd do something I never did before which was to have a match between backs and forwards for five minutes. Nobody was trying too hard but Seánie seemed fine, but we knew that Limerick were going to hit him on the shoulder. It was Colm who said that he'd strap up the wrong shoulder. Practically the first thing that happened was that a Limerick forward crashed into Seánie's shoulder. There was a terrific outcry from the crowd, but it was the wrong shoulder! Seánie was outstanding in the Munster final.

George Martin was the fifth Beatle. The fifth member of the Clare backroom team was the county secretary.

We were lucky in a lot of ways. Pat Fitzgerald was on the county board. He is one of the most intelligent, constructive and progressive administrators in the GAA. He is a brilliant man, a member of the board of Aer Rianta. He has a progressive vision of the future which very few administrators would have.

Pat was a terrific support to me. He was almost like a selector. He never refused me anything. He was cunning, but everything he did was for the good of Clare hurling. I regarded us as being terrifically fortunate to have him as county secretary when we were there. We went through some desperately hard times together, but we looked on them as challenging. He was brilliant at meetings: he was able to think on his feet, he was fantastically articulate, and could handle any situation and was excellent at organising and planning.

There was one more essential piece of the Clare jigsaw.

Sponsorship of county teams took off in the early '90s. The Clare county board were trying desperately to get a sponsor but found it virtually impossible because Clare's hurling fortunes were so low. It ended up with a farcical situation whereby Aeroflot, the Russian airline based in Shannon, sponsored the Clare team. They had their name written, in the letters of the Russian alphabet, across the jerseys of the Clare team. It was a reflection on how hard things were that nobody wanted to get involved in Clare after five or six years of really poor results in the Munster Championship. It was when things were at an all time low that Pat O'Donnell came along as sponsor of the Clare team.

Pat was born and reared in Crusheen and went to school in Flannans and had gone up to Dublin, set up a business and had great success, but had always kept in close contact with Clare, through his involvement in the Clare Association in Dublin and frequent visits back to Clare. Pat O'Donnell became involved after Len Gaynor's first year, just for love of Clare. He was interested in raising standards. He came before the tide turned in Clare and put his money where his mouth was, so he wasn't one of those who jumped on the Banner bandwagon.

From my point of view, the great thing about him as a sponsor was that although he was always involved in terms of attending training sessions before big matches, the matches themselves and team holidays, he never interfered in any way. He came into the dressing room before big matches, but in a very unobtrusive way. He has very strong beliefs and people mightn't always agree with them but they respect the sincerity of his convictions. Everyone who knows him knows that he is a very honourable man. When we made the breakthrough in '95, it seemed appropriate that the team was sponsored by such a passionate Clare man.

THE BUSHMAN FROM FEAKLE

Another thread was woven into the rich tapestry of hurling when Clare won their first All-Ireland in 81 years. Starved of success for so long, the Clare fans were more happily sated by the special excitements of Croke Park. Loughnane was to discover that some of the Clare officials who had been the most unenthusiastic about his appointment as a manager were now suddenly speaking about their lifelong admiration for him and declaring that they always had confidence in him. These included a few who had given the impression that they would rather walk barefoot over hot coals than allow him to be manager.

'Lying in the arms of Mary.' Loughnane with his wife
Mary at the reception after the All-Ireland final in 1995.

One of Loughnane's most memorable media performances was in the aftermath of the '97 All-Ireland when he took grave exception to the comments made by RTE analyst, Eamonn Cregan. Two years previously there had been a more serious outburst which was never covered by the media. Where others might have baulked at the prospect, Loughnane had no problem tainting the happiness that suffused the entire occasion.

People often speak to me about my comments in '97 but it was very lucky there were no cameras in '95! What I said about Cregan was only in the ha'penny place compared to what I said about the county board. After winning the All-Ireland, we had a reception in the Berkeley Court. As you would expect, there were a lot of speeches. I got up and fairly laid into the county board.

Brendan Vaughan wasn't sitting up at the top table. He was relegated to one of the peripheral places. I told them straight out, 'We wouldn't be here with the Liam McCarthy Cup only for Brendan Vaughan and the courageous decision he took with the county board'. After I finished, there were a lot of people's whose jaws had dropped. One man said to me, 'You shouldn't have spoiled the night by saying that.' I replied, 'The truth is often bitter but it has to come out.' I thanked Vaughan for what he had done. He always did things what he saw as the best interests of Clare hurling – whether it was wrong or right. He was often wrong and we had ferocious arguments.

Once at a schoolboy match between our two schools, we nearly came to blows. There were two coats down as goalposts. There was no crossbar. He was umpire at one side. I was umpire at the other. A head-high ball came in at one stage. He said it was a goal. I said it was a point. After a full and frank exchange of views, he looked at me disdainfully and uttered the immortal words, 'Get away you bushman from Feakle'!

To the outside observer, it is hard to comprehend why the county board were so unwilling to endorse Loughnane.

I find it difficult to understand why they didn't want me. I suppose it's the old story, 'One of your own couldn't possibly do it.' That's a country thing. It comes from the way we were brought up. It was always someone from outside. If somebody came from far away, especially if he had a briefcase, he was your man. One of our own couldn't win.

I believe they appointed me begrudgingly knowing that they could have got rid of me in a year or two anyway and get somebody else. They'd have preferred if Len Gaynor stayed on, if not Len then somebody else. They never had the confidence that somebody from within the county could produce the goods, whereas I was totally confident that I could organise things so that Clare would be successful.

3

The Ten Rules of Leadership

We never made a rule about drinking or eating. The players always knew that they could have a few drinks and that was it. One night going into training, coming up to a big Munster Championship match, we found out that one of the panelists had been out drinking the night before. Not alone was he drinking, but he was drinking heavily. It was just not on. Every player knew the boundaries and that there were certain lines you did not cross. All the other players knew he'd been drinking and were keenly awaiting our reaction. I heard the news as I was going in the gate and I decided immediately he was going off the panel. I spoke with Mike and Tony and we decided that before we would drop him we were going to punish him.

We went out on the field on a stifling, roasting evening and had a hard hurling session. After this, we decided we were going to do ten 200-metre sprints back to back. Up and down they went. The sweat was pouring out of the man who had been drinking and he was gasping. After the ninth sprint, he couldn't run anymore. I pulled him over and I said, 'You were out drinking last night.'

He replied, 'Oh, I was but there were other lads drinking too.'

'I'm not talking about other people. I'm just talking about you. You were drinking last night?'

'Yeah. I was.'

'You're off the panel. Tog in and go home.'

Cruel? Maybe, but that's the way it was. I wasn't happy just to let him go. I wanted him to see that this was a betrayal of his comrades and everyone else. A thing like this could not be tolerated. It also sent out a strong signal to everybody else.

23

Fear had nothing to do with it. I would say a lot of players feared me. No doubt about it. But you don't motivate anybody through fear anymore. A leader is someone who has willing followers not fearful followers. In an amateur game, you wouldn't get fearful followers because they won't stay. At, the same time, everybody knew they must produce the goods. Somehow the players found contentment in that set-up. Any time we came across a huge obstacle or a big challenge, there was always electricity between the players. You wanted to be in the middle of it. You felt totally energised by it. The players felt a confidence that they were indestructible. They'd go out and do everything for Clare to win. I had to be prepared to do the same for Clare and take whatever tough decisions were necessary.

RULE ONE: BE DECISIVE

The first law of leadership is to be decisive. Once you have made your move, you have to stand by it. The world of the hurling manager depends on minutiae: split-second decisions that mean the difference between winning and losing, landing on your feet or on your head.

Duty has no sweetheart. The best way to unlock the secrets of Ger Loughnane the man is to walk with him, in the softness of the western mist, through the fields in Feakle bequeathed to him by his late father. A hint of a frown is replaced by a boyish smile, and he seems to shed years in an instant. This is the place from which his heart can never be removed. This land furnishes all the answers about his history and identity, and goes even further to some secret compass point which directs him to the inner core of his being – crossing boundaries where memories of sadness and joy meet so dramatically. Walking these fields, Loughnane listens to secrets of lives gained and lives lost. The melody which enters his consciousness is a melody of tradition and pride in one's place. In these fields, people long dead live again, somehow speaking to years that belong to people not yet born. The ghost of his father will always linger in these fields. Without understanding the pride and passion Loughnane feels about Feakle, it is impossible to understand how excruciatingly painful two choices were for him. Disappointment is etched all over his face as he speaks about them seven years on.

In my first year as manager, I was faced with two very tough decisions. I had to let two of my former teammates from Feakle off the panel. I had played with Tommy Guilfoyle for Clare. In the '86 Munster final, he was marvellous and he was the one who had kept Clare in the game. He started training with us in the autumn of '94 but he had a problem with his hip and wasn't up to the pace, and I reluctantly had to let him go. That cost, and continues to cost, me a friend or two in Feakle.

To have to release one friend, neighbour and teammate is bad enough, but I had to let go a second one as well. Worst of all, he was a huge hero in Feakle. Val Donnellan had been on the panel for all the League games in 94-95 and he had trained really, really hard all through the winter. I always thought that he'd be ideal for Croke Park because it was a smaller pitch and, although he hadn't great pace, he had fantastic skill. I always had it in my mind that if we needed a goal in Croke Park, he could come on and get it for us, and that would be the day we would use him.

There was one game that brought matters to a head. We didn't bring him on for the last League match in Cork. A few days later, I got a letter from Val. I never opened it. I knew straight away that it was telling me that he was pulling out of the panel. I gave it to Tony Considine to read and when he did, he said, 'Isn't that terrible?' I never asked him what was in the letter but Val was off the panel. That was it. These were two men who had won a county championship with me in 1988, but they had to go. We needed people who were going to give themselves completely to what we decided. They had to have faith in what we did.

Victory in the 1995 Munster final had ended Clare's barren years. But for the revival to be sustained, it needed an exceptional talent to carry the banner. The Clare renaissance found its ideal artist in Ger Loughnane. He had much more than motivational ability to fit him for the role. His toughness as a competitor equipped him to take Clare back to the Promised Land. With such commitment, and the less easily defined capacity to establish a rapport with players together with an instinct for their individual and collective needs and abilities, he was a force to be reckoned with. He was at his best when the stakes were highest, with the adrenaline flood that sharpens the senses. He was a man who looked at the tide of defeatism and relentlessly forced it back. Self-pity is not in his lexicon, self-help is.

The great managers are often not easy men. They have to be driven by an endless quest to avoid the inevitable, to minimize risks and to maximize potential. Loughnane cites an example of a manager with these qualities.

In 1974, Clare were playing Dublin in a National League hurling match in O'Toole Park. When we arrived, the Dublin footballers were already training and we watched them. It left a lasting impression on me. The

Clare players went out on the sideline. There was a match going on between two teams of footballers. On the sideline was a man in an anorak. He came down along the field and you could see he was serious about what was going on. There were no words spoken but, as he came down, everyone instinctively started to move back because this man in the anorak had the teams out on the field in a mental grip. The exchanges were absolutely savage, physically. But you knew that the man in charge was the man in the anorak.

Kevin Heffernan taught me that day the greatest lesson of all time for a coach. When you are coaching a team, YOU are in charge. Players don't want a committee. They always want a man in charge. There must be one voice. When I went out on the field with a whistle in my hand, nobody had any doubt as to who was in charge.

'Winning isn't all-important, it's the only thing,' said the American coach, Vince Lombardi. Loughnane transformed the culture of the Clare team. Only winners would survive. Easier said than done, and it required a manager who could look at a match, assess the whole team performance, and at the same time see ways of foiling the opposition game plan. Not all players would immediately see this bigger picture.

Loughnane was harder on himself than on anyone else. The impression he created was of a man who knew his way round, but did not feel it necessary to be unnecessarily tough to prove it. Yet he was strong enough to use any hint of a threat to his authority to proclaim publicly that his word was holy writ. In those moments, the strength of his command would activate a seismograph. The players knew he was not a man to trifle with when he was intense, and in the moments when a glacial sternness came over his features.

In 1997, Colin Lynch was not named for our Munster Championship clash against Cork. I knew that Colin was very upset by this but we weren't sure if had the temperament for the big occasion. He went to Anthony Daly and his basic theme was: what did he have to do to play for Clare?

One night shortly after, in Cusack Park, I gave the panel a lecture about trust. I looked everybody in the eye, especially Colin Lynch, and I said: 'We won the All-Ireland in '95 because ye trusted what we did. Never doubt a decision we make. Here there is total trust. We have total trust in ye. Ye have total trust in us. Anybody who hasn't that attitude is out the gate.' I looked Lynch straight in the eye. You could hear a pin drop. There was no more complaining. Everybody knew who I was speaking about – Lynch. The players were as close as could be. They all knew the slightest move in the camp. It was the same rules for everybody. That's the way we all are. We all trusted each other. By chance, Lynch did play and he was brilliant. He was outstanding in the Munster final and in the All-Ireland final and won an All-Star that year, but even brilliant players have to understand the message that you fall into line or else.

RULE TWO: HAVE VISION

We expect a lot of our heroes. A lot of the time they disappoint us. Occasionally, as in Nelson Mandela and Ger Loughnane, they are even better than we expected. The 'Loughnane project' was not just for Clare to win a long overdue Munster title, but to turn Clare into the Offaly of Munster, where they would be up there with the traditional powers as one of the major forces in hurling. Proof that he was not indulging in flights of fancy was provided each time he went on the training pitch. He brought an inspirational zeal, almost a sense of joy, to his task.

People, though, can only be led where they want to go. A leader rides the waves, moves with the tides, understands the deepest yearnings of his charges. His purpose must resonate with the mood of his underlings. His task is to focus the people's aspirations, to articulate them in simple terms, to enthuse, to make the goal people already want seem achievable. Confucius claimed that while the advisers of a great leader should be as cold as ice, the leader himself should have fire, a spark of divine madness.

Leadership has a lot to do with timing. The leader must arrive when people are crying for leadership, as Parnell did in 1880, as Roosevelt did in 1933, as Churchill did in 1940. The great leaders offer a simple message, and leave no room for ambiguity when it comes to the solution they offer. Parnell stated that 'the land of Ireland belongs to the people of Ireland'; Roosevelt boldly informed the American population that 'the only thing we have to fear is fear itself' and Churchill told his followers to expect 'blood, toil, tears and sweat'.

A leader must stand out from the crowd. Loughnane came with a simple, uncomplicated message. His diagnosis of, and prescription for the problems of Clare hurling were rooted in his own playing days.

When I came on the scene first the late Matt Nugent was manager. In 1973 and '74, Clare had good under-21 teams that both got to the Munster final. A lot of people felt if those players were 'minded', it would be possible for Clare to make a breakthrough. Fr Harry Bohan had founded the Rural Housing Organisation and, although he hadn't a huge hurling background, the then chairman of the county board, John Hanly, felt that Harry would be the man to take us places. It was the beginning of the cult of manager with Kevin Heffernan and later Mick O'Dwyer. Harry was the man who turned things around for Clare. We started winning League games and got to the League final in '76 where we drew with Kilkenny but were hammered in the replay. We were hammered in the Championship as well, but people felt a start had been made.

In '77, we made real progress and beat Kilkenny in the League final. It was a massive breakthrough. The celebrations were not quite as good as when we won in '95, but they were really great. By this time, highlights of League matches were shown on television so we developed a great profile across the country. That year we beat Tipperary in the Munster Championship after a replay and got to play Cork in the Munster final. The hype was unreal. Everyone thought this was going to be the big breakthrough. The game started off at a great pace with great scores. Then a row developed and Jim Power was sent off after hitting Ray Cummins with his head. The whole scene came crumbling down for us. Everybody blamed the referee but he had no option. There was a massive outcry and all the sympathy was with Clare. I think Clare made a huge mistake after the game, and Waterford made the exact same mistake in '98. We failed to appreciate that the pace of our game was short but nobody wanted to admit that. Everybody wanted a scapegoat. It would've been better to have faced up to it and say, 'Right the pace of our game is too slow. We'll correct that and take them on next year.'

In '77-78, we went through every match in the League unbeaten, including the final against Kilkenny. Then we qualified to play Cork again in the Munster final. The build-up to the game was something you rarely experience. The level of tension was unbearable and there was a terrific air of expectancy within the county. What happened the previous year was behind us. Now we had to deliver. There was such tension that one of our players hadn't slept for three nights before the game. In the dressing-room before the game, you could see some players almost visibly shrivel. When we went out on the pitch, the tension was everywhere. However, it was a terribly flat game. Most players seemed to be paralysed by the occasion. If you saw it now on video you'd ask was hurling that bad back then. When the real challenge came, the confidence wasn't there and the occasion got to us. We shrivelled up completely. I'd say only one or two of us played up to scratch. At half-time it looked as if we were going to win and as we came off the pitch the Clare supporters stood up and cheered us. They were certain we were going to win. We had been playing against the wind but were only four points down. We held their forwards in the second half but we couldn't score.

That was the end. Nobody said it was the end but we all knew. The day had come for us to make the breakthrough but we hadn't. From then on, we were going backwards. The door was open but we didn't go through. Waterford were the very same in '98. The door was open for them four times that year: in the League final, two Munster finals and an All-Ireland semi-final, but they didn't go through.

We had some magical times in those three years. We'd go so far, but when the real test came, we would fail. We could beat Kilkenny on the wet days in spring, but we were caught out by Cork on the fast days in Thurles. We were as strong and tough and willing and dedicated as the rest of them. But Cork and Kilkenny always believed they would win. We never fully did. I was never as good a player again. I was only 25.

Where you'd notice it most was coming up to a big match. A month beforehand, everybody would be flying. Then the doubts began to emerge in both the players and the mentors. Did we really believe we were going to win? If Harry Bohan had a fault – and let's remember we would have been nothing without him – it was that he didn't fully believe. I think it's absolutely vital that the manager believes and that you as a player can see this. As manager, you must transmit to the players your total conviction that nothing is going to stop you. But we had great players on that 1977-78 team, and when the final whistle went in '95, they were the first people I thought of.

By the time he became manager of the Clare team in '94, Loughnane had a very clear vision of what was needed: a group of mentally tough men who could play at pace. The gospel he was preaching once he became manager was that Clare hurling was too slow – players were not moving the ball fast enough, and were playing at a slower pace than the top counties like Tipperary, Kilkenny and Cork, and he reversed that. The basis had to be a frugal defence and a lean, efficient style.

RULE THREE: MENTAL TOUGHNESS

Loughnane never had the opportunity to play in hurling's showpiece. Two League medals were the comparatively meagre rewards for his prodigious exploits on the playing field. Hurling provided an ideal context in which to express his combination of cerebral gifts and extreme competitiveness. The hurling field was an exhilarating arena where he could pitch his abilities and his nerve against the opponents. His achievements as a player were not enough in themselves to warrant confidence in him as a manager, given the number of great players who have not successfully made the transition to inter-county management.

From the beginning, there was no doubt that here was a man with an obsession. All champions are dedicated. All new managers come in saying they will give it their best shot, but few ever had quite such a sense of destiny as Loughnane. Right from the start, it was clear that there was a commitment quite daunting in its intensity.

The contradiction in me is that outside of hurling I'm a totally different person than when I'm with a team. When I'm at home, when I'm at school, I'm really easy going, but when it comes to hurling, especially when it comes to the Clare team, I'm totally obsessive. You're not going to win anything unless you have that obsession. Players will forgive anything. They'll take anything when they see that you have a genuine passion for their welfare.

'Tunnel vision'. Loughnane's legendary concentration was never more needed than in 1998.

Loughnane may have been seen in certain quarters as the Messiah, but was never worried about behaviour that might see him labelled as an antichrist.

In Clare, the biggest deficiency we had was a lack of mental toughness. We were always playing not to lose, rather than to win. Mayo always gave me that impression too. And my theory is that the best time to confront that is while lads are training, fully warmed up. I would go straight up to a player and eat the head off him if I saw him backing off, because that was our biggest problem: players backing down when the challenge really came. So I would expose him in front of his buddies. Not downgrading him, just telling him a straight truth.

Players cannot leave their character in the dressing room. It goes out on the field with them. If genuine, stellar talents could not be found, lesser performers were processed to play the part. But did they have the mental toughness to be champions? In his playing days, when the big games came along the Clare players had already surrendered. They had grown comfortable with the idea of being a 'nearly' team. Although many of the players were exceptionally skilful, more than capable of bringing a touch of élan to the proceedings, they were guilty of flitting in and out of big matches, rarely taking them by the throat.

We met Tipperary in the League in '95 in Ennis and it was a watershed game. Tipperary had their full team including English, Fox, Aidan Ryan, Declan Ryan and all the stars that had demolished Clare in '93. We had won all the matches in the League up to that. We had started off by just scraping wins over Antrim, Galway and Kilkenny and then it came to Tipperary. I said to them in the dressing-room, 'This is the day you have to stand up to them. We have to make a statement. They've come with all their big guns and today we're going to put them down.'

Not alone was it a hurling battle it was a verbal battle as well. The message was sent out loud and clear: you might have demolished us two years ago but you'll never do that again while we're here. That's what they told them up to their faces. We might have got a reputation later for dishing it out, but we really dished it out that day! Clare really stood up to Tipp. It was a terrific game and our lads saw that for the first time they could outhurl them. The Tipp lads really wanted to win. I saw Nicky English after the game and he was really disappointed. We beat them and after that we felt something big was going to happen.

People say that the League isn't important, but some games at some times are vital. That was the crucial day for us. Cyril Lyons missed a free from 30 yards out and I belted the wire behind me in frustration that, like so often before, we'd let a crucial match slip away. We knew everything was at stake that day. It's very hard to make progress when teams are shattered and the least thing can cause a psychological meltdown. It's like someone who has a phobia: you have to confront the phobia to beat it. I rate that Tipperary team of the '80s and early '90s as the side with the most exciting forward line I've seen, but our lads drove them back every way: physically, verbally and hurling-wise. Every team that's going to go places needs to make a statement. You can even afford to take a step back after that. That was the really vital day.

The Babyface Killer

The manager's jobs pulsates with compromises and negotiations. In the early months, Loughnane had little time to ruminate on destiny. His priority was on the talent at his disposal. Individually and collectively, there had to be a total focus. Moping was improbable behaviour for players who found themselves in Loughnane's vicinity. One player typified the mental toughness he was looking for.

There are men and there are men and then there's Seánie McMahon. You just couldn't have greater regard for a person than you'd have for Seánie. If you had a daughter and she brought Seánie home, you'd be really, really delighted. You'd think, rightly, that here comes the nicest, most sociable, most humble and intelligent person you could ever meet. Put him on a field and that is his demeanour, but inside is the mind of a predator! He's the Bertie Ahern of hurling, 'the most cunning and most ruthless of them all'. He'd do anything to win. If Seánie was in the mafia, he would be a killer. He'd be a babyface killer. He's a fantastic person above all else, and in spite of what I said he's a very ethical person, a terrific hurler and a real leader. The substance and depth in Seánie is such that you meet in very few people in life. That is the really, really great thing to admire about him. Whenever things were at their worst Seánie always did something to redress the situation. In the All-Ireland final in '95, who got Clare's first two points? Seánie McMahon. When chances were going astray, he showed the way with a 65 and one from play. Look at all the vital scores he got from frees in the most pressurised of situations.

He's from a wonderful family. His father, Michael, is chairman of Doora-Barefield. His sister, Maria, is a wonderful camogie player. Seánie's a special man. He's a religious person. If you were listing all the best qualities you would want in a person, you'd find them in Seánie. But when you want a job done, Seánie is the man. For his skill, his character, the inspiration he gives in the dressing-room, his loyalty and his mental toughness, I admire him as much as I admire any person in the world. He was a leader off the pitch and a Colossus on it.

*If there was one example of Seánie's mental toughness, it has to be the Munster semi-final against Cork in '95. He broke his collar-bone and we'd already used three subs. I said, 'F**k it, Seánie you're going to have to come off.' He replied, 'I can't go off. We can't play with 14. I'll go corner-forward.' All I could say was, 'fine'. Up he went to corner-forward, holding his shoulder. With a few minutes to go, Timmy Kelleher got the ball in the Cork backline. Seánie went towards him to put him under pressure and Kelleher sent the ball over the sideline. Fergie Tuohy,* *who I'd never seen in my life taking a line ball, took the perfect line ball and Ollie Baker put it into the net. From the puckout, Alan Brown got the ball out near the sideline and went for a point. His shot hit the post and fell straight into the hands of a Cork forward with a goal at his mercy. As he threw up the ball, out of the corner of my eye I saw Frank Lohan coming out of nowhere and he flicked the ball away and cleared it out. It came to Fergie Tuohy and the final whistle blew. Clare had won by a point.*

Claws

For 81 years, Clare teams had to suffer scepticism about their ability to deliver the big performance on the big day. Loughnane and his mentors sought players who were like a Formula One racing car – nothing fancy, all business. Conor 'Claws' Clancy fitted that mantle perfectly.

I couldn't figure him out. He just kept to himself, but he was relaxed and couldn't be intimidated. He's the definition of courage. He's so brave that he'd put up that hand anywhere. The punishment he's taken would kill anybody else. He's broken so many bones in his body but he keeps coming back for more because he's such a great competitor. He lacked pace and real skill in fast shooting, but nobody ever starred when they were marking Conor Clancy. If Clare had him in 2001, they'd definitely have beaten Tipperary because he'd be in there holding up the ball and hassling the full-back.

He was highly regarded by all of us because of his wholeheartedness. His battles with Lohan in training were legendary. Conor gave you absolutely everything and then more. Somebody was needed to mix it up and there was none better than Clancy. He was the man who made the openings for Jamesie and the Sparrow. He threw himself at everything.

Asked whether his team were too willing to mix it, if he had a win-at-all-costs mentality, Loughnane chose to illustrate his answer with an example.

Going into the Munster final against Cork in 1999, we were totally flat. Jamesie's arm was broken so he was ruled out. Bad and all as things were going Ollie Baker took the game by the scruff of the neck and it looked like he was going to win the game on his own. Then he went over on his ankle and had to go off. Then, with two minutes to go, we got a free, 21 yards out in front of the posts to level the game, but sent the ball wide. There was only one result after that: we were going to lose.

Strangely enough, there was no sense of desolation afterwards. We were still in the Championship. All of us liked Jimmy Barry Murphy. We congratulated him with real, genuine feeling. We were truly glad after what he had gone through in the previous years. He had suffered at the hands of Clare, and now Cork had won a Munster final.

That's a lot of what sport is about. People say it's about winning at all costs. No. It's about doing everything you can to win and pulling every trick you can in order to try and win, but when the game goes against you, you sincerely congratulate the team that beats you.

Loughnane has radically revised his views on the mental toughness of the master executioner of hurling.

There was a lot of talk before the 2000 All-Ireland when DJ Carey wasn't on the Team of the Millennium. I was of the opinion that he didn't deserve it, because he hadn't proved himself in an All-Ireland final. The test of a really good player is to produce the goods against a top-class player on the really big occasion.

In '97, before we played Kilkenny in the All-Ireland semi-final, I was asked in an interview what I thought of DJ. He had been absolutely brilliant in the All-Ireland quarter-final in a thrilling game against Galway in Thurles. He practically beat the westerners all on his own. I said, 'DJ will prove himself to be an outstanding player when he plays really well on one of the best players in the country in a big match. Next Sunday he will be playing in a really big match against Brian Lohan and if he plays really well against Brian Lohan, he will prove himself to be a really great player but I won't regard him as great player until he does it against somebody like Brian on the big day.' Nicky Brennan was Kilkenny manager then and he taped the interview and played it on the bus on the way to the match. According to the version I heard, and how true this is I don't know, he said, 'Listen to what that c**t Loughnane said about one of our best players.' Eddie O'Connor is supposed to have piped up, 'He's f**king right!'

In 2000, we went to play Kilkenny down in Gowran on DJ's home pitch. He put on an exhibition. I never realised he had the skill, the pace and the wit to the degree he showed that night. All that night, he was on a different plane. He left Brian Lohan totally and utterly stranded. I met Brian Cody coming off the field and he said, 'He's something else.' I answered, 'He's a wizard.' In 2000, I was delighted that he played a great game in the All-Ireland. Look back over his record and the difference between him and everybody else is the goals he's got. I think, though, that what people underestimate about him is his courage. When you look at his face and his hands, you see all the injuries he has picked up. Yet his nerve has remained as good as ever. His one instinct is to go for goal no matter what kind of punishment he is going to be subjected to. Under every category of defining a great player, he is without doubt the finest player of his generation, if not ever. There's no doubt about it, he's the finest player I've ever seen.

RULE FOUR: MORAL COURAGE

All the really great leaders were people of moral fibre. One of the defining images of Loughnane is of him patrolling the sideline on match days, wrapped in stern concentration, fist clenched. Everything about him said he was not a man to be crossed, but when it came to moral courage, he would not be found wanting either.

I was a selector with the Clare under-21 team ten years ago. Seamus Durack was a manager at the time. We were playing Galway in a challenge match in Athenry. Just as the game was over Seamus asked the referee would he play a few extra minutes because we had just brought on a few subs and we wanted to give them a run out.

A ball came in from far out and our corner-forward came across the square and pulled on it and he hit his own man on the jaw – our full-forward Gary Logue. It emerged later he had broken his jaw in four places. Brian Feeney, who went on to become a big star with Galway, was playing full-back that day and he waved frantically for play to be stopped. I shouted at the ref to stop the play and he did. The problem was that as Gary went down, and I can still see it vividly, his body jumped and hopped. People rushed in to investigate. The game was over and I collected the hurleys that were lying around, not appreciating the seriousness of Gary's injury. As I walked to the square, there was a big crowd around Gary but everybody pulled back. It was like the tide going out. 'What's wrong?' I asked. There was an ambulance driver there from Ennis, Patrick O'Malley, and he said, 'He's going.'

I said to Louis Mulqueen, 'What's wrong?'

'He's swallowed his tongue and we have to open his mouth. If we don't open his mouth he's gone,' he answered.

I remember as clearly as could be: there was blood coming down his nose and coming out his mouth. He took in this deep breath but nothing came out. I said, 'Louis what are we going to do?'

'We've got to open his mouth.' There was a scissors in Louis's bag. I can still see it before me. I grabbed it and pulled back his lip. He'd the strongest teeth I ever saw and I drove the scissors through his teeth as hard as I could and I levered his jaw down. You don't actually swallow your tongue: it falls back into your throat. Louis flicked back his tongue

and when he did I saw the breath returning to near normal. He was unconscious for four hours.

We went back to the mart in Athenry for a meal but nobody ate. Everybody got the shock of their lives. He came so close to death. Everyone was touched by young Michael Murphy's death in April 2001 during a hurling match in Clare. There is something shocking about a 20-year-old dying on the field of play. What would it have been like for me to have to go to Gary's parents and say, 'Your son was playing for Clare and he's dead'?

I saw what people did, though, in that moment of crisis. Everybody, except Louis, faded back. Nobody wanted to take responsibility. They didn't want to be there when he was going to die. It told me everything about human nature.

A recurring feature in any lengthy Loughnane analysis of hurling is the word 'manliness'. It is a term which he often uses interchangeably with moral courage. He has a very strong views on what it is not, and illustrates with an example from his playing days.

The Munster final in 1978 was a huge game between Clare and Cork. It was a crunch game in front of 65,000 people in Thurles. The atmosphere was electric. I was hurling really well. At one stage, the ball was going wide, and Gerald McCarthy struck me with a hurl right in the balls, and disappeared out the field straight away. Lucky enough, the umpire spotted the incident and McCarthy was booked by the referee. That was the nastiest belt of a hurley I received in my playing career. I didn't like that hit-and-run type of player. I don't mind a player who plays it hard, but is man enough to face the consequences of his actions.

RULE FIVE: PERSISTENCE

Hanging up on a wall in Loughnane's home is a the following quote from Calvin Coolidge: 'Nothing in the world can take the place of persistence. Talent will not; nothing is more common than unsuccessful men with talent. Genius will not; unrewarded genius is almost a proverb. Education will not; the world is full of educated derelicts. Persistence and determination alone are not omnipotent. The slogan "press on" has solved and always will solve the problems of the human race.'

Loughnane's playing career is a testimony to the value of persistence. As a player, he would be the first to admit that the long, hard apprenticeship he spent honing his natural gifts set him apart more dramatically than might once have been the case. All along the way, nature was assisted by plenty of self-sacrifice. His skills, athleticism and immense physical authority were sufficient in themselves to separate him from the mass of modern hurlers, but equally vital was his conscientiousness and discipline as he assiduously developed his gifts. His appetite for adding to his knowledge of his craft was insatiable. Most of his stories about his playing days are distinguished by wry self-deprecation.

> *I was an average player, but I was able to play at my best in the big games. So many players play way below their best when big games come around. The bigger the reputation of the player I was marking, the better I played. I made the most of what I had. I had a very poor left-hand side. I wasn't great in the air but I was able to disguise my faults and to make the most of what I had. As time went on, I developed very good skill by consistent practice. Whenever we went into training, I played as if it was a championship game. A lot of players would be pucking around but I believed in doing everything at the maximum pace.*

Sometimes there is a pared-down practicality about Loughnane's utterances that does not lend itself to lyrical evocations of glorious deeds on the hurling sod. It is more about dark dressing rooms through which light enters as stealthily as a burglar. Yet if he is nudged persistently enough towards memories of his playing days, the recollections that emerge are affectionate, vivid and entertaining. Persistence was a quality he encouraged in other players. In the 1976 League final replay, Eddie Keher got a head injury and the blood was pumping out of him necessitating a long delay while he got attention. Loughnane, ever helpful and compassionate, went up to him and said, 'Jaysus Keher would you ever get up and get on with it. Sure there's nothing wrong with you'!

As a new manager, Loughnane swept in like a gust of fresh air, but he would need an ability to put an optimistic spin on the bleakest situation and a willingness to stick with his team through what could be a long, sometimes frustrating process of renewal. He reached the top because his assessments, his strategy and his organisation were more instinctively accurate, more directly arrived at, and more meticulously effected than those of any of his rivals. But some energy has to create and drive this. The mystery lies in the man. Success has only been achieved by taking each move, each decision seriously. Maybe too seriously for some. Unnecessary risk was to be eliminated.

There was no place for sentiment in the Loughnane scheme of things. He had to be ruthlessly analytical in his assessment of players and the state of hurling. For the ugly duckling to be turned into the swan, he knew an obsessive belief in the virtue of perseverance was needed with some players more than others as he pulled together the sinews and nerves of resolution.

> We didn't select Ollie Baker for the Munster semi-final against Cork in '95. I'd seen him play first for Clare under-21s against Cork at wing-back. He was on Brian Corcoran that day and he beat him, but it wasn't through hurling. It was through sheer physical presence. He was badly lacking on the skill levels at that stage. Ollie would come into training, and I would do an exercise with him for three minutes where the ball would be continually coming straight at him and he'd have to collect it and strike it. He'd miss three out of four. We persisted and persisted with it because he had so many other great attributes. He improved at a rate of knots and 12 months later was unrecognisable from the player we started off with.

RULE SIX: INSPIRATION

For years, defeat had jostled the Clare team's elbow and dogged its steps, imposing unbearable strain on their fragile spirits. Once Loughnane was at the helm, the injection of his unique spirit and his talent for inspiring people brought meteoric progress. It does not require special perception to detect the solidity of the confidence behind the man.

The romance of sport is its unpredictability. Sport is the only arena where David can still defeat Goliath. It is surprising that nobody has done a Ph.D. thesis on those victories, because in this respect sport can teach society an invaluable lesson – there's no need to overpower when you can outsmart. Loughnane knew that if he was to win things with Clare, he would have to pull enough strokes to put even the most manipulative politician to shame. In this respect, he was not found wanting.

He had the good fortune to attend national school in Feakle. His teacher, Seán Harrington, was one of the old-style teachers, but always got great results from his students. Loughnane was one of many students from the school to win a scholarship to St Flannans. It was there that his hurling education really began.

> I was so lucky that when I went to Flannans that Willie Walsh and Seamus Gardiner, who were young priests at the time, decided to become involved in the hurling coaching.

> They started at under-15 level with a squad that included John Callinan, Colm Hohan and myself who later played for Clare. They had a new way

of coaching: with a ball between three, developing skills and then playing games. Every fine evening we were out hurling. They really gave great encouragement.

In second and third year, we played for the junior team and in fourth and fifth year, we played on the Harty Cup team. Getting on the Harty team in Flannans gave you a huge profile and status within the college. Extra meals were provided, time off study and travel to exotic places like Limerick and Thurles were huge perks at the time.

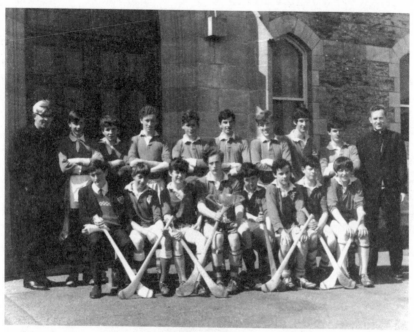

'The best days of our lives.' Loughnane (back row, third from right) proudly wears the Flannan's colours. Two future Clare stars, John Callinan and Colm Hohan (front row, second and fourth from left respectively) also feature. The team is flanked by trainers, Fr Willie Walsh and Fr Seamus Gardiner.

Loughnane was denied the ultimate dream of every young player – to win the Harty Cup. In the process, he learned an invaluable lesson about the value of an inspired tactical ploy that would remain with him throughout his managerial career. He could not have learned from a more astute teacher.

We played in a Harty Cup final against St Finnbarr's of Farranferis. The opposition were trained by Fr Michael O'Brien, who brought Cork to the Liam McCarthy Cup in 1990. He came up with a master stroke which cost us the match. He had this midfielder, Dan Dwyer, a wonderful player who never really fulfilled his extraordinary potential, primed to win the game for them. Just before the puckout, Dan would stand at one sideline then take off and just get to the other sideline as the ball landed there. It was a brilliant tactical move. Michael O'Brien was pulling stunts like that all his life!

After the Munster title victory in 1995, the Clare fans acquiesced happily enough in the fanciful efforts in certain quarters to persuade the non-believers that this team was a legend in the making. Loughnane knew this talk was premature and some rabbits would have to be pulled out of the hat if Clare were to dethrone the reigning All-Ireland champions.

Before the All-Ireland semi-final in 1995, we went up to Croke Park for a training session to familiarise the players with the place, and Eamonn Taaffe pulled his hamstring. He had pulled one of his hamstrings earlier on. That ruled him out of the semi-final. He was back training a few weeks before the final. He was off the pace. He wasn't even listed among the subs, but we said we'd bring him along because if we needed a goal there was no better man to get it.

We needed a goal! We brought on Taaffe and he was playing terribly. Worst of all, he was marking Kevin Kinahan. At one stage Eamonn was coming out for a ball that he should have won but Kevin Martin cut in ahead of him, grabbed the ball, went on a solo run, and opened up a massive gap. He took a shot but thanks be to God it went wide. I turned to Pat Fitzgerald and said, 'Eamonn Taaffe is going off and Alan Neville is coming on.' The slip was written out. I had it in my hand as Frank Lohan was fouled coming out of the defence. Dickie Murphy awarded a free to Clare and Anthony Daly took it. Dalo aimed for a point but the ball hit the post and came down. I was looking out on the field to see where the referee was to see if I could come on to make the switch. The next thing I saw the Clare flags hitting the sky at the canal end. The ball was in the net.

I thought it was Fergal Hegarty who had scored the goal, but my mind immediately switched to other things. My first concern was to stop the game no matter what to give our lads time to settle. The most dangerous time for a lapse in concentration is after you score a goal. This is when defences who had previously been so organised can lose concentration. So I wanted to stop the game. I ran out to the referee, Dickie Murphy, and as I was about to hand him the slip of paper, I pulled back my hand at the last second forcing Dickie to stop in his tracks, but at that precise moment, Dickie said, 'Don't pull that one on me Ger.' He knew what I was up to straight away. He grabbed the piece of paper and ran away.

The one thing I didn't want to happen, happened straight away. The puckout was taken quickly. An Offaly player was fouled. A free. Johnny Dooley pointed. Offaly were level and right back in the game.

That's why Eamonn Taaffe came off when the goal was scored. Eamonn would not have been taken off only that I wanted the game stopped to give everyone on our side a chance to regain composure, but Dickie outwitted me. Fair play to him. When Eamonn was taken off, it became a joke and I let it go. That's the real reason he came off so quickly.

One of the people best placed to comment on Ger Loughnane is Bishop Willie Walsh. With amiable openness, and an enthusiasm for hurling that remains dew-fresh, in conversation with this writer he spoke about the cocktail of inspiration and luck that constitutes a good tactical change:

'One of the things that always struck me in hurling was about the strange ways positional switches were made in a match. Straight away I think of the 1990 All-Ireland hurling final between Cork and Galway. After about fifteen minutes, I was wondering what the Cork selectors were going to do about Jim Cashman. Joe Cooney was destroying him, and I couldn't understand why they left Jim there. They went in at half-time and I said, "Well Jim Cashman won't be centre-back in the second half", but amazingly he was and he went on to win his battle with Joe Cooney in the second half and Cork won the All-Ireland.

'I went back to Clare and some people said to me, "Ah, you can't beat those Cork guys. Now if that was Clare, we'd have panicked and taken Jim Cashman off but the Cork guys were wise and knew what was best." Of course, that was a bit hurtful to me as a Clare selector so I went down to Cork a month later and I went to Dr Con Murphy and I said, "Up front now, what happened with Jim Cashman and why didn't you change him?" So he replied, "Well, we all agreed that Jim was being beaten and we'd have to change him. The problem was that none of the selectors could agree on who we would replace him with. So we decided to do the usual thing and give him five minutes in the second half."

'I remember in 1994 we were playing Tipperary in the Munster Championship and we were being beaten in midfield, and Ger Loughnane and myself had an argument on the sideline. Ger wanted to bring Jamesie O'Connor centre-field but I felt if we did that, we would be robbing Peter to pay Paul. We had to get a few more points to beat Tipperary and Jamesie was the one forward who would do that for us. Eventually, we called over Len Gaynor and both of us put our case to him and let him make the decision. Len favoured Ger's option and made the switch. Within a few moments, Jamesie had scored two points and lifted the whole team and we won the match. Afterwards everybody said, "Ah that was a great change ye made" without knowing it was a toss of the coin. Often a match hangs on a thing like that. The day it works, you're a hero. The day it doesn't, you're useless.'

RULE SEVEN: LUCK

Napoleon famously said that the only generals he wanted were lucky ones. In his later years, Loughnane's luck appeared to desert him but in the early years he was blessed with it when his team needed it most.

People often say to me, 'Ye were very unlucky not to win three All-Irelands.' I always say in return, 'Do you realise how lucky we were to win two All-Irelands?' You have to have luck to come from where Clare did to win two All-Irelands. Tony Considine is the luckiest man I know. Everything he's involved in, he's a success at, be it with his team, or in business. Even if we even go playing golf, the day is always fine.

I think back to the match against Cork in the Munster Championship in '95. We should have been beaten out of the gate, but we weren't and we went on to win the All-Ireland. It could be said we picked the wrong team against Cork. We didn't start with Ollie Baker. We picked Stephen Sheedy who had been a brilliant under-age player but he had a lot of problems with injuries. He didn't play well on the day. If we had lost that day, the Clare officials would have had the perfect excuse to bury me. It's a very fickle thing.

With the benefit of hindsight, Loughnane can now see that some of the apparent setbacks were actually huge strokes of luck.

In '95, Tony Considine and I were coming out of the dressing-room after losing the League final to Kilkenny. We saw their captain, Bill Hennessy, going out with the cup in his hand. He just dumped it into the boot of his car. I said to Tony, 'Imagine if we won the cup. It would still be floating around.' If Clare won it now, we'd throw it in the boot of the car as well, but not back then. It would have been a massive victory but the worst thing that could have happened to us, because everybody's ambition would have been satisfied. '95 was just a magical year. What was wrong was right. In '98, on the other hand, what was right was wrong! We were lucky to have lost the League final in '95.

There were a number of myths that gained popular currency about Clare's freakish training methods. This avalanche of almost Homeric accounts accelerated when it was discovered that the players were training early in the mornings.

The reason the early-morning sessions came about was by pure, absolute chance. 1995 was the best summer we ever had. It was very hot training in the evenings. One Wednesday evening, I said we'd train on Saturday morning. I knew the Sherwood opened at nine in the morning and we could get breakfast then. The players mightn't have liked getting up in the morning for a 7 a.m. training session but it was an outstanding success. They loved the fact that they had the whole rest of the day off, and from then on, it took on a life of its own. A myth built up around about us training at all hours of the morning running up hills, but it was just a practical response to a particular situation.

I got hurleys made that were twice as heavy as a normal hurley and we did wrist work with them. They were like shovels. Everything was new and combined to give a newness and freshness to proceedings. It was the pace we played our games at that led to our victories.

Luck is often the happy alliance between preparation and opportunity. If one of his players made a mistake, Loughnane sometimes used that to forcefully accentuate a point. If the player in question had to suffer some discomfort, that was a small price to play. One man to suffer in this way was 'Fingers', PJ O'Connell.

In the run-up to the '95 All-Ireland semi-final, I had emphasised over and over again the importance of not getting distracted by crowds or noise or by anything. On the morning of the final, we trained in the ALSAA complex, near the airport. While we did a very light workout, there were planes flying over us constantly. At the end, I called the players together around me. Just as I was about to start talking, another plane came in and PJ looked up at it. I saw my chance, so I let fly! I roared at him, 'If you are distracted here, looking up at a plane, what will you be like in Croke Park with 60,000 people roaring down at you? Are you going to look up at everyone of those?' I can tell you that when the next plane came in, no one moved their eye upward! I couldn't have planned it better. It was a lesson in distraction not just for Fingers, but for the whole team. In all the years after that, nobody once looked up when a plane came in!

Loughnane's stewardship of the Clare team brought him the most unlikely and captivating vistas. One of his most glorious triumphs was viewed from an unusual angle and achieved with a little help – albeit completely unintentional – from one of his friends.

With about 20 minutes to go in the '97 All-Ireland final, I went along the sideline and I overheard Len Gaynor telling Michael Ryan to stay inside. I decided immediately to bring on David Forde. I went to Mike and Tony and said, 'We'll bring on Fordy but we'll play him as an extra wing-forward.' They looked at me, but I told them to trust me. A comical situation then developed with Len telling Michael Ryan to stay inside and I telling the man he was supposed to be marking to stay out! This meant that Forde was totally loose. He won that All-Ireland for us. He scored two points and set up another one by playing as an extra wing-forward.

The Eyes Say it All. No words are needed as Len Gaynor and Loughnane exchange handshakes after the '97 All-Ireland.

David Forde is a really lovely guy. If you had a daughter, he's the sort of man, like Seánie McMahon, that you'd like to see her with. There was none better when it came to training. Fordy's at his best when he's sprung from the bench, like the Munster final in '97 when his wonder goal won the game for us. Afterwards, I said to Len, 'Jesus how did you leave David Forde loose?' He answered, 'I was afraid of my life that Jamesie would come in from the wing and score a goal and that would be the end for us.' It was a lucky break which we made the most of. Sometimes you have to think on your feet.

RULE EIGHT: ATTENTION TO DETAIL

In Loughnane's playing days, the story of Clare hurling in Championship games alternated between the admirable and exasperating: a mixture of sometimes honourable failure and Sunday afternoons on which the supporters could find nothing to praise but the weather. On one of those days, Loughnane learned a lesson he would never forget.

In the League final replay in '76, I was marking Billy Fitzpatrick. At one stage the ball was in the far corner with Mick Brennan. Billy took off down the wing. I said to myself, 'I'll let him off, I'll chance it.' Billy caught the ball coming across the square and stuck it in the net! The lesson stays firmly in my mind to this day. You can never take a chance against a good team. One moment of laziness can be the losing of a match.

Hurling is an inexact science, but as Clare manager Loughnane planned to keep the inexactitudes to a minimum. One of the most interesting discoveries of a trawl through his records is a set of notebooks which contain his personal ratings for each player for each game in each year.

Very often, training can be deceptive because you can forget that a guy flying in training may not have done it where it really mattered, which is in matches. People judge things over the short term, how a player played in his last match. I gave each player a rating out of ten after every game. Coming up to the Championship, I was able to look back over the entire season to see who had done what. Then, at the end of the year, just for my own curiosity I'd add them all up to see who came out as the player of the year. It was usually very tight between four or five players.

In accepting the Clare job, Loughnane knew that his job would have more to do with hard work on raw evenings than afternoons of triumph at Croke Park. Demonstrating again the spirited optimism that is essential to a modern hurling manager, he felt that to be given charge of a bunch of players like this was a small miracle that warmed and brightened the whole of his existence. Winter training was an important ingredient of Clare's success, but there were times when his players were the victims of such inclement weather that the most robust dog-sled teams would want to remain inside.

Exuding a vitality that helped ignite others, Loughnane had a fantastic capacity to take a training session and get players to train very hard and at the same time enjoy it. Every training session was planned to the last minute, and it was always clear he knew what he was doing. This gave added confidence to the players.

Attention to detail was crucial to our success but I didn't emphasise being spot on time in training. Players get caught in traffic and so on, so laying down strict laws about it was absolutely crazy. The only objection I had to players being late was that they were missing out on the warm-up.

Attention to detail was most important on the day of Championship games. I think no international soccer team planned their day better than we did. The planning depended on where we were. If it was Croke Park, most people say: 'ye're 150 miles away, ye have to travel the night before', but we never did. We always ensured that the players stayed in their own beds the night before. On Sunday morning, we met at 8 a.m. at a hotel in Shannon. I always made a point of almost bouncing out of the car, and always gave the message that I was really fresh and had slept very well, even if I hadn't slept at all. Tony Considine would come whistling along and tell a few jokes. Everything was upbeat. You were giving off positive energy straight away. We then got a bus to the airport where Pat Fitz had everything arranged. There was no checking in. All that was done the night before. The bus took us straight to the plane ramp. Nobody else was allowed travel on the plane. When the plane landed in Dublin, a bus was waiting for us on the runaway and it took us straight away to the hotel. We always had breakfast at 10 a.m.

Then the players went to bed for two hours. I always had two to a room, with two players who were playing near one another on the pitch like Dalo and Ollie Baker, or an inexperienced player with an experienced one. We usually put an inexperienced forward with Jamesie. It was always a sign someone was going to play if they were in the room with Jamesie. We'd ask Jamesie when they came down if the other player slept and was all right. This also happened when we went to Cork.

Lohan and Mike O'Halloran are as close friends as people can be. They always roomed together but in '98, Hallo didn't make the team. Brian Lohan came to me and said, 'Hallo isn't playing. I want to be in the room with somebody who is playing.' Lohan will be best man at Hallo's wedding, but this was business. It showed how professional Lohan was.

After the rest we went out on to the field for a puck around. This was when we closely observed the players to see who was sluggish and who was looking lively. Very often, this was what decided who would play. This is where the build-up to the game would start. Mike would start off with a slow warm-up and stretching exercises. Then I would take over with a short meeting, reminding them of what was ahead and the challenge we faced. Then we would hurl at half-pace, building up to three quarters and finally, 30 seconds at full pace. Daly would then take them on a lap of the pitch – all closely knit together with Dalo and all the other natural leaders on the team laying it on the line. By the time the lap was finished, everyone was ready for the battle. We went back to the hotel. We had calculated exactly how many minutes it took to get to the ground so that we wouldn't have too much time in the dressing-room. Every eventuality was catered for.

Loughnane was adept at picking up the tiniest clue about the opposition's weaknesses and using it to the team's advantage.

Offaly had defeated Kilkenny in the Leinster final in '95. I think it was the game of the nineties. Offaly were tremendous. They were so good they'd frighten you. The All-Ireland semi-finals that year were a double header on a scorcher of a day. We were playing Galway. They were only playing Antrim, but they looked totally exhausted. I was talking to Brian Whelahan afterwards and he was totally jaded. He said, 'It was very hot out there.' That told me they weren't fit enough. We knew we had an advantage there.

There were times when Loughnane's attention to detail led to unorthodox practices.

In 1997, we had 16 players in the photo before the All-Ireland. One of the best ways of raising money was selling the All-Ireland team photo. Our objective was to destroy the chances of people selling unofficial photos and making a fortune for themselves. It rendered the photo useless for them.

In '95, five days after the All-Ireland, a guy from Tipperary came to my home, not realising who lived there, selling a plate with a picture of the Clare team on it and the score of the match. People cleaned up selling clocks and all kinds of mementoes. In '97, we decided we weren't going to let that happen again. We were always scheming and trying to stay one step ahead of the posse, be it officials, journalists or anybody else. When one avenue was cut off, we found another one.

Loughnane's attention to detail was also highlighted by his tendency to always have a Plan B. Given his often fraught relationship with the GAA authorities, such contingency plans were occasionally necessary.

In the '98 All-Ireland semi-final against Offaly, I had received a one match ban from the sideline for previous 'offences'. On the morning of the game, I asked Pat Fitz in the lobby of the airport hotel if it was okay for me to go out on the pitch before the match. He thought it would be okay, but I told him to make sure because I needed to know before the game. As we were travelling on the bus to Croke Park, I got a call from Pat telling me that I wasn't going to be let out. I said, 'You tell them that unless I'm let out on the pitch they're not going to get a team sheet.' They knew that the team announced wasn't going to be the real team. I said nothing to Tony, Mike Mac or any of the players. After we got to the *dressing-room, Seán O'Laoire, a prominent official in the GAA, with three men in green jackets stuck his head inside the door and asked for the team sheet. I answered, 'Get the f**k out.' We went into the warm-up, and just as I was about to give the team talk Pat Fitz came in and said I could go on the pitch before the game if I gave them the team sheet. I said that was fine. It was brinkmanship, but it was vital for me to keep the link with the players on the pitch right up to the throw-in and in so doing keep the distance between them and the crowd. This is the routine they were used to, and I wasn't going to allow it to be breached by any official. I wouldn't have given them the team if I hadn't been let out.*

If it had come to the crunch, how far would he have pushed the issue?

I went up to the stand for the game but nothing was going to stop me from getting on the field before the match. If they said no, I was going to put on a helmet and a track-suit and walk out behind the team!

A Bird's Eye View, Loughnane, flanked by Colin Lynch and Brian Lohan shares a last-minute chat with Tony Considine before the first chapter of the Offaly trilogy.

The other two rules of leadership are the building and maintenance of a team and motivation. As these issues are so central, to the success of the Loughnane project we will consider them separately in the two following chapters.

4

There's No Me in Team

In the All-Ireland semi-final against Galway in 1995, Brian Lohan damaged his hamstring. He was on Joe Cooney and Cooney had got a couple of points off him. I went down to the sideline and looked at him. I did more than look at him I needn't tell you! He started to hurl out of his skin. Lohan said afterwards, 'I saw Loughnane coming down the sideline and decided it was time to start hurling!'

In the All-Ireland final that year, with about 20 minutes to go, he pulled a hamstring and he gave a signal. We had built up such an understanding that at any time, whether it was in a dressing-room or out on the field, a look was all it took. There was no need for words most of the time. It was the look, and especially how you sent the look, that sent the message, especially with players like Daly, Seánie, Lohan and Doyler. It showed the terrific understanding there was between everybody and that applied with the selectors as well.

Colm Flynn said to me, 'Jesus, his hamstring is gone!'

'Tell him, he's not f**king coming off', I replied and turned my back and walked in the other direction. Colm went in and broke the news to Brian. No reaction whatsoever. He just got on with it and pretended nothing was wrong with him. When you talk about mental toughness, what Lohan did in the All-Ireland was out of this world. It would never happen in soccer. If a player pulls his hamstring in soccer, the stretcher is brought in and there's a big exit. In the last 20 minutes, he used his head, stayed goalside of John Troy and whoever else came on him and played away with a torn hamstring. He wasn't able to train for three months afterwards. For those last 20 minutes, he held out by sheer guts. For a Clare player to do that in an All-Ireland final was incredible and said everything about the difference between the team I played on and the team I managed. There's no way I'd

have done that when I was playing. Lohan got through it by cutting down the angles. It was a measure of his courage and his intelligence. He used his head to survive with a torn hamstring. He was willing to go through the pain barrier because the team needed him to do so.

As a manager, Ger Loughnane's single greatest achievement was the creation of a team greater than the sum of its individual talents. Loughnane had a mission. Short-term solutions would remain just that. He wanted to create a team. Nothing unusual about that, but he wanted a particular type of team where selflessness was the driving force. To achieve this, he needed to create a structure that would empower everybody on the team, not only the All-Stars, to grow as individuals as they surrendered themselves to the group effort. Loughnane was as much a nurturer as a coach: rather than trying initially to inspire breathtaking flights of creativity, he was cultivating a spirit so that the players could blend together effortlessly.

Many companies spend small fortunes to be told that teamwork is a social engineering problem: take group A, add motivational technique B and achieve result C. A waste of time and money. What sport illustrates is that the key to building a team is to blend individual talent with a heightened group consciousness. Sport teaches us that we need to expand our minds and embrace a vision in which the group interest takes precedence over individual glory: to move from thinking about 'me' to thinking about 'we', because the most crucial lesson sport teaches us is that selflessness is the soul of teamwork. There is no me in team.

The Masterminds. Tony Considine, Mike McNamara and Loughnane.

The Loughnane mantra was primarily a spiritual one: seek the power of oneness instead of the power of the one. That was the secret of overcoming the cult of the star player which had ruined more gifted teams. A hurling team is like a band of warriors, a secret society with rites of initiation, a strict code of honour, and a sacred quest – the drive for an All-Ireland title. Rituals were used to accentuate the sense of oneness.

> For all the big matches, I would sit on my own, about two seats from the front, on the coach from the airport into Croke Park. All the players were at the back. Every two minutes, I'd look straight back at them but not a word would be said. Then I'd turn around again.

Hurling is a sport that involves the subtle interweaving of players at full throttle to the point where they are thinking and playing as one. To maximise their potential, each player must trust the other, and know instinctively how their teammates will respond in pressure situations. Even the most skilful player can only do so much on their own. If he is out of sync psychologically with the other squad members, a Munster title would remain as elusive as ever. The star players had arguably a bigger challenge: to share the spotlight with their less illustrious teammates so that the side could grow and flourish. With intuitive leaders on the team like Daly and Lohan, it was easy to spread the gospel that it was not brilliant individual displays that would make a great Clare team, but the whirlwind that would be released when players put their egos aside and work towards a common goal. The Clare team would never become a great team unless each one, without exception, surrendered the 'me' for 'we'.

Loughnane always encouraged his players to air their views, in part because it strengthened the collective mindset, the sense of 'we'. As a Clare player, that had not been his experience.

> I first played for Clare, with Enda O'Connor, against Tipperary in 1972. What struck me most when I first went into the dressing-room was that the Newmarket-on-Fergus players were on one side and the Clarecastle players on the other, and there was no communication between them. I made myself as small as I could in the middle and said nothing!

If a school report had been written on the Clare team Loughnane starred on, it would have read, 'good potential but underachieving.'

> I played on a really terrific team. It was very similar to the team that won two All-Irelands. Harry Bohan was a charismatic figure. Justin McCarthy came to coach us and both gave us a high profile. The half-back line was particularly well known. Seán Stack was centre-back, I was

on one wing and Seán Hehir on the other. We understood each other's play very well. For its time, we were a terrific half-back line, but I wouldn't compare us with the team we have now. Liam Doyle was better than me, Seánie is a better player than Seán Stack and Dalo is a better player than Seán Hehir. Seán Stack was the most talented of the three of us. He had fantastic stick work, Seán Hehir and I were more of a manufactured talent. Seán Hehir had a real hardness about him. He was a man who would get the job done and wouldn't let his man past him.

Seamus Durack was a great character. He was the very same as Fitzie, totally self-centred which you have to be if you're a goalkeeper. He's had fantastic success in business and I've terrific regard for him.

The best character of all on the team was Noel Casey. He was known as 'The Case.' He'd turn up for training and he'd belt a few balls into the net from the 21 yard-line. He hardly ever did any serious training but he got vital scores for Clare in big matches. He had this charismatic personality that drew people to him. Harry and himself got on great. If it was another person in charge, he'd be dumped out the gate and never get another chance, but he was a character every one really, really liked.

Jackie O'Gorman was an inspirational figure. He was the first Clare player I ever met who was always totally confident. He would talk down an opponent's strengths to the degree that you'd think you were playing a Junior B player of 44.

Most of the rest of us were the one age like the two O'Connors and John Callinan. John had lightning pace and was a great man to score a point. He played a lot of great matches for Clare but although he was terrifically talented he had the same hang-ups as your normal Clare hurler at the time. He didn't have the inner arrogance you need. He's a brilliant person, with the highest ability and he is an exceptional administrator.

Loughnane was determined that the Clare team he managed would not underachieve. Some mentors feel threatened when players start asserting their independence, but he felt it was much more effective to open up the decision-making process to everybody. Each match brought its unique challenges and there were no automatic answers. Moreover, the players had their own tactical nous because they were right in the thick of the action and could pick up instinctively the opposition's strengths and weaknesses.

Clare players were required to look through a less self-centred lens and Loughnane had to understand the situation from their point of view.

Otherwise he would have to spend his time babysitting fragile egos. He needed to turn his players into dreamers, to expand their vision of their potential achievement. He taught them that to be a good team member was more important than trying to be heroic individually. The team he managed would be smarter, more alert, and much less easily intimidated than the team he played on, which produced some occasionally dazzling but infuriatingly inconsistent hurling. The muddy pitch at Crusheen, an unlikely repository of sporting dreams, was the setting for an epiphany where the spirit of the team he managed took form over the severe winter training. The players' lives were dictated by the rhythms of training. On a soggy, mucky training pitch, the mystery of life was played out night after night. Everybody literally mucked in.

Given the commitment required, Gaelic games at the highest level are increasingly young men's games, and even more so single men's games. The team transformed before his eyes, invigorated by the cult of the 'we'. Loughnane's views on teamwork were shaped by his experience coaching at under-age level.

I was a totally different person as a player than when I managed a team. In my playing days, I never pulled any big tricks. I always tried to out-think my opponents and outhurl them but from the very first time I was put in charge of a team at school level, I just became a totally different person. When I was a player, I just had to think of one person. When I became a manager, I had to think for 15 people at the one time. I found myself playing every ball, making every tackle and arguing every decision.

I first got a taste of managing from a schools team in Shannon. I remember once we were playing in Newmarket. The referee, a teacher from the other school, got so annoyed with me that he threw the whistle over the line and walked off the field! He said, 'I've enough of this lunatic', and disappeared!

I then became involved with Wolfe Tones at Shannon where we had brilliant days at under-age level. Having won numerous under-age competitions, I set my sights on winning the under-12 county championship in Clare. I then trained them for two years, winter and summer, with the aim of winning the All-Ireland under-14 championship. At the end of June each year, the Feile na Gael under-14 championship is held. It is a totally underrated competition. This is, in effect, an All-Ireland championship with the under-14 champions from each county taking part. Matches are run off over one weekend. It is a fantastic experience for young players, their parents and their clubs. In

1986, it was held in Clare for the first time. We set our sights on becoming the first Clare side to win the competition, especially as it was being held within the county, and we won.

During the competition, people would make a point of watching us play. We played a very similar game to the Clare senior hurling team in '95. It was a war of attrition. You closed down the opposition, you crossed the ball, you followed your own man and you were totally disciplined. That was the essence of it. It was really picture book stuff.

None of them ever became great inter-county players, but when they played together as a team, they were absolutely unbeatable. It gave me this idea that with any good group of players, you could have success if you developed them properly. That's where I started, but the referee and the mentors on the other team suffered listening to me!

Loughnane knew that no leader can create a successful team alone. Each member of the squad, regardless of whether they were a fringe player or the most august member of the celebrity contingent, should feel that their voice counted. Unity could not be imposed from the top down but must be won at the level of hearts and minds. In the Loughnane system, anyone could shoot, anybody could score, anybody could make the pass. The system facilitated anyone with an available opportunity. This required the manager to be very sensitive to non-verbal communication, to pick up the subtle messages that players sent out and pick up the subtext in the silence between the words.

My son, Barry, worked in a pub up the road. A new manager came in and brought all the staff together and said, 'We're all a team now.' They only laughed at him. You can't go into a crowd and say, 'We're a team.' You have to build a team. You build with blocks. When all the blocks are together you have the house.

When you are building a team, you build the players individually. You build their confidence. You show you have confidence in them. You motivate them individually and then, when you have them individually motivated, you can start with the collective effort.

That's where so many companies make their mistake. They bring in their whizz-kids who have charts and videos on what motivation is. Afterwards, everyone comes out feeling very good but it's not lasting. A house is only lasting if the blocks are well built. That's how you build a team. You get a link between them, but first of all, you build up every individual to be strong. It is literally building a team. Going into a dressing-room saying 'we are a team' gets you nowhere. You then find a thread to bind the team together and you make that thread stronger and stronger and the strength of that thread will eventually decide how good a team you have.

It's not as simple as people think. All the quick-fix solutions people come up with are rubbish. They'd be better off if they attended to the individual needs of the workers. Take, for example, a worker whose wife is sick. You tell him take the day off and come back when she's better. When he comes back, he might work twice as hard. If he doesn't, and you know he's useless, get rid of him. If any player ever betrayed my trust, he was out the gate, and not alone out the gate but well punished.

HALLO

Increasingly, the Ireland of the Celtic Tiger places a high premium on individual achievement. Against such a backdrop, it would be easy for players to be blinded by their own importance and abandon their fierce interconnectedness, the essence of teamwork. Though fans might tell players how good they were, the media can be the most alluring temptress of them all, turning heroes into superheroes. The Clare boss was never going to let that happen.

What the Clare team needed was an unshakable desire to win that would reach to every corner of their bodies and souls. There are a number of variables that dictate a team's level of performance: one of them was fitness. Loughnane decided that was not going to be a factor for the Banner. Clare were simply going to be the fittest team in the country. Another variable is the ability of a team to rise to the big occasion. Loughnane and his mentors sought to eliminate this from the equation by seeking out a particular type of player – men who would respond to pressure in the correct sort of way.

It was all very well for him to have his own idealised vision of how the team should play, but he was pragmatic enough to know he had to work with what he had got. Otherwise, the Loughnane project was doomed to failure. Unless the team, built on rich talent though it was, took ownership of the plan, everyone – above all the manager himself – would end up with shattered dreams. However, his vision was based on a brutally candid assessment of his available resources.

We looked into what was there already to see who would fit into the category of what we regarded was needed for county level: total commitment, dedication, athleticism, a desire to achieve, a willingness to listen and above all mental toughness, the sort of player who could withstand any kind of aggravation or anything that is thrown at them. We felt that if we had that, we could mould them into a team. You can develop the skill of a player over two years if he's got the right attributes. The only thing that really annoyed us was when players started making excuses. Once you start making excuses, you're on a rocky road. They knew we had no interest in excuses.

When you think of Tipperary, you think of their tradition. When you think of the great Cork and Kilkenny teams of the past, they all had identity. We wanted to have an identity. We wanted men who would stand up and be counted – men who would make something happen and not wait for things to happen. That's why we chose players like Baker, Fergie Tuohy, Conor Clancy, Colin Lynch and Michael O'Halloran who had been left out by other people. We knew they would stand up. Talent is not everything. The only thing that really endures is character.

The only way you can test that out is on the training field in order to see who will survive and who will buckle. When you see anybody buckling in training, you know they will buckle when the big day comes. It's as simple as that. That's as true a law as the law of gravity. That's why when the games were on in training, if someone went down injured, the game went on. There was no notice taken. It was up to them to get help from the sideline or get up again. It was all about breeding that real toughness that would be needed when the Munster matches came on – something that Clare were lacking for years and years.

There is no doubt but there was never any defence better than that Clare defence at their best, because of the way they covered for each other and the telepathic communication between them. If you add up the total score they conceded against great forwards, it was very, very low. The defence, Fitzie and midfield were the foundation stones of our success.

Mike O'Halloran typified the type of man we were looking for – who made us the team we were. When he got injured, it was the greatest loss to Clare of all time. He had gone to school in the Comprehensive school in Shannon and they'd gone on to the Harty Cup final where they played Flannans. Many of them were the lads I had as under-14s in Shannon – but two subs on that team were Hallo and Brian Lohan.

The first time I met Hallo was when he came into Flannans for an under-21 trial. He was marking Jamesie, and Jamesie went to town on him, and Mike was never heard of for a good while. Then in '94, I'd heard that he was playing really well for Sixmilebridge and brought him onto the Clare panel. He played in front of his own crowd in Sixmilebridge against Kilkenny in a League match. It was the hardest possible start for him and he didn't play well. The following Sunday we played Kerry in a tournament and he lined out at corner-back and he was absolutely brilliant. I told him, 'Now you're right.'

He was very friendly with Brian Lohan and they formed an understanding between them that was almost telepathic. They could cover for each other unbelievably well. He was the sort of person that would do whatever had to be done for Clare to win and I like that sort of player. When all around were losing their heads, he'd keep ice cool. He had an assassin-like mentality.

In 1997, players, wives and girlfriends all had flown up on the plane the morning of the All-Ireland. The bus driver had taken all the gear back to the hotel we were going to stay in that night. I told the players to meet at 12.30 to go down for a puckout. When the time came, the bus driver still wasn't back. I said, 'Where's the f**king bus!' Hallo stopped me and said, 'Stay calm. It's only a short walk. We'll walk down.' That's the calm type of person he was.

When he went off the Clare team in '98 the full-back line was never the same, even though the players who came in for him did great jobs. A lot of people said he should never have been there in the first place because his skill level was limited, but he could do what had to be done. He was the unsung hero. I've the greatest regard for him as a person and for what he did for Clare. One night in training, he got a terrible accidental belt from a hurley which went through his helmet and his hurling was never the same after that.

Frank Lohan was another unsung hero for a while, but not any more. He's the best left corner-back I've ever seen playing. He's not good anywhere else, but he's an expert in that position because of the way he can cover back. He's like the boy with his finger in the dyke.

THE DUMMIES

It has long been part of the culture of big GAA games that spectators gather to watch a match to hear the famous 'fógra' and discover that a star player has recovered from an injury, in a miracle of Biblical proportions, and is to take the place of A.N. Other despite all the media stories to the contrary. Loughnane took the deception a step further by announcing dummy teams.

Nothing characterised the team spirit better than the switching of teams before games. There were articles written in papers about how their families felt and all this kind of rubbish. To me that was utter nonsense. The whole dynamic driving the squad and those of us on the sideline was that each of us would do everything possible for Clare to win. When we switched around teams before games, everybody understood that. We used every tactic possible to outwit the opposition in order to win.

Everyone on the panel understood that. It was the people outside the panel who didn't understand.

The idea of the dummy teams came about from the temperament of certain players who, if they knew they were expected to play, would get nervous and over-excited and not do themselves justice on the big day. We had a meeting before the '97 All-Ireland final and someone said we can't start Niall Gilligan because he started against Cork in the Munster semi-final, played poorly and was taken off. We decided that we'd get around that by not naming him on the original selection – so that he'd be on but wouldn't be on!

It worked really well with Gilligan. He was going to be on Paul Shelly who had a big reputation and everyone would be telling him what Shelly would do to him. He didn't know he was going to be playing 'til a few hours before the game which meant that he was so unfazed by the occasion that he scored two points before Shelly knew where he was. Niall was very young and inexperienced and maybe if he had known he was playing he wouldn't have performed as well.

Also, if you have a hot, sunny day when the game is going to be very fast, it will suit a certain type of player, so picking your team on the Tuesday night when you don't know the conditions is absolutely nonsensical to me.

The dummy teams worked so well that we decided to use it for other players. After a while, the players started to like it, because they knew that any combination of six forwards out of nine would play. This meant that everybody had hopes of playing until the day came. Often, I didn't tell the players until we had the puckout who was on and who was off. It worked extremely well and never caused dissension except that one time with Colin Lynch. I always said that once they had a good game from the start, you could let them go. After Gilligan played well in the '97 final, you could pick him from the start.

SUBBING THE SUBS

Team sport requires individuals to surrender their self-interest for the greater good. The Clare players understood that winning meant giving up something for themselves so that the team could triumph. All were prepared to sacrifice themselves for the betterment of the team. Winning a Munster title, let alone an All-Ireland, was a prize that surpassed individual stardom. The Clare project was teamwork in its purest form. It was not enough to have players who wanted to win: they had to be prepared to do what it takes.

Not alone did the men from the Banner play better and win more, they also became more attuned with each other. The collective satisfaction they experienced working in harmony in itself provided a more potent motivating force because it came from within each and every one of them. It was not dependent on the demented coach screaming from the sidelines.

Loughnane broke the mould in many areas. One was in his use of substitutions. There was no room for sentiment. Players not performing were taken off very early in matches. It was not uncommon for players who came on as substitutes to themselves be substituted later on, sometimes very quickly, notably Danny Scanlan in the third match against Offaly in 1998.

> *All egos had to be subordinate to the good of the team. For Clare, to win was the only thing that was important. When the game was over, all the paraphernalia had no appeal whatsoever for me. All that mattered was what happened on the field. Winning was everything.*

> *My concentration on the '97 All-Ireland was such that I never even knew there was a big screen in Croke Park. I didn't notice it, but if a player wasn't doing his business on the field I noticed it quickly and he was gone. What would be the point of having him on and to have us lose? It was better for him to come off and we win. It was part of the deal that you had to sacrifice all interest in personal glory for the good of the team. There was nothing personal whatsoever about it. It was for the team and that was it. It wasn't an outing, or a social gathering. It was about going out to win a battle.*

In 1999, a desperate throw of the dice would yield a positive outcome. For many Clare fans, Jamesie O'Connor has somehow been transformed from a great athlete to a sports deity. Poet Paul Durcan once said that Cork hurling star Charlie McCarthy was a 'poet' and that his hurling was 'poetry in motion'. He might have said the same about Jamesie.

A thrillingly precocious talent in St Flannans, he would become his county's principal source of creativity. All-Ireland finals are often settled by explosions of effectiveness and nobody exploded more lethally or plundered more consistently than Jamesie. His mesmeric wanderings flummoxed many a defence and neutralised many a tactical plan drawn up to sabotage Clare's domination. You can teach a player many things but you cannot transmit natural talent. Jamesie's effortlessly exquisite touch, his blazing pace and the fluency of his every movement unfailingly troubled opposing defences. He was a forward who could consistently promise to fill the minds of hurling fans with glittering memories and delivered on that promise with a series of sublime performances. In 1999, like a beleaguered army greeting the hero who brings relief, the Clare players responded to Jamesie.

I would say that most of the substitutions we made were for the better. If there was anything I think we were really good at, it was making tactical changes during a game. We could improvise really well.

Bringing on Jamesie against Galway in the 1999 All-Ireland quarter-final was a psychological thing more than anything else. He had made a marvellous physical recovery from his injury, but was far from right. It was dire straits. We were nine points down and struggling in a lot of positions. When he came on, it was the effect he had on other players that ignited the whole scene and produced the final 25 minutes of absolutely electrifying hurling. Looking back though, at that stage we were well past our best.

STAR SYNDROME

Loughnane's dream was not just to win. Winning is ephemeral. It is wonderful but it doesn't make life any easier. You have to return to the training field and start all over again. Without a tightly-knit team, that was like inventing the wheel each time. He knew instinctively that the only way to win again and again was to give everybody, from the national stars to the last sub on the panel, a vital role in the squad, and inspire them to be acutely aware of the task that was demanded, even when the spotlight was on somebody else.

Of course, Clare had its stars. Seánie McMahon, for example, strode the turf like a giant, devouring yardage with a massive stride and terminating attacks with tackles of jolting finality. The capacity to amass epic performances while remaining stylishly fluent, apparently immune to the exhaustion engulfing others, came naturally to him. In attack he had verve and inventiveness and there were times it seemed that his determination alone would be enough to guarantee Clare a triumph.

When it comes to forward firepower, the big battalions of hurling are probably based elsewhere, though Jamesie O'Connor's name would have to feature prominently in any speculation about the greatest forwards available in hurling. O'Connor apart, the one element of the Clare forwards' armoury that was conspicuously unreliable was their capacity to crown their magnificent teamwork with scoring finishes. It was the one component of their game where their standards could swing from the woeful to the wonderful. Although they dominated matches for substantial periods, they could not put away the opposition in the ebb and flow of action the way their possession entitled them to.

When Clare won the All-Ireland in 1997, they were the first team to win it without scoring a goal in the final since Tipperary defeated Dublin by a single point 0–16 to 1–12 in 1961. How does Loughnane react to critics who said that the Clare team did not have enough class in the forward line apart from Jamesie O'Connor?

> *That's probably a fair point, but they're missing one other outstanding forward, the Sparrow. His physical strength is that of a 14-year-old, but nobody could measure his courage – not to talk of the skill and the killer finishing instinct he had. The Sparrow was a truly great forward. I'd put him on any dream team as an outstanding forward. He was indispensable to the Clare team.*

Although Loughnane had the highest regard for the Sparrow's abilities as a player, it was not all mutual admiration on the training field.

> *He could be cranky and abrasive. We had frequent set-tos in training. I would totally dismiss his complaints, but it was all forgotten when the game was over. He was competitive to the point of peevishness. He was ruthless, clever, ambitious and had terrific self-confidence. He should be a great businessman.*

One incident encapsulates the qualities Loughnane valued in his star forward.

> *He had the heart and courage of a lion. He played for us once with cracked ribs. In the Munster semi-final in 1997 against Cork in Limerick, we were going to take off Stephen McNamara. The next thing PJ O'Connell grabbed the ball over near the sideline and sent it in towards the goal. The Sparrow got it, but a Cork player struck him with his hurl right into his balls. It was the greatest act of courage I ever saw on a hurling field. The Sparrow was bent over with pain, and had to go the hospital with the injury after the match, but he still had the presence of mind to pass the ball to Stephen Mac. Stephen still had a lot of work to do to get the goal. He had a striker's instinct for goal. It was a wonderful score, but if it happened two minutes later, Stephen would have been off. The goal won the match but it could have been disaster.*

> *I don't mind people saying that the Sparrow and Jamesie were the only two regular forwards we had. Teamwork was the essence of our success – everybody working for each other, no matter who came on. Everybody knew what their job was. On the big day, everybody said what would*

happen if Jamesie had an off day, but he had one in the '95 All-Ireland final and we still won. Jamesie got us to the final but others won it for us.

One day, Conor Clancy would be great, another day PJ O'Connell, another Fergie Tuohy. Niall Gilligan can still develop, but he hadn't the assassin-type mentality of the Sparrow, nor the skill of Jamesie when I was there.

That is what a team is about, everybody working hard, so that eventually the break will come and someone will score. That was the basis on which we played. I agree totally we didn't have the perfect team, but what does that matter? It made it even better that our teamwork won five major titles.

CAPTAIN FANTASTIC

During a game, communication between the line and the field is almost impossible because of the noise. Loughnane had to rely on his players for leadership on the field. In this context, two key players were Anthony Daly because of his unbelievable, unwavering self-confidence and Brian Lohan with his massive work ethic. While Loughnane provided the leadership off the pitch, and there were a number of natural leaders on it, it was essential that the players could speak through one voice whenever there was a grievance. Again, Loughnane had learned the lessons from the way players were treated in his time.

When we were in Dublin, Johnny Callinan and myself would have to pay our train fare home and then try to get it back from the county board. That was a really tough battle. We learned to wait 'til the treasurer had five or six pints in him to ask him for the money! It was absolutely terrible. They wanted you down to play but they didn't want to pay for it!

Anthony Daly was the natural choice to be the team's spokesman. As a player, he deserved all the plaudits heaped upon him with a string of performances as captivating as the sport can offer. Opposing him in top form was like trying to defy a succession of breaking waves. Whenever danger lurked, he responded like a wounded lion. Daly had to be what he was, an excellent craftsman with a superb fighting spirit and the stamina of body and mind to cope with the long haul. While his famous speeches and innate media skills might have seemed to be his obvious credentials, Loughnane chose him for his ability in the dressing-room, given his flair to help players cope with frustration and disappointment. Dalo was adept at deflecting any anger by giving his teammates a chance to air their complaints.

Dalo knew moves before everybody else. I'd say there was never an occasion when Dalo didn't know who was really playing when we put out dummy teams. He was never told but he always knew.

If there ever was a grievance, Dalo would come to me. It was sorted out immediately. The players were treated exceptionally well which was the best way to prevent grievances from arising, but if they did come up, we dealt with them straight away. The fact that we had a holiday fund committee meant that we could do things for them that other counties couldn't do.

Never was Daly's role as captain more clearly illustrated than in the Munster final in '95.

Everybody in Clare was convinced that we had no chance of winning that game because two weeks before we had played Galway in a challenge match in Shannon. It was on a glorious, sunny day, and the previous day had been the very same. When we were inside in the dressing-room, I noticed that some of our players were sunburnt and I said, 'What the f**k were ye doing? Two weeks before the Munster final and ye come here sunburnt.' Clare were disastrous. Most of the crowd that were there went home at half-time, thinking we hadn't a chance in the Munster final. When the team came into the dressing-room, I gave them a fierce lambasting. We trained very well after that. On the day of the final, we stopped in the hotel in Cashel for a cup of tea. You could tell that it was very promising and that they were in terrific form.

We were on the way into Thurles and just as we came to the bridge, we could see the place was crowded with Limerick supporters. A few of them shouted at us, 'What a waste of time.' They were sure they were going back to the All-Ireland final. Straight away, Daly said, 'We'll f**king show ye whether it's a waste of time or not.' That had a crucial bearing. It was just the sort of little spark that the players really needed to liven them up. As everybody got off the bus, there wasn't a word. As the players went out of the dressing-room, I said to Pat Fitzgerald, 'If Clare don't win today we're never going to win anything.' Everything was just right. The rest is history, but the incident on the bus showed Daly's sharpness of mind. Top marks to him for picking it up. A small thing like that can make a big difference.

It is impossible to spend longer than ten minutes talking about Clare hurling with Loughnane without recognising the enormous admiration he has for Anthony Daly. Yet he had no hesitation about dropping him from the captaincy when he felt it was right for the team.

Cyril Lyons had come in for 2000. I was very conscious of making a transition to a new phase in Clare's history so that the changeover wouldn't be too dramatic. Apart from that, it is good from time to time to make a change. The big problem with a lot of teams is that they don't make changes either on the team or in the management in time.

Definitely, the time had come to make a few changes on the team and freshen up things. When I told Dalo I wanted to make a change in the captaincy he said, 'If you think it's for the best, that's fine.' It was no problem whatsoever. There was no drama.

In 1999, I faced a more difficult situation when I had to tell the Sparrow he would no longer be on the panel. He just said, 'I better bail out so.' That was it. When Brian Lohan became captain, Dalo still had as big an input as ever on match days. It wasn't like rugby where only the captain speaks. It was a co-operative thing. In the 10-minute warm-up, maybe eight or nine players, like Seánie, Dalo, Lohan, Jamesie and Liam Doyle would speak, but it would only be two or three sentences. That continued on. It was part of the ritual. Everybody had a say. That's the benefit of having so many leaders on the team and giving them the scope to take on responsibility.

SIMPLY THE BEST

Brian Lohan was the obvious choice as the new captain. When Lohan flexed that indomitable amalgam of physical strength and spiritual leadership, resilience and courage were never going to be a problem for the team. They could keep out teams that had superior firepower with the strength of one collective will. The players admired Lohan because not alone was he the impregnable fortress on the Clare backline, he was as tough as iron and steadfastly loyal.

I know that, in the fullness of time, Lohan will become a legendary character, even more than he already is. The characteristics he showed, the nerve for the big occasion, the intelligent play – I've never seen a full-back like him. In all aspects of his life, he's ambitious. He's driven to succeed but he is a totally calm, calculating person. His good points are too numerous to mention but anyone who has seen him play knows what they are. He is simply the best.

Loughnane's track record at predicting the future is impressive given his prophecy that Clare would win the Munster final in 1995. He makes one prediction with complete confidence.

The right manager for Clare is the man they have now. Cyril was the crucial appointment to bridge the gap to a new era while still having experience of the old. He needs a good, long term to put his own stamp on the team. I have no doubt, though, but Dalo will definitely be the manager of Clare some day. It doesn't always follow that a great captain makes a great manager. Steve Bruce was a brilliant captain with Manchester United but will he be a great manager? Dalo has all the attributes you need and will be a good manager in time. You need that bit of maturity. There are a number of potential managers on the current team like Seánie and Lohan. I know that from now on if Clare have the players, they will always have the proper manager.

LOUGHNANE LIGHT

Loughnane was looking for a bond between his players that went way beyond solidarity on the field. He wanted what might be grandiosely described as a psychic fusion on the field so that everyone would be aware of the other's situation and be ready to immediately cover up any deficiencies or exploit any opportunities.

Timidity is not part of Loughnane's nature! Although he could, and often did give speeches that would terrify Hannibal Lecter, he could also bring a touch of humour to proceedings. Some of his happiest memories are not of the glory days in Croke Park but of the training pitch.

Some of the best games we had were when there was no audience there. It is something that will only be remembered by the players. We had great fun. It was like a family. We all rallied together.

There were moments which provided the cue for Loughnane to show the softer and more mischievous side of his nature.

In '95, we went to Thurles to train on the pitch ten days before the Munster final. The man who normally supplied food to us after training gave us his van to take food down to Thurles with us. I volunteered to take the van, which may not be the cleverest idea as I had never driven a van before! I had my son, Barry, with me and we were to pick up Frank Lohan on the way. We collected Frank and put Barry in the back of the van which was nothing but a freezer, because all the food was frozen. When we got to Tipperary town, we stopped because it was so hot, and we decided to get a cool drink. We went back and opened the door for Barry. He was nearly frozen alive!

We were flying as we trained in Thurles. There was a kind of carnival atmosphere. When it was all over, I brought them into the middle of the field and said, 'Right lads, look around at all the seats. When we come here on Sunday week, it will be the very same, except all those seats will be full of faces, voices and noise, but it means f**k all. All that matters is *that patch of grass in here. When ye come back on Sunday week, imagine there's nothing here but noise, and out here is where all the action takes place.'*

On the way home, we had a race back to Shannon between us in the van and Jamesie and Seánie in another car. It was that kind of atmosphere that lightened up the whole thing in the run-up to the Munster final.

Loughnane was adept at turning any unusual situation into an opportunity for a good laugh.

Before the All-Ireland in '97, our team sponsor, Pat O'Donnell, made a presentation to the panel and management. He gave each of us a blue and yellow towel and tiny silver bell. The morning of the All-Ireland, Tony Considine was fuming. 'The dye from that f**king towel ran. I'm f**king blue all over.' He was quickly told, 'It wasn't the dye from the towel that ran. It was the dye from your hair!'

TUTS

The Clare team was not short of personalities who could lighten the mood in the dressing-room. There were times when Loughnane found it to be a mixed blessing.

Fergal 'Tuts' Tuohy was a real character, though not one that would always endear himself to me or me to him! He was always a sub in St Flannans, Clarecastle and Clare. He had great qualities, good physique, blinding pace and could score points from the most unusual angles at the most unexpected times. Whenever the players had time for the craic, he was always the most popular and the most wisecracking. He was great with the media because he could bring in a new angle and would be relaxed and funny.

He was infuriating at times in training. Three weeks before the '95 All-Ireland, we had a practice match. The Sparrow and Tuts were making no progress whatsoever in the game. Tuohy started acting the fool. He was playing very badly himself, but he was telling everyone else what to do. I blew the whistle. There was silence for ten seconds. Then I said, 'Tuohy and Sparrow would ye ever f**k off to the far end of the field and don't come back 'til ye're ready!' He was a bit like a talented schoolboy who had no interest in study. He was entertaining and even when he was infuriating he was still interesting. You had to keep him down, otherwise he'd take the lightness off the field, where it was welcome, onto the field where it wasn't welcome.

To wind him up to play in a big game was the most challenging thing of all. You did that by not letting him know whether he was playing. Then you let on to him that you had great suspicions about his work rate and application. He will always be remembered for scoring four points in the '95 All-Ireland. Fergie was our top scorer. He was a mountain of contradictions but, having said that, he never complained when he was dropped and he was our most dropped player. He gave a great service to Clare. When he was good, he was very good and when he was bad, you whipped him off straight away. In spite of his rebellious streak, he always realised that the team came first. There was no sulking. I liked him. He'd pass a few smart remarks but it was nothing personal.

HEGO

Tuohy had a few serious rivals for the position of clown prince of Clare hurling.

Fergal 'Hego' Hegarty came out of nowhere in 1995 from the under-21 side. If ever there was a 'made hurler', it was him. He was very athletic and his job was to win possession and move the ball on. He did massive work in '95 and '96 and was great in our first All-Ireland win. In '96 against Limerick, he was easily Clare's best player and almost held the game for us. He was chasing Ciaran Carey for that final point and only he fell, he might have stopped him.

After that, his form went completely. I still can't figure out why. I tried everything but maybe I was too cutting with him. That's always the problem with a made hurler. You knock the best out of him while you can but you know that it won't last. He's a fantastic character in a pub and is a wonderful mimic – mostly of me!

We had desperate set-tos in training as his form declined, and he was always complaining to Dalo that I was too hard on him. There was one night we nearly fell out. I was making the point that a good player needs to be a good thinker. He got his wires crossed and went to Dalo afterwards and said, 'Did you hear what he said to me? He called me a tinker'. Dalo had heard what I actually said and thought it was hilarious!

ALL FOR ONE

Loughnane and his mentors formed a cocoon around their team that was difficult to penetrate. Once the players had gelled as a unit, a powerful sense of collective identity emerged which transcended the manager's ideas or those of any individual on the team. When his team reached that state, Loughnane could step back and let the match itself provide the motivation for them. There was no real need for power pep talks when he would froth at the mouth or smash hurleys on the table. All he had to was to let them loose and let them take their place on the stage.

The real secret of the Clare success was that they had such a sense of team. Their brilliant organisation, dedicated commitment, intense concentration, defensive efficiency and rich resolution was more than a match for teams with far more glittering individual talent. Everyone loved playing with each other so much. Players accept injuries as natural punctuation in their careers, but Clare players took their place on the pitch when they could barely do more than walk. What did intense physical discomfort or pain matter? Otherwise they would miss out on something wonderful. The fear was not of being injured but of being found wanting. Their collective philosophy was an adaptation of the three Musketeers' philosophy – alone we might be nothing but together we can do anything.

Loughnane believes that the Clare team took on some of his own characteristics.

> A team reflects the coach's personality and attitude, but this takes time to build. The crucial point is that deep down the players must know you care about them. Deep down, my players knew I cared about them. I could never get away with what I did to them if they felt I didn't care. They always knew, in the long run, I was in their corner. It amazed me that we had such an adventure together and such a bond between us, and it still amazes me. So many people said and wrote so much nonsense about the secret of the Clare team but they missed the fundamental point. When you came on to the Clare panel, you ceased to be an individual and became part of a team. There was such a unity there that the players themselves didn't matter. All that mattered was the team performing to the maximum of its potential. That was the ethos all the time.

To create such a sense of team in the first place required a manager with extraordinary motivational powers who could knit wonderful, subtle talent with a ferociously competitive psyche.

5

All in the Mind

Ollie Baker was different from Anthony Daly, Seánie McMahon and Brian Lohan. They were the three front-line warriors. Ollie had no inhibitions whatsoever, which was both his strength and his weakness. They were his strength on the field, his weakness off it – because he could be easily led by other people into not taking it as seriously as he should.

Two or three weeks before the All-Ireland in '97, we arrived in Ennis one night for training. The pitch was flooded, and lucky enough we got the Gaelic Grounds in Limerick instead. It was the first time we had anybody watching because I never let anybody watch us train. If I had, they'd be going home with stories about what I said to players. If you took what I said to players literally on the training field, not alone would all the players be offended but all their relatives would never speak to me either.

Baker had been taken off in the All-Ireland semi-final. He was absolutely brutal. He needed to up his game because he's so important to Clare. In order of importance to the Clare team you would put Baker in the top three. It was vital to get a good display from him in the All-Ireland final, considering how good a team Tipp had.

One night in training, we discussed what we could do to motivate Baker for the final. We decided the three of us would berate him at every opportunity in order to bring out the stubborn streak that is in him and wind him up for a huge display in the All-Ireland. We would line up in every part of the field all during training from warm-up to the end, and one of us would be constantly on to him.

That night in Limerick, the abuse we gave him was unreal. The Limerick under-21s were training after us and they were watching us on the sidelines. Not one of them spoke among themselves. They couldn't believe *that Baker would have listened to, let alone take the abuse we gave him. I can still see the look on their faces. They were gobsmacked.*

Baker was furious, but he'd always take it. I always realised though that it was a short-term thing. You couldn't possibly keep treating a player like this, but while you had a psychological edge on him, you could do it. I always felt that he would have a short inter-county career, because he had to be pushed so hard to get the best out him.

He was vital to the success of Clare, because of his physical presence, his power, the way he guarded the whole half-back line, and above all he was totally uninhibited on the big day. The bigger the day the better. It seemed to thoroughly inspire him. He didn't care about Croke Park. He didn't care about anything. He was just the sort of player we never had in Clare when I was playing or that I never saw in Clare before.

He was brilliant in the All-Ireland final. Tipperary got a goal to go a point ahead with only minutes to go. From the puckout, Baker got the ball and stroked it over the bar. He just threw it over as if it was a training session in Cusack Park and walked away afterwards as if it was only a challenge game.

Not a man but a giant. Ollie Baker soars highest.

S ome managers walk into a dressing-room and the air goes out of it. A select few walk in and everybody starts to walk a little taller and think more boldly. Even his sternest critics, and he has many of them, would concede that Ger Loughnane had exceptional powers of motivation.

To Clare people, Loughnane is the man who brought them an orgy of trophy-collecting. For decades, they had experienced hurling misery and emptiness. The Clare team Loughnane played on could not cope with the swirl of anxieties sufficiently to concentrate on the job confronting them. The silken skills readily displayed in the League asserted themselves only sporadically, and the deep uneasiness that inhibited them betrayed itself most tellingly in the white heat of the Munster Championship. The brisk purpose, incisive surges and explosive hand speed was much less in evidence for the summer hurling. Like most glimpses of the Clare team's mental state, it was enough to make a psychiatrist lie down on her own couch with a damp flannel on her forehead.

Michael Jordan famously said, 'I've failed over and over again in my life, and that is why I succeed.' Failure can be a tremendous motivator for success, but equally it can be a self-perpetuating misery chain. One of Loughnane's biggest contributions to Clare hurling was to replace the psychology of defeat with the psychology of victory.

JEEPERS KEEPERS

Once it had fully bloomed, the Clare team was unlikely to be a wilting flower. Cultivating and nurturing it was going to be the problem. There was one player who provided a litmus test for Loughnane about his team's psychological state.

> I always judged things by David Fitz's face. His face reveals everything. When you see his face before a match you know if everybody is up for the game or not. People outside judge by the way he comes out onto the field. Whenever he bounces into the goals and draws a lash, you know everyone is up for the game. After the League final in '95, I could see Davy was very down. He had lost another final by a big score. Would it ever be any different?

Clairvoyance is one of the lesser known talents of Ger Loughnane. After losing that match, his prediction that Clare would win the Munster final was widely quoted in the media the next day. It had not been a sight to cheer the heart. If he was right, a lot of critics would have to eat their words, but for a team yet to establish a champion's credentials, this remark appeared to be a hostage to fortune.

> *That was one of the greatest flukes of all time. When we got back into the dressing room, Liam Horan of the* Irish Independent *must have been there, but I didn't see him. I didn't want any journalist to hear what I had to say.*

> *The Clare players had lost a Munster final in '93, a Munster final in '94 and a League final in '95. Even the most optimistic had their head down. Instinctively, I decided that something different had to be done.*

> *I jumped up on the table and I spoke for two minutes. I said, 'Listen, ye're all very down but this is only the League. Everyone look up at me now.' I held up my finger and pointed around the room and said, 'This year we're going to win the Munster Championship. Get that into yer heads. This year we're going to win the Munster Championship.' They all looked at me aghast! I think they picked up on the conviction in my voice but I never suspected there was a journalist in the room.*

It is difficult to keep a positive attitude in the face of criticism or negative feedback. Negatives sometimes seem more powerful than positive feedback.

> *That's what happened to Clare after the League final in '95. It reinforced all the feelings of failure even though there had been so many positives in the previous six months. They were going to be wiped out. It is very easy to lose confidence if you start to focus on the negative. When the setback came that day, I had to do something different. I couldn't allow them to leave the dressingroom the way they had left so many times before.*

Though players' passions would sway, Davy Fitzgerald was a pillar of rectitude throughout Loughnane's stewardship of the Clare team.

> *He has nerves of steel. He would never show the slightest fear in a competitive hurling situation. He would have faced a pride of starving lions. His nerve in facing John Leahy right at the death in the All-Ireland final in '97 was something to behold. He has cat-like reflexes. His save from DJ Carey's penalty in the All-Ireland semi-final in '97 was the greatest save I've ever seen. When Kilkenny got the penalty, I was right behind the goals telling our lads that they were going to stop it. DJ Carey connected with it perfectly and hit it magnificently. Ninety nine times out of 100 it would have been a goal but Davy Fitz made a stunning save. He wanted it and was defying DJ to hit it as hard as he could. In saving it, he blocked it away from his own goal so that no in-rushing forward would score on the rebound.*

Keeper of the Flame. Loughnane gives instructions to Davy Fitz before this famous save from DJ Carey.

You never had to worry about his physical and mental preparation. He has his own goalkeeping routine. The greatest saves he ever made were in training. We'd line up 20 players who would bombard him with shots. The saves he made were absolutely breathtaking. Often the saves were so good that no goal would be scored out of the 20 shots. He's been very hard-done-by in the All-Star selections. He should have got a lot more.

As a person, he is the most charming and popular of all the players, especially with young people. He's a massive ambassador for the game. Crowds gather around him and like him instantly. The contradiction is that he's totally self-centred like most goalies! His own performance was paramount.

I used to give Fitzie a desperate time in training. The very odd time he'd let in a soft goal and I'd eat him. But I'd always be killing him about his puckouts. I would never say anything quietly to a player because I wasn't just giving a message to him, I was always giving a message to the whole team. I was always in the middle of the field so everyone would hear what I said and my criticism was always laced with outrageous language.

There was one night in Cusack Park I gave him a particularly terrible time. I went with him to Castlebar in June 2001 for a golf classic and he confessed that on that night he had called me every foul name under the sun. I told him I knew that because my son, Conor, was standing behind him all night and reported everything back to me. He went pale and all he could say was, 'Oh, f**k.'

MIND OVER MATTER

Loughnane brought drive and organisational ability to the manager's job but above all else a capacity to get the best out of players. He tested players all the time to see that they were up to the job and often seemed to know exactly the right thing to do at the right time. A serious man engaged in serious business, he knew that if their self-belief was not ravaged, their collective will would still enable them to prevent 15 men, who might be better hurlers from beating them. This was a tribute to his capacity for extracting maximum effort from players with very different personalities.

He effectively made his players distinguish between self-awareness and self-consciousness. The two terms are often confused, even though they describe different states of mind. To be self-conscious means that we look at ourselves from the outside, and worry about how others see us. When we are self-aware, we do not think about the self at all, but about our role in the performance of the task.

> When Clare players went out on that field, they were not self-conscious. They didn't care what the crowd thought about them. When the game was over, self-consciousness returned, but it was the banishment of self-consciousness on the field that was crucial to our success. It meant that on the big day we could produce a big performance. The best way I can explain it is that you have to dance like there is nobody watching. That was at the heart of our success. It was all about casting off the inhibitions of the past.

> On the night before big matches, the players were relaxed. They knew that all the preparation was done. If you haven't reinforced them in the belief that they are the best prepared team, then insecurity sets in. If insecurity comes in at the last minute, then you're gone. That's what used to happen to Clare in my playing days. At the start of the year, everyone was talking about winning the All-Ireland, and just around the last training session, you'd see players beginning to shrivel and on the morning of the game you'd see them shrivel even more. If we had met the Saturday evening before a big game when I was playing, you'd have seen and felt the nerves. When the late '90s team met the night before a big match, you always believed that you were going to win.

Like Tony Blair, Loughnane continually kept his players 'on message'. Old habits were hard to break but they were the habits of losers and had to be ruthlessly eliminated. In training, the squad had to acquire new habits. Repetition was the key. It was a painstaking, time-consuming process but his players had the maturity to recognise what was needed.

They knew that the side with the greatest dedication, desire, drive, and determination invariably ends up winning.

At our next training session after losing the '95 League final win I told them I had a plan for winning the Munster title: we'd got to up the pace of our game. I always drilled that into them. We had to have a faster, faster pace. Everybody realised that the League final wasn't a normal loss. It shows this fallacy of Clare running around fields was all rubbish. Our training methods were much more sophisticated and designed to achieve a specific objective. The secret of our training sessions was that every activity and every skill was performed at a lightning pace.

The training sessions in Ennis are part of legend, mainly because nobody outside the team saw them. There would be at least two matches played a week with an intensity that you would not see in most Championship matches. There were no lineballs. If there was ever a game when the pace was slack, I stopped it straight away. I'd rather an eight-minute game at lightning pace than a 45-minute game at average pace.

People thought that fitness was all we were interested in. Much of that we orchestrated ourselves. But that was also sending a message to our own players that their physical wellbeing could never be better. There was no reason for them to fail. If you believe that you've done everything possible on the physical and mental side, that every facet is covered, that reassures their conscious mind that you've done everything. Then players just had to switch themselves on in the match and let it happen. Each player knew what to do and believed they could succeed. They were so focused on their task, there wasn't enough attention left over to worry about themselves or their problems.

Coming up to the Munster final in '95, the one thing I emphasised was that all the losses in the previous years had nothing to do with us. We were living in the now, playing in the now and we were going to win now. On the day of a big match, we could block out everything: the crowd, media and all the distractions that were the bane of Clare teams in the past. The heat of the pitch during the All-Ireland semi-final against Galway in '95 was unbelievable. Unless players could disassociate themselves from that and the noise of the crowd, they were lost.

We entered into a collective state of mind. There was an invisible link between the team, Tony, Mike, Colm and me. We saw nobody else except each other, the opposition and the field. When you enter that state, it is total freedom. Anyone from outside who tried to enter that zone was chopped off immediately. If people properly understood what we were doing, they would have understood why we didn't want media people in our zone. We had to do that to make up for the deficiencies in the team.

Nicky English has often said we had some of the greatest players that ever played the game and this is true, but we also had some very average players. When you are in this state, you see every move on the pitch in slow motion. Without that collective focus, we wouldn't have won anything, because we were often up against teams of superior talent.

Hurlers could learn to block out external criticism, but the most difficult voice to silence is internal.

The toughest voice to block out is the one inside your head. That was always the biggest problem in Clare – to blot out the voice that said, 'Ye can't win. Ye won't win.' You can only get rid of that voice when players are convinced that you absolutely believe that you will win. If you do, gradually that voice in the player's minds melts away. The old Clare wanted to win, prepared to win but they couldn't block out the voice of self-doubt. In the '97 All-Ireland final, we were four points down at half-time but we could get each other to believe we would win. It's something I'll never be able to do again, to hold a group of men in such a vice-like mental grip.

In this zone, everything else melts away. Nothing else matters. The roar of the crowd only intruded now and then. Otherwise focus was never lost. Crucial to this sense of focus was mental rehearsal. The more a plan for a big match was rehearsed ahead of time, in training and simulated match situations, the more automatic it became. This helped keep the players' minds on the task because it takes discipline to follow the plan when it really counts – when the pressure is on during the big match. You reinforce it again and again when the training session is at its height and when a player is exhausted. That's what makes him get up. You were always reminding them of who they were playing on and telling them the worst case scenario if they weren't prepared for their task.

If we were training to play Kilkenny I'd be saying to Brian Lohan when he was beaten for a ball, 'Carey will roast you if you're playing like that. He'll have three goals scored against you in the first five minutes.' Next ball that would come near him, Lohan would thunder out and clear it. That kind of mental preparation meant that they were always ready for it.

The '95 All-Ireland was a case in point. I had noticed that Offaly players were brilliant at finding a loose man whenever they were tackled. If I ever saw two players on the one man in training I'd shout, 'Get the f**k on the loose man.' There was a brilliant photo taken during the All-Ireland of Brian Lohan and John Troy going for the ball. Instead of looking at the two of them, Anthony Daly was in shot looking for the loose man. It was driven home again and again. It's not the man in possession you watch, but the loose man. That was how we kept Offaly down to 2-8 in that match. With all the talent Offaly had, that must have been a record low score of points for them.

IT'S MORE THAN WORDS

Loughnane's tonsils took great punishment during his stewardship of the Clare team as he exhorted and screamed his team to victory. For all the intensity of his passion and desire to win, he could stay calm and focused during a match and could offer a penetrating analysis of the team's performance at half-time. Never was this talent needed more than in the 1995 Munster final when Clare trailed Cork by four points and faced the wind in the second half. Loughnane defiantly told his team, 'The ship has sprung a leak but we are not going down!'

The show looked really over, especially as we had been beaten badly in the League final. I was praying for half-time. It couldn't come quick enough and I clearly remember as I spoke, Mike O'Halloran, who was as mentally tough as anyone on the team, looked at me for the first time straight in the eye. He knew immediately it wasn't the normal half-time 'Come on now, lads' speech. It struck a chord even though we went seven points down in the second half. It was if something magic had occurred – even though we were playing against the wind and Seánie broke his shoulder.

The half-time speech was central to our revival, but important as it was, going in on the pitch to drive them on was equally crucial. That was the first time the players ever saw me doing that. I can still see the look of surprise on Liam Doyle's face when he saw me coming on. I could almost see him thinking, 'Christ, there's something big going on here.' I was up and down and across the field, talking to players, encouraging them, telling them the tide had turned, and that we were going to win even though we were seven points down. This set the scene not alone for a marvellous victory but established the pattern for the years ahead.

A pensive Loughnane plans and schemes.

Loughnane had an uncanny ability to turn the most unlikely scenario into a motivational ploy.

I think Winston Churchill put his finger on the core of leadership when he said that the leader is the one who enthuses others to rally to the cause.

Morale was at an all-time low when we took over in September '94. Clare had been hammered in two consecutive Munster finals. Partly to build up morale, we went for a weekend to Kerry at the end of the following March just before the real hurling began. We had four training sessions and a match against Kerry and a bit of fun as well. We found a corner in a small pub in Killarney on the Saturday night. Everyone was drinking away and eventually a sing-song started. A night like that is so enlightening because you see another side to people's personalities. Dalo and Fergal Hegarty are brilliant singers. At about one o'clock in the morning, I was pressganged into singing a song. They all expected me to sing a silly song but I had just done a poem with the kids in school, 'The Band Played Waltzing Matilda'. I'd heard it sung by Ralph McTell and I knew the air of it, but it wasn't for the quality of the song I chose it, but because of the message I wanted to get across.

I started the song and coming to the end I stopped and said, 'Now listen carefully to the next bit. These lines are about ye coming home for the last two years after the Munster final, but it'll never happen again.'

'And the band played Waltzing Matilda
as they carried us down the gangway

Nobody cheered.
They just stood there and stared and turned their faces away.'

Then I said, 'Do you recognise that? That's never going to happen again.'
You could hear a pin drop. They never forgot it. It had such an effect on
them. You could see the goosepimples rising. It happened by fluke but it
was a defining moment for us.

THE BIG MAC

Most players prefer a hands-on manager, one who communicates with
them. Some players need a supportive arm around them, a reality that a
manager fails to appreciate at his peril. Those with fragile egos need
soothing words to make them perform. The best managers talk to the
players they are not picking. They offer words of encouragement, 'get
your head up in training, try hard and maybe you'll be off the subs bench
for the next match.'

At times, the great manager requires a touch delicate enough to catch
butterflies without damaging their wings. Sometimes less sophistication
is called for. Loughnane's profound enthusiasm for hurling has been
constant, but as a manager, the fruits of his commitment showed in a
capacity to blend mastery of the classic fundamentals with soaringly
imaginative improvisations. His motivational powers were something to
behold – preferably from a safe distance!

A speech just before, during or straight after a game rarely means
anything. It's what's done in the weeks leading up to it that wins a match
for you. It was a speech well before the final that won us the All-Ireland in
'95.

We were inside in Cusack Park. Usually spectators were allowed in to
watch. We were playing a challenge match between ourselves. None of the
players were paying much attention to what was going on, because they
were looking at the crowd. Anytime someone got a score there was a big
cheer. I stopped the match and I said, 'What the f**k is wrong?' They said
they were tired. I said nothing but played out the rest of the game.

The next night the gates were firmly shut and nobody was allowed in. I
said to Mike Mac, 'You take them for a warm-up and do one round of the
field, and after that take them into the dressing-room.' He did, and
everybody knew there was something up. When they came in, I closed the
door and laid into them about being tired. Towards the end, I went to
absolute town about the importance of winning the All-Ireland and how
the Munster title meant nothing.

There was one incident I will never, ever forget. I said, 'Do you know what pain is? Pain is coming out of Croke Park with your head down after losing the All-Ireland.' Stephen Mac was beside me, and I caught his head and shoved it right down on the floor. He tried to pull up his neck but I wouldn't let him up. I continued, 'With your f**king head down on the ground after being beaten by Offaly in an All-Ireland final. That's what pain is.'

They went back out training and the pace of it increased by 200%. Tony Considine and others often said to me afterwards that the Stephen Mac speech was the single most important factor of all.

As the '95 All-Ireland was such a new experience for them, getting the team up for a big game was not going to be a major problem, but was it not difficult to keep the players calm?

There was never any fear of them not being relaxed. Daly was brilliant at that. The great thing was that there'd be fierce clashes in training, Lohan and Clancy would be flaking each other, and then they'd go across the road to eat and everybody would be sitting around laughing and joking. There was no need to ever say, 'Lads don't get uptight.' There was never any problem that way. The night before the '95 All-Ireland, we met them in Cusack Park just to tell them the arrangements for the following day. You wouldn't believe how relaxed they were. They were confident.

I always believed that the last serious training session set the scene for what was coming up. The last training session before the All-Ireland final in '95 came on the Saturday the week before the match. I blew the whistle early and they wanted to go on for another five or ten minutes but I said I wouldn't let it go on. When they want more, you know you're ready. We could always judge how ready they were. Tony, Mike Mac and Colm Flynn were brilliant at that as well. They always knew when things were exactly right, when to push and when to pull back.

Buried deep in the collective subconscious in Clare was a nagging doubt. But Loughnane was always looking for an opportunity to stress that this team were not for turning or rolling over.

The morning of the All-Ireland in '95, we were driving out to the airport from the Oakwood Hotel in Shannon. We had met there as usual at 8 a.m. Instead of turning in the yard, the bus driver decided to drive right around the hotel and come out via the back exit. When we arrived there, we found the gate was locked. The bus driver said he would turn around. I told him no. Tony, Mike Mac and one of the players got off the bus with me and we lifted the gate off its hinges. A clear message was being sent out to the team. Unlike Clare sides in the past, we were never going to turn back and no obstacle was going to stand in our way. That was the message.

WHAT GOES UP . . .

Though Loughnane's motivational qualities were undoubtedly extraordinary, in 1996 he could not save his team from a blunted appetite. Clare would re-acquaint themselves with the emotional turmoil of a losing team.

After an All-Ireland win, especially in the aftermath of an emotionally sapping campaign, the dilemma is how to do the consolidating, and when to begin the shedding. Could the Banner brigade, playing on a shared memory and understanding still produce hurling as thrilling as in the year of glory?

Historically, team managers tend to favour the team that won the All-Ireland the previous year on the reasonable assumption that if they were good enough to win it once, they would be good enough to win it twice. That logic fails to consider the loss of hunger that may come once the cherished All-Ireland medal has been secured. The never ending round of celebrations that lasts the whole winter also takes its toll, puffing egos and eroding physical condition. This could be the team's real undoing – trying to regenerate the sheer passion and commitment of the previous year.

For any team that wins an All-Ireland, the following year is always very difficult. To get back into the same physical shape is hard enough, but the real problem is to get back the same mental shape. To get the same hunger back was impossible, especially in Clare where the celebrations were extended and everybody was feeling so satisfied. You can be starving for ages, but when you get a big meal, you forget what it was like to be hungry. I would say the same hunger wasn't there.

I knew things weren't right. Six or seven weeks before we played Limerick, we played Laois in a challenge match and struggled to beat them. We probably trained as many times from January to June as we had the previous year, but all of us weren't pushing ourselves the same way. The afterglow of the previous year was dazzling us. We were still in the comfort zone from winning the All-Ireland final and we didn't have that same fight. In the Munster Championship, Clare pulled three points clear five minutes from the finish. It looked as if we might triumph again, but Limerick came with a late surge to get four points in an amazing finale.

That game was one of the great days. I went to Limerick that morning about eleven o'clock to have a look at the pitch, just as the hawkers were setting up their stands. It was a lovely sunny morning and even though there were only about 100 people there, you could feel the atmosphere. You just felt this was going to be something else. When we came in later, there was just a river of people in white shirts and in the Clare and Limerick colours, in a kind of shimmer of heat.

In Limerick, the crowd is right in by the sideline so there was a brilliant atmosphere. The game was very even throughout. It was tough and hard but there was no rancour. With about six or seven minutes to go, we seemed to lose all our energy. That was epitomised by Liam Doyle. Barry Foley came on as a sub and scored two points off him. At one stage, Liam had the ball in his hand but let it fall and Foley popped it over the bar.

Near the end, when we were two points up, I met a Limerick selector, Liam Lenihan, and he said, 'Jesus if we beat ye, it will be total robbery.' I said, 'Ye are going to beat us.' I just felt that the tide had totally turned against us. Then they went level and Ciaran Carey scored the point that is now gone into folklore. It was the sort of wonderful score that deserved to win a game. It was a brilliant day and that match will always stand out as one of the great hurling clashes for me.

Loughnane's unflinching ambition would nullify that reverse, but as he lights the lamp of memory and looks back on the game with affection there was a post-match incident which left a slightly bitter taste.

I went into the Limerick dressing-room afterwards to sincerely congratulate the team on their victory. It had been a terrific occasion and a wonderful game, and even though we were beaten, I felt enlivened.

It wasn't the usual atmosphere after a team wins the Munster semi-final. I didn't get the warmest reception. They were talking about bones having to be picked – whatever that meant. They seemed to have the attitude that the record had been set straight after '95. I had a totally different attitude going out of the Limerick dressing-room to that coming in. My own mind was firmly set that we would really set the record straight the next year.

When I got back into the Clare dressing-room, all the top GAA journalists were there from the main newspapers and standing around waiting for something dramatic. Although nothing was said, there was a feeling there that this was the end of the road for the Clare team, which seemed to reflect what the journalists were thinking. We were a flash-in-the-pan and now we were gone. They were just waiting for the epitaph.

Unusually for him, Dalo got sucked into the atmosphere that these journalists had created by their presence. He said that he had the time of his life and if he never did anything else in his career, he would cherish the experience and he thanked everyone. It was up to me to respond. I said we would have a meeting the following week to discuss what happened that day. It was a total anti-climax for the journalists but I wasn't going to show my hand in front of them.

The following week, we had a meeting in the Clare Inn. I told the players to enjoy the summer and not to resent who won the Championship because we would get our chance again the following year. After what happened in the Limerick dressing-room, I was determined we would come back again. The players had picked up the vibes from the Limerick team and wanted to get revenge. Ideally in '97, we would have beaten Limerick, Cork, Kilkenny and Tipperary, but maybe it was better to beat Tipperary twice than Limerick once!

I went to the All-Ireland final that September. In normal circumstances, I would have been passionately shouting for Limerick but when the final whistle went I, and at least three Clare players, instinctively jumped up with joy. It wasn't because we had a great love for Wexford! It was just a reaction to the atmosphere in the Limerick dressing-room after the Munster semi-final.

Hopes rise, hopes are crushed. It will always be thus. But there is one abiding, redeeming feature which all sport shares. Every morning, the hopes are there. Motivation, though, becomes tougher after success. It is like climbing Mount Everest. Once you have reached the summit, it is very hard to motivate yourself to do it again. Motivation is not something that happens five minutes before a big name. The motivation to win the first All-Ireland was obvious. Getting the team to draw from the well a second time was a whole new challenge, but the old seductive dream of glory came knocking on Loughnane's door again.

Now that the curse of Biddy Early had been put to rest, the road ahead could be equally tough. One All-Ireland would not lift them into the pantheon of great teams. It was inevitable he would have to try again. Should he fail to deliver what was long the county's holy grail a second time, his team would be denied the unquestioned greatness they craved. The route to the promised land the second time would have a detour. Those who remained a dissenting minority amid the eulogising clamour around the 1995 team felt vindicated by the defeat to Limerick the following year.

That autumn I went to Ballincollig. It was a question-and-answer type of thing. Billy George was the chairman and the panel included Mick O'Dwyer, Jason Sherlock and myself. At one stage, Mick was asked what did it take to be a great team. His reply really spoke to me, 'Any team can win an All-Ireland but it takes a great team to win the second one.' It rang a bell in my mind immediately.

We had been beaten by Limerick in '96, but once we started training for the '97 Championship, I drove home the message that no one would ever remember us unless we won the second All-Ireland. We played Kerry in the first round of the Munster Championship in '97 and although we scored 3-24, we were terrible. We played absolutely dire stuff in the first half. At half-time I told them again, 'We'll never be remembered unless we win the second All-Ireland.'

AN FEAR CRUA

In the old days, win or die was the code. That kind of approach, though it often gets the blood boiling, interferes with concentration. Loughnane appreciated the fine line between playing hard and playing angry. When individual players were matched up against someone with superior skills, the message was 'We'll give you any help we can but you're going to have to be the door that doesn't open.' Sometimes a few words like that were all that was needed.

Clare played Tipperary in a League match in May 1997. It was the kind of game you rarely get to see. The game had to be put back 15 minutes so that everyone could get in. I went in to tell the ref that the match was delayed. He was actually shaking in the dressing-room. Everyone was caught up in the tension because it was in Ennis and it was Len Gaynor's first match against the team he had trained. When the game started, it was the toughest match I ever saw. Everybody knew the chances were that we would most likely meet in the Championship later on. There was a lot of 'sorting out' going on by both sides.

Tipperary had this young corner-forward who was supposed to be a player of the future and had played a great game shortly before against Kilkenny. He was marking Hallo, Michael O'Halloran. After about 10 minutes, this young Tipp player gave a bit of 'attention' to Hallo. The next thing we heard O'Halloran giving his response. We didn't see it but we actually heard the thump of timber on flesh. The Tipp player was substituted later. Hallo got the reputation then of being a 'hard man'. He didn't deserve it really, because he got hit first and he was settling the score in this highly charged atmosphere – where there were unreal physical exchanges all over the field.

It was a brilliant hurling game. John Leahy came on in the last 20 minutes and Tipperary won narrowly. I went into the Tipperary dressing-room afterwards and they were absolutely delighted. It was like as if they won the Munster final. Len came in to our dressing-room and he could see how disappointed everyone was. It was like a funeral scene.

It came to pass that Tipperary met Clare in the Munster final, and surprise, surprise, this time Tipperary had a new corner-forward, Philip O'Dwyer. Just before the national anthem, I saw Len Gaynor calling him over to the sideline and he started to adjust O'Dwyer's helmet. Hallo followed him all the way onto the sideline. When I saw this, I was immediately suspicious. I could be wrong, but I thought that Len was worried that Hallo was going to strike his man, before, during or after the anthem. Len was looking straight at Hallo. I went up beside them and immediately the national anthem started. O'Dwyer was right beside me and I sang the anthem as loud as I possibly could into his ear. He looked as if he was going to turn into absolutely jelly! Not a word though was exchanged between any of us. Then, when the anthem was finished I let out an almighty roar to Hallo. O'Halloran hardly gave O'Dwyer a puck of the ball and the Tipp forward was taken off. He would have been a lot better off if he had stayed where he was before the anthem!

Loughnane and his mentors insisted that his team be inoculated against slipping standards. He spoke with unmistakable conviction that complacency in hurling is not an enemy that attacks head-on but an insidious, slithering infiltrator of attitudes. He had no peers when it came to finding new persecution complexes to motivate his team, and was able to tap into that psyche superbly and use it to fuel his players with extraordinary determination. Yet he knew too that if you send out a team with tears in their eyes, they will not even see the ball. He tells a story which illustrates this point.

In the build-up to the 1997 All-Ireland final, the rivalry between Clare and Tipperary was to say the least, 'intense'. In this classic case of nouveau riche versus old money, Clare were four points down at half-time. The Clare boss did not shout and told his team they were playing badly but they could win if everyone took responsibility. He was the last man out of the dressing room and, as he walked out, the Tipperary team passed him by. He was called every name under the sun.

I knew at that moment that Clare were going to win. The Tipp lads were in too much of a frenzy. In my mind, I said, 'Continue on like that, lads.' The bigger the rage they were in, the better I liked it.

I always believe that the best thing to do is to whip up the opposition into a total frenzy. Before that All-Ireland, that's what I did. Deep down, I really feared that Tipp would pull one over on us. I knew the way Len operated. He's an emotional man and I knew he'd go absolutely ballistic over some things. I put out the story that Tipperary thought nothing of Clare and that Len Gaynor told us that when he was with us.

A singer from Ennis, Ciaran McDermott, brought out a song coming up to the match and one line was: 'We'll stop in Nenagh to really rub it in.'

Before the final, Des Cahill came down to interview me. He asked me something. I paid no attention to the question but I brought up the issue of how Nicky English had insulted Clare in '93, and how that was really motivating me to manage Clare and to really sock it to Tipperary. The whole thing blew up again and it was driving Tipperary mad!

In his playing days, Loughnane had witnessed a scene where a fire-and-brimstone speech had produced a more robust response than had been envisaged.

I went on an All-Star trip to America in 1978. We were hammered by about 14 points by Cork in the opening match in Boston. The Cork half-back line was absolutely outstanding. After the match, we were told by the management that we were a 'disgrace' and unless we upped our performance in the next match in San Francisco, there would be 'severe repercussions.'

Pat Hartigan was team captain and he gave a speech in the dressing-room before the second game. He threw his jersey on the floor in the middle of the dressing-room and said, 'Any one not prepared to die for the jersey, throw it in there and get out of here now.' Our wing-forward was Pat Delaney from Offaly. He went on to become an outstanding player, but at that stage he was, shall we say, a little 'impetuous'. He was marking Denis Coughlan. The first ball that came into him, Pat let fly and accidentally struck Coughlan on the side of the head and split it open. Pat then moved into the centre to mark Johnny Crowley. The next ball that came his way he let fly, barely missing Crowley and accidentally struck his own man, Tony Doran. The game was only five minutes old and he had sent two men to hospital! There was an immediate cry, 'Get that Offaly player off.' Pat was substituted immediately. He was very disappointed afterwards but not in the way you might expect. He said, 'What harm! If they had just left me on another minute or two, it would have been great. I was just going to move over and mark Dermot McCurtin.' He had taken it on himself to upset the entire Cork half-back line!

TOUGH LOVE

When his players failed to perform, Loughnane had no difficulty telling them they had let him down.

After the draw against Tipperary in the Munster semi-final in '99, I took the players into the dressing-room in Cusack Park during a training session and said, 'If I took the 20 people I most admired in all the world, at least 12 of them are right here. To let yourselves down like ye did last Sunday is so disappointing.'

The resourcefulness which enabled Loughnane to free himself and Clare from a tragic hurling history would reassert itself. If you can rescue a county from 81 years of losing, winning a replay is much less daunting. The soft-spoken put-down that day was more effective than a fire-and-brimstone speech. The results were to be seen in the near perfect display Clare produced to win the replay by 1-21 to 1-11. The importance of this match to Loughnane is revealed when he is asked about watching the videos of his glory days.

Not alone did I never watch the videos when Clare were playing, I haven't since I retired. Other managers spend lots of time watching videos of their games. I didn't do that. I've seen bits of games, but the only game I've ever seen in its entirety on video was the '95 final. I feel uneasy watching them and I think if I did, I'd only be looking out for mistakes the players made and I wouldn't enjoy watching them. The one game I wanted to see was the replay of the Tipperary game in 1999, and by chance, a friend of mine got it and he hasn't given it back to me since. In that sense, I have no nostalgia whatsoever.

In sport, the twisted valleys of fate make assumptions dangerous. Loughnane was always vigilant for anything that would represent the wrong sort of motivation.

In 1999, our sponsor, Pat O'Donnell, asked if he could make a presentation to the team three nights before the Munster final. He came along with a nice silver-framed photo which said, 'Munster final '99 three-in-a-row Clare.' Talk about tempting fate. I got them out of the way quickly.

Clare's two All-Irelands were in every sense the culmination of a dream, for Loughnane, his backroom team, his players and the fans. But All-Irelands are not easily won, and Loughnane was not an easy man to impress. Even the great and the good were subjected to Loughnane's withering tongue.

In training, I drove Brian Lohan to distraction. When I wanted to improve a forward like Barry Murphy, I always put them on Lohan in training. Indirectly, I was given him the line that he 'cleaned' Lohan. Then I'd say, 'Barry, move around. He's slow. He won't be able to keep up with you.' Lohan would be growling. Then I'd say something, 'Don't let him forward. Drive him back. He's not able to hit the ball when he's going backwards.' All the time, I was giving messages to Lohan. I never told him directly what his weaknesses were. Any message I wanted to give him was via somebody else and then he'd go out and prove me wrong. To Conor Clancy I'd say, 'Catch the ball. Lohan can't catch it. He's no use in the air.' Brian would be fuming inside, but he'd never say anything. He is one of the most loyal people you could meet. I just can't find the words to praise him enough. We'll never see his like again.

LITTLE BROTHER

Loughnane is a contagiously optimistic man and, as he talks about some players his face is animated by the genuine joy he derived from his work.

People say Frank Lohan is a totally different person to Brian but he's actually very similar. He's ambitious in the very same way and is even more calculating and ruthless than his big brother. If I was going into battle, Frank would be one of the people I'd send for. Frank will do what has to be done. He's blessed with great pace, fantastic vision and an unparalleled instinct for spotting the danger before it comes. He's the perfect corner-back. He's one of the most likable and honourable people you could meet in life. He has a sense of fairness and right, and would never do an injustice to anybody off the field – though he could take out a forward going for goal. If you wanted someone to typify the ideal modern young person in Ireland, it would be Frank. He's tough on the field and yet has a great heart.

The two Lohans are just brilliant men and it was such luck on my part to be there when they were at their prime. They have a typical brothers' relationship. They're seemingly constantly at loggerheads and yet you'd know they'd die for each other. Two of my favourite photos, they're nearly identical, are of the two of them closing in on Johnny Dooley in the All-Ireland final in '95 and on Michael Cleary in the '97 final. When one of them is closing in you can be sure the other isn't far behind. They had an incredible bond and Hallo was part of that as well.

Any mistake that would be made in training, you'd know it would be Frank that would be blamed for it! Without doubt the most common saying in training was, 'For f'*k's sake, Frank.' Whenever he made a mistake, that's what I'd say to him. Whenever Brian gave away a score, he'd say the same to Frank only he'd say it with even greater venom than I! Frank would never complain or say anything back.

BAKER STREET

After '95, with so many people telling his players how great they were, Loughnane was always going to puncture any inflated egos. The relationship between a trainer and his squad is fraught with possibilities for conflict, as the coach is constantly critiquing each player's performance. Loughnane recognised that by focusing on a system, it would depersonalise the criticism. The players understood that he was not attacking them personally when seeking to correct a mistake, but only trying to fine-tune their knowledge of the system. From time to time, though, his plans came unstuck.

> We took off Ollie Baker in the '97 All-Ireland semi-final. We were beating Kilkenny very easily, but Baker was playing very badly and I wanted to take him off to teach him a lesson before the All-Ireland. When I took him off, the whole thing seemed to collapse. I suppose it explained the importance of Ollie to Clare. He formed the barrier between the forwards and our half-backs who weren't noted for their pace but Baker eliminated that factor. He made the half-back line because whenever a wing-forward beat one of our wing-backs, invariably he would find Baker waiting for him. Anthony Daly always played way better when Baker was outside him.

> We were 10 points ahead and they pulled us back to three points, but Jamesie scored a point to give us a four-point victory. Baker's substitution was a huge influence on the game. If Kilkenny had got a goal and won the match, it would have been a massive, massive blunder to have taken Ollie off.

Loughnane's basic exuberance is unquenchable but Baker did put a strain on it at times.

> Ollie was the bane of my life! I don't know what my relationship with him is now, but it was always fraught when I was manager! We'll never be great friends nor great enemies. You could talk to him for a half hour but you never knew what he was thinking.

> When I think of him, I think of constantly nagging, threatening and verbally abusing him. Although he wanted to be a good hurler, he loved the good life too. In order to achieve anything in hurling, he had to develop his skill enormously. When he came training first, he'd miss two out of every three balls. Shortly after I took over, we played against Kerry and that was the first time I saw his presence in midfield, especially under the high ball, being able to win it, striking it too slowly but showing his potential.

Another vivid memory I have of him is in a League match against Laois. On that morning, Baker had buried his grandmother and we presumed he wouldn't be available. We were in the dressing-room before the match and Ollie sauntered in. He had arrived too late for the team bus and then thumbed to Laois and played as if it was the most natural thing in the world to thumb to a match.

I particularly remember one day in 2000 in Milltown. Ollie was very overweight with eight weeks to go to the Championship. I was giving a talk to the players as he arrived and he made the error of standing, leaning against the door. It was a big, big mistake. He was the only one standing. I outlined the programme for the coming eight weeks. I finished by saying, 'we haven't a hope of winning anything unless one person gets down to business and loses weight. Unless he's hurling fit we all might as well stay at home. And that's the man standing at the door.' Baker looked around for a place to hide and everybody looked up at him. I really didn't mince my words. I said unless he got fit the 30 of us there were going to suffer and worst of all Clare were going to be out of the Championship. He did try but it was too late and was taken off against Tipperary and Clare lost.

In some respects Loughnane found himself dealing with the problems of Clare's success in the latter years of his management, as the hugely influential trio of Seánie McMahon, Baker and Jamesie O'Connor were centrally involved in Cushendall St Joseph's Doora-Barefield back to back All-Ireland club final clashes in 1999 and 2000.

I'd say the only time Clare's success at club level damaged the county's ambitions was in '99 and 2000. At the same time, 'damaged' is the wrong word because it was just a terrific achievement for Clare sides to win so many consecutive Munster club titles and to win two All-Ireland club titles. That was fantastic. It's the old story that the rising tide lifts all boats. A lot of people were saying that because the Clare Championship was put off until so late, it would destroy club hurling in the county. The opposite was the case, as club hurling throve because of the county success. It's amazing the dominance Clare teams have had in Munster and reflects the confidence Clare's two All-Irelands gave them.

The downside was that Doora-Barefield were the one team you didn't want to win. They had Jamesie, Seánie and Ollie – three of the foundation stones of Clare. It definitely did take the edge off their game. It was unavoidable. I have no regrets that Doora-Barefield were that successful. It's something to be delighted about.

In the GAA, you've divided loyalty between the club and county. For the likes of Jamesie, Ollie and Seánie, the club is important as well, but we couldn't afford to go out and play in a big game without those three players in top form.

Whatever about any disagreements he had with Ollie Baker on the training field, Loughnane is deeply appreciative of the midfielder's contribution.

I've often said that we'd never have won anything without Baker. He could devour ground, devour opponents and was inspirational and indispensable. There was a massive improvement in his skill. He could lift the crowd and was a big-day player, but to get him ready for the big day was a nightmare. You often hear about horses that were impossible to train. Baker was like one of those. The amount of work he took to get him right was unreal.

Given the amount of cajoling, exhorting and bullying which the job seems to demand, do you have to be tough to be a manager?

I didn't regard it as being tough. I regarded it as doing what was right for Clare. It had nothing to do with me showing I was powerful. It was doing what was necessary for the team to win. A lot of people would say I was tough or severe, but I never looked at it that way. My view was that you've got to do what's got to be done.

6

Days of Innocence and Wonder

The scenes when we won the Munster final in 1995 were something to treasure. Although there weren't that many Clare people there, they were absolutely fanatical. Overjoyed is too tame a word to describe them. It was a feeling of surprise mixed with elation that there isn't a word invented for yet.

Bringing home the cup was absolutely incredible. Tony Considine was up at the top of the bus and he gave a concert for everyone. There was a wonderful feeling of achievement and togetherness. We came over the bridge in Limerick and that was fantastic, but we were on our own because there wasn't a Clare person in sight. We thought it would be just a bit of a celebration in Ennis.

When we got to Cratloe, we couldn't get through with crowds. It was such a scene of celebration and sporting hysteria. Tony Considine is a native of there. It took us three hours to get from Cratloe to Ennis. We couldn't even get to Shannon because we were so late getting to Ennis, but they had bonfires for us and everything. Clare FM was well established and it was putting out bulletins of our progress, so everybody knew where we were.

In 1992, the Clare footballers had won the Munster title and that generated great celebrations, but hurling was the game that had produced all the disappointments. This was a real break away from all that. You have to remember that when people talked about winning in Clare, all they meant was winning the Munster final. The All-Ireland final wasn't even contemplated because the Munster final had always been such a stumbling block. There was a total blockade in Newmarket, and we had to walk through it. I can't remember what happened for the rest of the night because I was just exhausted.

T he heart of all sport is the quality of experience it provides. There are moments that stand out from the mundanity of everyday as shining beacons. In the 1995 Munster final, Loughnane felt himself quiver with the excitement of a hound on the scent of a fox. Even when one major disappointment followed another, hope and dream always lived side by side in Clare. In 1995, Loughnane's team was poised to react hungrily to a disappointing first half of the year.

I think that after the League final in 1995, 90 per cent of Clare followers felt 'that's it': we can't take any more trouncings. You couldn't blame them. Although we hadn't been trounced on the scoreboard, in hurling terms we were. Coming out after the game, one supporter said, 'Kilkenny were a different class.' This massacre came on the back of major defeats in the two previous years. When I spoke about us winning the Munster final, none of the fans believed me.

There were less than 15,000 fans at our first game in the Championship and most of them were from Cork. Even when we beat Cork and the Munster final was jammed, it was mostly filled with Limerick people.

Before the team went out on the pitch, I did something I never did before. I held up a Clare jersey before the players. I reminded them of all the disappointments of those who had worn the Clare jersey down the years and all the heartbreak the Clare fans had experienced. Then, looking each one in the eye, I told them all of these would be cast away by five o'clock that evening.

We were out on the pitch first, but when Limerick came on to the pitch you could feel the whole place shaking. It was as loud a cheer as I ever heard. I was standing at the end of the tunnel and as Limerick's Steve McDonagh was coming out something inside me said, 'Will I flatten him?' It would have been an absolutely crazy thing to do. I wanted something to show them that although they had all the noise from the supporters, by God we were going to take them on that day.

We started off at a lightning pace. At half-time, we knew the chance was there. That gave the players confidence as well. In the second half, we took over completely but there was always the fear that something would happen because something had always happened before. Even with five minutes to go, we were still afraid that we'd be hit by a thunderbolt.

When the final whistle blew, it was such a relief. The hoodoo had been broken. It had nothing to do with beating Limerick. We were incredulous. It only really struck home when Dalo said in his victory speech, 'We'll go to Croke Park in our thousands.' I thought, 'Jesus we're going to Croke Park.' This was fantasy stuff. We had talked a lot about winning the

Munster final, but when it happened we couldn't actually believe it. Even when we saw the cup, we were wondering if we were dreaming and would it be gone when we woke up in the morning. There wasn't a huge sense of excitement because we just weren't prepared for it. Although we had won the match, the significance of the occasion hadn't sunk in.

The Munster final is one of the last genuine folk festivals left to us. There is no lens wide enough or screen big enough to take in its uniqueness, the ritual and razzmatazz and throbbing public excitement of it all. In all sport, there is nothing to match it.

Photo: Courtesy of Sportsfile

'The Winner Takes it All.' A triumphant Loughnane celebrates Clare's '95 Munster final win.

FINGERS

In the heady aftermath of their triumph, the Clare fans were ready to acclaim a new hero, a player who reached his zenith on that occasion. They were enthralled by his almost irresistible aggression which mixed animal drive with a frequently unappreciated mastery of the fine skills. His armoury included lightning speed, staying power and limitless heart.

PJ 'Fingers' O'Connell had a devil-may-care attitude. There was something about him that always stood out. His hair, his colouring and his walk made him an icon. He was the player who matured most through his involvement with the Clare team during my time as manager. He had blinding pace and a huge work rate. He was a 'made' hurler who knew his function and carried out instruction to the letter, but he suffered in tight, slow pitches. He was very popular with supporters. He is a most likeable lad and totally without malice. He's funny and loved by colleagues.

The first time I saw him was when he was sixteen or seventeen in his native Kilkishen. The local team, the Mills were playing Shannon. I'd heard about him before then because he was seen as a great prospect, but he was suspended at the time. To my amazement, during the game his coach was telling him to get ready to come on as a sub. I went over to PJ and said to him, 'Don't go out there no matter what he says. If you go on, you'll be suspended for a year.' PJ listened.

People had this idea that Fingers was a careless sort of guy when it came to training, but he'd be one of the first guys out. He'd always be on the training pitch 15 minutes before training started, pucking the ball. His nerve for the big occasion mightn't be quite as good others but he was a fantastic player to train. There was nobody with a casual attitude to training. Casual was out.

PJ is the free spirit of the team. The best game he ever played was in the Munster final in '95. He destroyed Ciaran Carey and was chosen as man of the match. He also played very well against Galway in the All-Ireland semi-final. '95 was his best year.

THE BANNER BRIGADE

Although it was only one step in a long climb which the team must make if there was any chance of surviving among the best in the country, Clare's Munster final victory was more feverishly acclaimed than any other in recent decades. Even when the small hairs stood on the back of his neck and the war-whoops of victory echoed all round him, Loughnane never imagined the attendant fanfare that might accompany it.

The following morning I was woken up by Pat Fitzgerald at 8.30. He said, 'Ye're going to have to do a tour of the county.'

'What?'

'Every club in the county has been on to me and they all want to see the cup.'

I met with Pat later that day and we drew up a schedule for the following three days to get into every parish. Throughout the day, we were getting this feeling that the whole county had been taken up with our success. It is most unusual to be doing a tour of the county having won just a provincial championship but these were unusual circumstances. On the Tuesday we began our tour. I'd safely say that no county that wins an All-Ireland experiences the scenes we witnessed as we travelled through

Clare as Munster champions. Remember this was the middle of the day or maybe eleven in the morning. Everybody came out in the middle of summer when all the farmers are supposed to be very busy.

Each parish was given a time when the team would arrive. We'd arrive into a village, bonfire blazing, the village thronged, most decked out in the Clare colours, flags, banners and bunting everywhere and a makeshift stand set up in the middle of the village. The team would get up on the stage for the speeches, followed by autograph signings, photographs, shaking hands and chat. Then it was time to move on to the next village. The big problem was trying to find something different to say in each place but it was an ideal opportunity to recognise the contribution of various people in the parishes down the years.

The highlight for me was when we brought the cup to Feakle. Feakle had supplied a number of players to the Clare team down the years. Dermot Sheedy, had played in the Munster final in '54 when Clare were hot favourites but were well beaten. We had Seamus Durack, myself, Val Donnellan and Tommy Guilfoyle, who had all played in Munster finals but had lost. To bring back the cup was really special. Everybody was there. All the older generation who had followed Clare all their lives were there. There is something really special about the GAA, that feeling of community it generates. People are interested in other sports but there is no other sport that produces a local pride like that.

My theory was that it wasn't going to be possible for us to stop the celebrations for the first few days anyway, so I decided to let them have a week of this. By the Friday, the players were nearly begging to get back to training. They just had enough of it. We went back to Clarecastle on Friday night just for a run, and on the Sunday we started full training again.

I think that tour was hugely significant and I think it was a brilliant idea to bring the cup to every village. We brought as many players as we could. When the Clare fans realised the kind of people that we had on the team, that was the start of the great bond that developed between the team and the fans.

A new ritual emerged at Clare matches with the appearance of 'the Clare shout' which introduced a whole new meaning to the term 'deep throat'. This was said to date back to the time de Valera came electioneering in Clare.

Loughnane had tasted the bitter pill of disappointment too often to get carried away, yet he found it impossible to conceal the swelling of hope his team engendered. The jury of experts was still out, but even after beating Galway in the All-Ireland semi-final, the team had as yet to prove themselves in Croke Park. The real test would come in the All-Ireland final.

On the day of the match, everything was very relaxed and I believe we made the right decision in flying up from Shannon that morning. If we had travelled up the day before and stayed in Dublin, we were bound to meet all the Clare crowds and run the risk of getting caught up in the 'occasion'. We had a work-out around 12 noon, doing a bit of stretching and pucking a few balls, before we sat down and talked with the players.

We left it as late as possible to get to Croke Park as it was no use arriving at the ground and hanging around. The first person I met when we got off the bus was Jackie O'Gorman, which I thought was a good omen because he had such a positive outlook and he was certain we were going to win.

I was the first into the dressing-room and Seán Hehir was there doing something for Radio na Gaeltachta. He was sitting up on the table and he gave me a long lecture about what we had to do to beat Offaly. I don't know what he said because my mind was elsewhere. I was hoping he would realise that I had other things to do, but eventually I had to say, 'Seán, we need to get ready now.' As he was leaving, Jimmy Barry Murphy and Dr Con Murphy came in to wish us luck. They had been there with the Cork minors that day and I really appreciate this very sporting gesture.

There was no discernible air of tension. We had been through the semi-final against Galway which, in a way, is a more difficult occasion to cope with. There were very few words spoken. We just told them that Clare people were there in their thousands and that people had come from all over the globe to be here, so a massive effort was needed. Above all we stressed that all the plans we had for Offaly were to be implemented and stressed the importance of work-rate, discipline and taking any opportunities that came our way because they would be scarce. We also emphasised that if they suffered any disappointment or setback they were to put it behind them. When they left the room, they nearly took the doors off the hinges they were so charged-up.

When the game started, everything was going grand. Seánie scored two great points to set us off. We were doing everything we planned. It was a war of attrition. We were blocking them and hooking them, putting them off their normal pattern.

Just before half-time, disaster struck. Michael Duignan came along under the Cusack Stand and he seemed to try and lob the ball over the bar

97

but it fell short. Fitzie tried to control the ball with his hurley, which was unusual for him, but the sliotar skidded off his hurley into the net. It looked like the classic sucker punch that could destroy us. If there was any fragile area in our make-up, that would undo us. Then the Sparrow scored a brilliant point from the sideline and instead of going in on a downer, everyone was in a different frame of mind.

In fact, Fitzie's mistake turned out to be a good thing because at half-time everyone was on to him saying, 'Not to worry. We're still going to win.' We held up the jersey in front of them and asked them to give every last ounce of energy for Clare.

Close your eyes and the years roll back. Great hurling matches refuse to be undramatic. If the form-book suggests predictability, there is almost always a sub-plot to send the blood pressure into orbit. In 1995, the outcome of the All-Ireland final seemed clear. As the historic contest entered its decisive final minutes, Offaly were travelling so smoothly that it seemed they should win as easily as a nun gets to heaven. Twelve months earlier, Limerick had outplayed Offaly throughout the All-Ireland final and held an apparently unassailable five-point lead with just minutes remaining, but they were caught by the Dooleys. Back-to-back titles seemed inevitable for the Midlanders, but the Clare team had a morale so tough that railway sleepers could be broken across it. People who witness miracles are wont to carry a detailed recollection of the event, and so it is with Clare people who witnessed the sporting miracle of the 1995 final.

Sweet dreams are made of this. Loughnane savours victory.

Managers are selected for winning matches, not for the quality of their post-match interviews. They have no obligation to produce either profundity or entertainment for the microphones and notebooks that cluster round them in the half-time interval. Yet at half-time, Loughnane had boldly told the television audience, hungry for direct evidence, that Clare were going to win, 'We're going to do it'. Cockiness is no crime, especially in a world where undue reticence is a recipe for being left behind, but Gaelic games is one of the areas where the penalties of overdosing on self-approval are especially severe. With five minutes to go, the manager's confidence had apparently been exposed as the creation of a romantic and deluded imagination.

Croke Park on a September afternoon, separates the strong, the enduring, and above all, the brave from the rest. In full flight in countless training sessions, Loughnane's team were something to behold and those recorded demonstrations of their talents implanted the thought that on a Sunday in September they would be just about unbeatable. Many a team had arrived for a final with unlimited potential, but Croke Park had ruthlessly exposed its flaws. Would all the endless training sessions prove justified? Would a momentary lapse of concentration get a great team beaten? Again. Maybe the team was more vulnerable than its most fervent admirers would admit. The questions dried the throat and brought a sharpness of anxiety that had nothing to do with mere All-Ireland medals.

> *The second half was tense. We were going well and then Johnny Pilkington scored a second Offaly goal. The ball should have been cleared. We had always said, 'For certain we'll make mistakes. For certain we'll have a lot of wides. But don't panic, stick to the plan and work, work until the last second.'*

IT'S A LONG WAY FROM CLARE TO HERE

As apprehension mingled with the ache of deprivation, the Clare shout was starting to spill over the line between the urgent and the frantic. It was an occasion of red faces, virile voices and nerves stretched to brittleness. The sense of what might have been lost reached achingly into everyone who had ever admired the Clare team. But it must have felt like a disembowelling knife to older fans for whom the imminent defeat was the latest in a series of disasters visited upon the Banner County. Yet whatever power allocates the disappointments in life should have learned by now that there is no point in trying to break the Clare hurling fans. They learned early and went on relearning how to live not only with losing but with losing painfully. They embodied the incomparable appeal of hurling, the blood-stirring excitement and democracy of ambitions which takes tens of thousands to Croke Park buoyed by the certainty that they are about to share not only hurling's greatest event but one of the most enjoyable experiences the entire sporting calendar can offer.

The prophets of doom had said the Clare team were fatally handicapped by inexperience. Success is impossible without opportunity and opportunity in hurling is the right blend of skill and character.

Loughnane's towering gifts as a manager, the priceless 'feel' for players and the commanding urgency of his voice, the cold nerve and iron determination, the judgement that springs a sub at precisely the right moment to suit their capacities, have never been better exemplified than in his icily patient delivery of the D'Artagnan of the big square, Eamonn Taaffe, in that final. With the clock ticking, Anthony Daly, a master at the height of his powers, lobbed the sliotar towards the square. The ball rebounded off the upright, Taaffe connected and the umpire was reaching for the green flag – goal.

> *It was from this point on that the game slows down in my mind. After Offaly equalised, Baker forced a 65. Dalo was facing up to it, though Seánie should have been taking it. Daly had made up his mind. There was somebody injured and the game was delayed. I ran into Dalo and said to him, 'Give it a right lash.' I'd say he never even heard me. He was looking at the posts the same as if it was Cusack Park. I was standing on the sideline and was shouting a point before it had gone half-way. Offaly came down the field again. They hit the post but the ever reliable Frank Lohan was there to relieve the danger. The ball was cleared and we got a 21 yard free which Jamesie pointed.*

The melodrama belonged in the last reel of one of the classic Western films in which John Wayne battled against the odds to snatch victory from the jaws of defeat. Loughnane's gifted team were suddenly buzzing and Clare were on their way to victory. Offaly had abruptly run out of reasons for celebration.

Across the nation, enthralled radio listeners were listening to the peerless Micheál O'Muircheartaigh, 'We're gone 45 seconds into injury time. It's all over and the men of Clare of '95 are All-Ireland champions.' As the game ended, radio and television crews tried to wriggle microphone and cameras through the scrum to bottle the naked elation and send it across the airwaves. Almost before the roars that greeted the final whistle, Loughnane was eulogising the talents of his young team.

The encircling group of Clare fans turned to each other and nodded at the wisdom. Fresh talent is the lifeblood of hurling. New shoots will spring up every season but it is only occasionally that you realise you are watching the emergence of a full new flower. That was the excitement of September 1995.

> I wanted to be back in the dugout with the other three mentors when the final whistle went. When it did, I thanked them for all they had done. Then the crowds descended on us. Every inch of Croke Park was covered with Clare people.

In decades of supreme contests, in a wide range of arenas, there have been few matches that have unleashed a greater flood of excitement and pleasure than the Clare victory. The fans whose incurable addiction to hurling readily survived the emotional haemorrhage attached to supporting the Banner county might have felt entitled to a small glow of vindication and a kind of dignified smugness. The haughtiest human denizens could no longer justify the slightest trace of condescension to Clare hurling.

Croke Park takes you like no other place, but add in Anthony Daly's famous speech to the emotional mix and it's a recipe for emotional release, 'There's been a missing person in Clare for 81 long years. Well today that person has been found alive, and that person's name is Liam McCarthy.'

> I will never forget the colour the Clare fans brought to the game. That's when it all really took off. Donegal had brought it first in 1992, but in '95 it really took off. We take it for granted now.

In the film 'Gladiator', Russell Crowe psyches up his troops going into battle by telling them, 'Whatever we do in this life echoes in eternity.' In his radio commentary, Micheál O'Muircheartaigh said it was easy to imagine the Clare hurling fans who had gone on to their eternal reward leaning over the bannisters in heaven watching the drama unfold.

Perhaps this match had not been the best showcase of the team's communal talents, but at that moment they were the happiest team in the world, and they deserved to be. As all round him were swept up in the madness, the manager looked out on the hallowed sod, lavishly garlanded on the day with thousands of ecstatic Clare people who spread out like a tree that blocked the sun, and quietly plundered its pleasures for himself. For the kind of man who can euphemise fanaticism as common sense, who can disguise obsession as the only sensible way to behave, his restraint was almost treasonable. From the peculiar terrain that champions inhabit, he was wearing the smile that only the vindicated know. His faith in his young team was magnificently justified, and it was right that the gods should refuse to throw a shadow across their dreams.

> When the cup was presented, it was just a thrill to stand there and soak it all in. It was surreal. Those players will be heroes forever and that is more lasting than cups or medals. The best way I can think of summing up the day is from the lyrics of a Paul Simon song, 'These are the days of innocence and wonder.'

POSTSCRIPT

Offaly on that day found themselves confronted by the sort of talent which knows few boundaries. He ensures a high rate of penetration, and his attacks are pressed home with a driving energy that few opponents can hope to withstand. He combines graceful economy of movement with fierce intensity of will and a dazzling repertoire of skills. Even pedestrian pundits predicted that with the passion and élan he brought to the hurling field, the inner need to express himself dramatically and his joy in virtuosity, he would really star in All-Ireland final. They were all correct but not until two years later. Nothing can tarnish his reputation, but the '95 All-Ireland final was not the climactic experience of an outstanding career that many anticipated.

> Jamesie missed frees which he normally would have scored in his sleep. Lucky enough, he had the honour of putting the ball over the bar near the end and we went two points up.

After the game he showed all his carefully hidden inner turbulence, in his uniquely gentlemanly way.

> He is a most unusual man! After the game was over, to escape all the crowd on the pitch, we went up into the VIP section in the Hogan Stand and had a cup of tea. Albert Reynolds and all the VIPs were there. Neither Albert nor any of the others were interested in us. We were just a sideshow.
>
> Jamesie came over to me and said, 'Jesus, I'm sorry I let you down today.'
>
> 'What?' I replied.
>
> 'I was shit. I let you down.'
>
> 'But Jamesie, we wouldn't be here with the McCarthy Cup if it wasn't for you.'
>
> 'I know, but I was useless today.'

He's so self-critical. That he came along at that time was such a dream. Without him, we would have won nothing. He was a pleasure to have in training. What he would do with the ball was spellbinding. He was always a huge test for the player he was marking in training even though they often did very well on him. He had this great self-belief, as had the other Doora-Barefield lads Seánie and Baker, that no matter how badly he was doing in training, he would always do it on the big day. He's a brilliant, brilliant man. The best thing I'd say about Jamesie is that if you ever heard anybody saying anything bad about him, you should be really suspicious of that person.

In the Munster final in '95, with four or five minutes to go we scored a point. I was walking up the sideline and he put up his fist to me. No word was said but yet the message was clear.

Jamesie was often shocked by things I'd say to him or other players and they never knew when I was going to rear-up on them, but when they went out on the field there was an incredible bond between us. You'd need a great psychologist to explain the links between us.

Jamesie always said to me that he never knew who the real me was. Once he was asked: 'What's Loughnane really like?' Jamesie's reply was, 'Sure I don't know!' There was always a bit of distance, that bit of a gap, but Jamesie always knew that I totally trusted and admired him.

Loughnane's relationship with Jamesie was a microcosm of his curious relationship with his team – a fascinating combination of closeness and distance.

When we got back to the dressing-room, we put the cup on the table and everybody chatted away. There was no jumping up and down. It wasn't like beating Tipp in '97. There wasn't that ecstatic feeling. It was nearly a feeling of wonder. Then we went out on the bus and with the cup up on the front we headed for the Berkeley Court. From then on, we knew we were All-Ireland champions.

THE CLARE CHAMPIONS

To understand where Clare is now in the hurling hierarchy, it is necessary to appreciate where it has been. Eamonn Cregan listed Clare's Jimmy Smyth as one of the top five hurlers of the last century. Smyth is ideally equipped to answer the question: what did Clare's breakthrough in 1995 mean to the older generation in particular?

'We had great teams in the forties and all the way up to the eighties, but, it was always the same old story - good management and back-up, commitment in training, but no delivery on the big day. Even on the days when we did deliver, as we did, for instance, against Cork in Killarney in 1986, it was the same old story. You could say it was almost a fear of winning and sheer bad luck. There were so many great players in Clare who would have won several All-Ireland medals if they were with other counties. Our predicament was that we had good hurling teams which were saddled with the sorrows of past years.

'Clare's record was poor and we had no tradition of winning. When you have a tradition, it seeps into the bones and the psyche. It breeds confidence and even makes a winner out of a loser. A fair team with a good tradition would always be confident of winning against a better Clare side.

'In the past, even the language of the supporters carried the wail and the woe of what was said and unsaid. I hated the question, "will ye win?" People knew the answer to the question when they asked you. What they were saying was: "We want you to win, we know you can, but you won't."

'Now we have broken that barrier at last. Winning and losing in the future will never be the same for Clare hurling. It's strange but I felt more peace than euphoria after we broke through in 1995 because the weight of the losses of previous years have been lifted off our shoulders. The win brought back esteem to Clare hurling.

'In hurling circles, a Clare hurler now means something: there are no question marks. We were All-Ireland champions and we couldn't believe it. We tested the locked gate for eighty years but the gate stood firm. We tested it again in the eighty first year, and to our amazement the gate opened. It was a fairy wand that cast a spell of happiness and contentment over the county and its people at home and abroad. When Anthony Daly raised the cup, I realised that the win was bigger than one person. It was more than self-fulfilment, more than seeing the net shaking, and more than the exuberance of fitness and health. It was on a place far higher than this. It was a totality: the merging of a collective spirit, a unification of minds that included every man, woman and child of a county unit at home and abroad. It brought life and confidence into the people and it was good to be alive.'

PEAK PERFORMANCE

Given the enormity of the '95 victory to Clare fans, it would be reasonable to assume that it was Loughnane's proudest moment. Reasonable but inaccurate.

I'll never forget our most thrilling victory. It was against Tipperary in Pairc Uí Chaoimh in 1997. We had set our sights on winning the All-Ireland in '97. We had great days in '95. Beating Cork in the Championship in '97 was wonderful, but from a purely hurling point of view, because of their great tradition and well-deserved reputation, to beat Tipperary in the Munster final was the day of days.

It was a beautiful sunny day. We had gone into the '95 All-Ireland in a relaxed frame of mind, but there was no relaxation that day. We went to Cork with a sense of going on a mission that was only recaptured when we played Waterford in the Munster final replay the following year. Everybody was totally up for it. When we met the bus outside the Shamrock Hotel, Frank Lohan was dancing from foot to foot. When Fitzie arrived, he was pale. There was none of the usual chatter. This was the day. There was an awful lot at stake and everyone knew it.

As usual, the team went to bed after breakfast and Tony, Mike and I went for a walk in the grounds of UCC. It was the first time I had been there and it's a really beautiful place, but all the time the thought was flashing in our minds: this is the day. Reports were coming in that the biggest Clare crowd ever had descended on Cork.

We went for a puckout in the Mardyke. Afterwards I called on the players and told them that they had done so much for Clare already but today we wanted a really special effort. I said in a soft voice, 'Everything we've achieved is at stake today. Our entire reputation rests on the match.' We went onto the coach and really the bus didn't need an engine to power it. Everybody was totally geared up. My last words to them were, 'Everything depends on today. Make every second of every minute count.'

I can't remember everything before the two All-Irelands, but I can remember every second of that day. As soon as we went on the field, we could feel the tension that was in the air. It wasn't a tension that drained you. It was a tension that enlivened you. For the first time, when the names of each of the Clare players were read out there was a massive cheer. The crowd was really up for it. There was an incredible sense of oneness between the team and the fans.

As soon as the game started, we were playing at 90 miles an hour. We led by 0-13 to 0-8 at the interval. Barely seven minutes after the re-start, Tipperary were level and playing with the wind. The Tipp supporters started singing Sliabh Na mBan. I immediately leapt to my feet and shouted to each of the players, 'Is that the sound you want ringing in your ears all the way home.' Clare lifted their game and regained the lead almost immediately when Seánie scored a point from a free. Suddenly the tide had turned in our favour again. We brought on David Forde and he scored a wonder goal.

*Clare were seemingly going to be beaten, after enjoying a huge lead.
Then we came back to lead again with that magic goal. We were still
winning by three points with minutes left. Then John Leahy broke
through and Tipp almost scored a goal in the last minute to tie the match.
However, he mis-hit the ball and Colin Lynch cleared it. I thought the
final whistle would never blow.*

*When the whistle finally went, I just lost the head. I leapt out of the
dugout and got a belt of a flag and my face was bleeding. Some lady
jumped on me. I was ecstatic.*

Photo: Courtesy of Leo McMahon

'Blooded but unbowed.' A bloody Loughnane savours beating
Tipperary in the Munster final in 1997.

*We won two All-Irelands, and they were brilliant. But this was unique.
People outside Clare would find it very difficult to understand just how
much it mattered. This was the dream for every Clare person for decades –
to beat Tipperary in a Munster final. Forget about All-Irelands. Had we
won six All-Irelands and hadn't beaten Tipp in a Munster final, it
wouldn't have been as good, but to win that day and go into the dressing-
room was sheer bliss.*

*I made sure the dressing-room was locked. The atmosphere inside was one
of total and absolute contentment. We're not supposed to feel it in this
lifetime. There was no need for a word to be said. The downside was that
you knew that there never would be a day like that again, but it is a feeling
that will last forever.*

*You didn't even want to go out among the crowd afterwards. You wanted
no patting on the back. We had all that when we won the All-Ireland in*

'95. We just wanted to sit back and share that among ourselves. We didn't want to leave the dressing-room because the magic was inside. It was great going out and meeting our relatives and everyone else in Clare, but even though the fans felt brilliant, they just hadn't felt what we felt in the dressing-room. Only those who were in there could ever understand what it was like. You just couldn't get it anywhere else and that was the magic that was Clare.

The '97 Munster final is the treasure of all treasures. You ask yourself did it ever really happen. Everything that day was just bliss. It wasn't the All-Ireland final but the Munster final that was more important to us. That's what people don't understand. Munster is magic because of the local rivalries. Whatever changes are made in hurling, the Munster Championship must stay. You look at the Munster Championship and see the passion it generates. Croke Park is business. There is something spiritual about the Munster Championship.

It took us four hours to get home that night. All the towns we went through, like Charleville and Buttevant, were thronged with Clare people and Limerick fans delighted for Clare. It was such a pleasure. No night coming home from any All-Ireland final could match it. The only night that matched it was coming home from the Munster final in '95. We felt we really had arrived as a major hurling power and we just sat back and savoured it all.

If it is true that when we die, major moments of our lives are replayed before our eyes as we enter the pearly gates of heaven, then the immediate aftermath of the 1997 Munster final will be one of them for Ger Loughnane. It is difficult to talk about it in anything less than sacramental language, 'the peace that passes all understanding.' Even if that could never be repeated, to get a glimpse of it just once was enough. If it is not too melodramatic to describe it in religious terms, there was almost a sacredness in the spell of contented silence that fell over the dressing-room. The undiminished status of the Munster final has withstood all assaults on its uniqueness since it was first contested over a century ago, but this victory was all the sweeter because it meant that the '93 beating had finally been thoroughly avenged.

OUT OF THE DOLDRUMS

Loughnane, having engendered an era that was often spellbinding and gratifying, always wore his heart on his sleeve. Enthusiasm for hurling still shines in his eyes and, not surprisingly, the glint intensifies when victories over Tipperary surface in conversation. There was one Clare-Tipp contest that was a sight to put a permanent tingle in the blood.

> *In the Munster semi-final replay in Páirc Uí Chaoimh in 1999 against Tipperary, we gave the most perfect performance the team ever gave. I always longed for the day that the team would give a display I'd be totally and utterly satisfied with. That was the display. It was so commanding: we overpowered them, outwitted them and were more skilful. Every aspect you could possibly judge a good performance on, that one had. Afterwards there was a great feeling that this was the ultimate collective performance.*

> *One of the smartest managers I've seen is Nicky English and he came into the dressing-room after Clare had beaten Tipperary in the replay and said, 'Ye could win the All-Ireland this year if today hasn't taken too much out of ye.' He was dead right. It had taken too much out of us, though we didn't realise it at the time.*

> *We were too satisfied afterwards. If the first day we had beaten Tipp by a point and everybody said, 'Ye no more deserved that', which we wouldn't have done, we might have won the All-Ireland. Everybody was too satisfied about beating Tipp. Now whether you'd swap winning an All-Ireland for giving Tipp a good trouncing is another thing!*

A week later, Loughnane would discover that his attire on that day was not acceptable to the authorities.

Cumann Lúthchleas Gael

ÁRD STIÚRTHÓIR: LIAM Ó MAOLMHICHÍL

Páirc an Chrócaigh, Áth Cliath 3
Guthán: 8363222
Fax : 8366420

SÓL/TNíR

19 Meitheamh 1999

Gearóid Ó Lachtáin Uasal
F/Ch Pádraig MacGearailt Uasal
Baile Caisleán Crainn
Sixmilebridge
Co An Chláir

Maidir Le: **Guinness Munster Senior Hurling Championship**
An Clár v Tiobraid Árann (P. Uí Chaoimh) 06.06.99/12.06.99

Gearóid, a chara

Coiste Riaracháin na gCluichí at it's last meeting considered six (6) reported unathorised incursions by you at Páirc Uí Chaoimh on 6 Meitheamh 1999 and five (5) reported unauthorised incursions in the replay in Páirc Uí Chaoimh on 12 Meitheamh 1999.

You have three days to submit a written explanation or to seek 'by writing' an oral hearing.

In the event that you request (in writing) an oral hearing, the hearing will be granted at the next meeting of the Games Administration Committee at Croke Park on Wednesday 30 June 1999.

Should you wish to attend can you do so at 8.00pm.

The Committee also asked me to point out the need to have 'Bainisteoir" on the jersey/polo shirt.

Is mise, le fíor mheas

Seán Ó Laoire
Bainisteoir na gCluichí

cóip mar eolas don Runaí Contae

Enjoyment is the most well-remembered and treasured aspect of the experience. Ultimately it is how much we enjoy rather than how many trophies a team accumulates that really matters.

Your goal is to get the very best out of players. When you achieve this goal, you're in right trouble. In '99, people said it was tiredness. It had nothing to do with that. We produced the perfect display in '99. There was no hill to climb after that, even for me. It enhanced it because it was against Tipperary, but the performance was everything I strove for since I first trained a junior team. Once you do get to the pinnacle, there's no place else to go. Even when you win, there are always flaws, but not that day. It's a lot better than winning an All-Ireland because you can win an All-Ireland and play badly.

The whole thing left me with a treasure trove of memories. The thrill of it all is there when you are sitting down somewhere and the memory of a match like that will come back to you. That's what made it all worthwhile. But it was deadly draining.

Especially in 1998.

7

Forgiven Not Forgotten?

It is very hard to describe the atmosphere that prevailed in the '98 Munster final replay. I've often tried to figure out why the players reacted the way they did. My comments were part of it but I think the big thing was what the players said among themselves. It was like going to war. You just didn't care what was going to happen to yourself individually. All that mattered was that you were going to fight for the players beside you. You were going out with a tunnel vision. You were going to give of everything you had to put them down. Once we got to Thurles, you could feel the hostility in the air. I still can't rationalise what happened and why Waterford felt the same way. It was a two-edged sword.

Pat Fitzgerald had told me it was raining outside so I told the players to put on their track suits 'til the match started. Many of them did but some of them didn't. Somebody handed me a wet suit to put on but it was soon on its way, flying through the air. We were going into battle and this was no place for any creature comforts.

It was a day when there was really no need for any words in the dressing-room. I held up the county jersey again and told the players that they had shit on it the first day and anyone who was going to allow that to happen again should stay in the dressing-room and tog in. The jambs of the door nearly went flying with them on the way out. They hit the field like an absolute tornado that day, but the fact that they were wearing tracksuits aroused suspicion. I learned afterwards that when he saw them, a journalist in the press box asked, 'What's the bastard done now?'

In the drawn game, one of the Waterford mentors stood in front of our dugout. It was total and utter intimidation. Wherever we walked, he walked in front of us so that we couldn't properly see what was happening. The second day we detailed Mike Mac to mark him. The plan beforehand *was, if a row broke out he was to 'look after' him, Tony would look after the other selectors and I would 'look after' Gerald McCarthy. It was every man for himself after that.*

Before we went out on the pitch, I stared right into each player's eyes. They'd have taken on the German army. It was the only time I ever understood how soldiers could go out into battle and not be afraid of dying. The cup meant nothing. This was personal. Waterford were not going to be allowed to humiliate some of our players the way they had done the previous Sunday. We wanted to put them down.

I admit completely it was war without bullets.

The clash of the ash.

Those who make history can afford to ignore it. In 1994 when he became Clare manager, Ger Loughnane could not have known that his name would become the most instantly identifiable and, in several senses, the most emotive in the recent mythology of hurling.

His is a fame shot through with many subtleties of feeling. It evokes deep affection but he has been called unflattering names in his time, as his extreme determination has been interpreted as ruthlessness. There was, for a start, more than a whiff of controversy that was never far from his name from the time he first arrived as a manager to challenge the sensitivities of senior GAA officials. He often caused the raising of voices as well as eyebrows by his willingness to take on the authorities. When it comes to officialdom, 'diffidence' is not part of the Loughnane lexicon. His team selections were sometimes inclined to be a shade more enigmatic than the Dead Sea Scrolls. He rewrote the training manual, but many believed that a few of his opinions swept across the borderline between the outrageous and the indefensible. His relationship with the GAA authorities became explosive in 1998, but there had been trouble the previous year.

> Initially, I had no problems with the GAA whatsoever. Clare were the new kids on the block and everyone wanted them to do well. The first sign of trouble came in the '97 Munster semi-final when we played Cork. Stephen Mac had just scored a late goal which put three points between the teams. Cork got a line ball up near our goal but Frank Lohan had his back to the ball. A Cork player was going to strike it and I was roaring at Frank but he didn't hear me. I was walking along the sideline so I kicked the ball away. Of course I was totally wrong. All hell broke loose. The Cork crowd went wild. Frank Murphy was very annoyed on the sideline. That was the start of my confrontations with the GAA.

> From '95, I had been running in on the pitch but everyone else was as well. In the '95 All-Ireland, I spent more time on the pitch than any player! No one said anything because Clare were on a roll. In '97, the thing changed completely and they started to say we better get mentors off the field.

The affectionate response evoked in 1995 was remarkably absent two years later. It was time for Loughnane to demonstrate again the resilience that has enabled him to overcome previous crises. Yet he was sometimes the architect of his own misfortunes.

> In the Munster final in '97, there was a lot of travelling across the pitch and I had one memorable confrontation with John Leahy who said to me, 'Get off you f**ker or you'll get the same as Maughan.'

(The then Mayo manager John Maughan had been knocked to the ground by a punch to the face, following a punch-up between players from Mayo and Leitrim in the Connacht semi-final on June 29 that year.)

I said, 'From you is it?'

Leahy just kept running by. That was the great thing about him. He could take it as well as he could give it and there was nothing more about it. The thing with him is to give it back to him twice as hard. It adds to the whole aura of the game. You laugh at it when its over.

 # COMHAIRLE NA MUMHAN C.L.G.

Nollaig Breathnach, Cathaoírleach
Seán Ó Ceallaigh, Leas-Chathaoírleach
Déaglán Ó Maoláin, Cisteoir
Dónal Ó Nialláin, Rúnaí
An tAth. S. Gáirnéar, Oif. Chaid. Poiblí

Árd Aoíbhinn,
Baile Nua, Aonach Urún,
Co. Thiobraid Arann
Fax/Guthán 067/31594

28/8/97 . . . . 199 . . . . . .

Gearoid Uas. O Lachtnain,
Bainisteoir Foireann Iomana Sinsir An Chlair,
Fe/Ch. Padraig Uas. Mac Gearailt,
Runai C.L.G.,
Bothar Caislean Crainn,
Droichead Abhann Ui gCearnaigh
Co. An Chlair.

Re: Breaches of Match Regulation No.8(a)

Gearoid, a chara,

Following a decision taken at our last Comhairle na Mumhan meeting of 11/7/97, at which Breaches of Match Regulations No.8(a) in recent games were discussed, I was instructed to request your attendance at our next Comhairle na Mumhan meeting on Friday September 5th, in the Limerick Inn Hotel at 9.15pm to explain your numerous unauthorised incursions on to the field of play at Pairc Ui Chaoimh on 6/7/97 on the occasion of the S.H. Final and also, on the occasion of the Clare v Cork game at Limerick on 8/6/97 when you interfered with play by kicking away the sliotar after it had been placed for a sideline touch by the linesman near the end of the game..

Trusting that you will be able to be in attendance at the appointed time of 9.15pm.

Mise le meas,

Donal O Niallain.

After the Munster final, I got a warning from the GAA about running on to the field, but it was after the All-Ireland semi-final against Kilkenny that I really got in hot water. I made numerous transgressions onto the field that day because we had built up a huge lead and we were letting them back in, and just to keep them going I had to speak to different people to wake them up. With Kilkenny, there's always a danger they'll come back. I was barred for the All-Ireland and had to sit on the famous green bench.

What happened to me was fine, but what happened to Len Gaynor was a total disgrace. Len hadn't gone into the field in the All-Ireland semi-final. In one match earlier that year, Len had gone in to take off Brendan Carroll and for that he was banned to the dugout for the All-Ireland. It was just a balancing of the books exercise. If I was in the dugout, he was in the dugout.

During the All-Ireland, they had a man watching me to see how many times I was up off the green seat. The seat was way back at the start so we pushed it right up to the sideline. That was the first move. I was watching Gaynor and he was watching me. We both stayed sitting down for a while but Tipp went four points up and that was the end of the seat! We parted company for the rest of the game! I couldn't sit down in an All-Ireland. Len was the same. It was in and out the field, up and down the sideline, behind the goals, everything.

Towards the end of the game, I crossed the field to wake up one of our forwards. We were two points up and Tipp had a 65. Dickie Murphy ran across to book me. Then a bottle from the old Hogan stand flew across and just missed me. I picked it up and threw it to safety. I was just back on the sideline and Eugene O'Neill scored a goal. Not a very bright move! It was an intervention that didn't work. From the puckout, Ollie Baker got the ball and equalised.

I was standing beside the goal when Jamesie got the ball. There was a kind of gloom in the sky and the only question once he hit it was would it have the distance. When it went over the bar, the umpire seemed to have vanished. I thought about getting the flag and putting it up!

In his own unique style, Micheál O Muircheartaigh captured the moment magically in his radio commentary. 'Colin Lynch, the Lisseycasey man, Colin Lynch flings it to the wing to Jamesie. Jamesie is 60 yards out, Jamesie is 50 yards out, he tries a shot from way, way down the field, it's over the bar and the man who snags it is Gerrrrrrr Loughnane.'

For one horrible moment, it looked as if his celebration was premature.

I didn't want to cross the field again so I went back to the dugout the long way and when I looked up, John Leahy was on the 21-yard line. He drove the ball low and hard to the left corner but Fitzie made a spectacular save and Dalo cleared the ball.

I was called to Croke Park after that. I was barred from the sideline for the first game in the Championship in '98 but Clare appealed over the winter and I was given a final warning and was let back on the sideline.

Loughnane speaks wistfully as he looks back on his one big disappointment from the '97 All-Ireland final.

When the game was over, I didn't go over to where the presentation was being made. I saw Colm Flynn's two bags and I knew how precious they were to Colm, but in the heat of the moment he abandoned the two bags so I collected them and went to the dressing-room.

On my way I met two Clare people and asked, 'Is there any chance ye could take my bench and bring it home?' They agreed, but some official in a suit stopped them and took it away. I was hoping to have it as a souvenir. It would have become a tourist attraction!

However, Loughnane would not escape the wrath of officialdom. He was summoned to account for his indiscretions.

Len Gaynor and I were called to a meeting about incursions into the field. I had no difficulty with being punished for my actions as long as other people who did the same thing in Munster Championship matches, like Eamonn Cregan, got the same treatment, but that didn't happen.

Pat Fitzgerald, the county chairman Robert Frost, and I appeared before the Munster Council. The Chairman of the Munster Council at the time was a Clare man, Noel Walsh. He raised the incursions onto the pitch. I said, 'Hold on now. How come Len Gaynor and I are the only ones here, when others who committed pitch incursions are not? I can give ye a list of them.'

Walsh replied, 'We're here to discuss your incursions, not anybody else's.'

'Hold on a second now. We'll discuss mine when ye discuss everyone else's as well.'

There was silence. Then we moved on to the kicking away of the sliotar. I apologised and explained it was not premeditated and I gave him an incident of a Cork official who, in my opinion, had made an unauthorised incursion onto the pitch against us in order to try to slow down play. Frank Murphy was incensed about that comment because of the man's commitment to Cork hurling. I said, 'I'm not saying anything about his character. What I did was wrong. I admit that. In my opinion, what he did was wrong too. I've been called to answer for my actions, why wasn't he?'

With that, it started back and forth between myself and Frank. Eventually Noel Walsh called a halt and said, 'We'll stop it there and we'll discuss it among ourselves.' As I walked out the door, the chairman said, 'I suppose we should feel privileged that he came at all.'

Later that year, Loughnane would again be carpeted for pitch incursions.

ONE RULE FOR CLARE – A DIFFERENT RULE FOR THE REST

No one in Clare will object to everyone being treated equally. Ger Loughnane had no problem with the decision to ban him from the dugout for the 1997 All-Ireland Final. He felt however that Len Gaynor was very harshly treated.

Let us now compare how the rule was applied in the case of Paidí Ó Sé:

> *On 24 August 1997, during the All-Ireland semi-final between Kerry and Cavan Paidí Ó Sé made a number of intrusions onto the pitch and was involved in an altercation with a Cavan player. He was summoned to a meeting of the GAC which was held on the same day as the All-Ireland hurling final. The decision of the GAC was to allow Paidí off and not suspend him. Many people were shocked by the decision of the GAC but I wasn't. In fact, late on the Sunday night while celebrating our All-Ireland victory in the Alexander Hotel, I was told what the outcome of that meeting would be and how it happened.*

All of us have had experiences of having being involved in instances when least expected, the memory of which are forever etched in our mind. It may have been the death of a loved one or a catastrophic event such as the 11 September 2001 in New York where every detail is easily recalled.

> *Dramatic and exciting as the All-Ireland victory of 1997 over Tipperary was, and unusual as the altercation with Eamon Cregan on live television may have been, it was an encounter later that night that outraged me and left me with a feeling that will stay forever in my memory. It's funny the little details you remember like having one leg resting on a chair, it was however the look on the face of Tony Garry that surprised me.*

> *Tony Garry is Chief Executive of Davy's Stockbrokers, but it was as a Clare supporter and contributor to our Holiday Fund that I knew him. Following the banquet and speeches, I was looking forward to the enjoyable part of the evening which is meeting our supporters and enjoying the craic. So there I was with my leg resting on a chair at the back of the function room, when I was approached by Tony Garry. Being the intelligent person that he is, I was expecting some cryptic comment about the match. I was completely taken aback when in a serious mood he said 'Ger, it's a disgrace.'*

> *'What's wrong with you?' was my immediate reply.*

> *'It's a bloody disgrace,' he repeated.*

'You and Len Gaynor in the dugout today when Paidí Ó Sé is going to get away scot free tonight.' 'How do you know?' I asked. Tony then told me the story that had happened earlier that day naming names and strategies employed.

Tony told me that on that weekend of the All-Ireland final, a long standing Cork-based friend came to visit him. He drove his friend, a leading GAA figure in Cork and closely associated with Cork teams to the All-Ireland hurling final in Croke Park. During this journey, his friend made a mobile phone call to Paidí Ó Sé and outlined from a prepared document the approach and strategy he was to adopt at his meeting with the GAC that day.

If successful, this strategy would enable Paidí Ó Sé who was to make a personal appearance before the GAC that evening to escape the Loughnane and Gaynor type of punishment for the upcoming All-Ireland football final against Mayo. Having contacted Paidí on the phone, his friend began to read from the document very slowly, line by line, carefully outlining the strategy that Paidí should adopt when he faced the GAC. This included stressing his high regard for the GAC and its rules and a guarantee that it would not happen again. This strategy was so detailed that it involved Paidí going into the meeting twice, the second time was to mention something important which he didn't refer to the first time.

The outcome of the GAC meeting was that even though Paidí Ó Sé made many incursions onto the pitch and had an altercation with a Cavan player, he was not suspended. Shocked at what he was hearing in his own car on that journey to Croke Park, Tony Garry enquired as to where this strategy document came from, he was shocked by the name quoted in the reply as the Mr X named was well-known to me. To me this was the shock of shocks.

During the final preparations for this book, I contacted Tony Garry on 28 September to again discuss this issue with him. Without any hesitation, Tony Garry confirmed everything as he had done on that September Sunday night in Dublin and also during a holiday chat in Lahinch in 1998. He agreed the story should be told. On the day before the famous radio interview in 1998, I met with Tony at his holiday home in Lahinch when he was then captain of Lahinch Golf Club. My aim was to try and persuade him to allow me to use the story in the interview on the following morning. We went for a walk around the perimeter of the golf course and Tony repeated the story to me and still appeared angered by what he saw as the injustice of it all. However, he asked me not to use the story as it could jeopardise the long standing friendship between his family and his friend's family. He has no sympathy for the person involved and would have loved to expose him but friendship came first. Reluctantly, I relented, even though at a time when Clare were being vilified by the media and GAA officials, his help would have been welcome.

We agreed to meet for lunch in Dublin on Thursday 4 October 2001 to discuss the matter again. To my great shock, I received a phone call from Tony Garry on Monday 1 October. During this phone call he indicated that he would now prefer if the story wasn't in the book and if it was, he didn't want his name mentioned. He confirmed that he had contacted his Cork GAA friend who had made the phone call to Paidí Ó Sé. Some other comments made to me in the phone call of 1 October really shocked me. Needless to say, he also cancelled the lunch appointment arranged for Thursday 4 October in Dublin. As Tony Garry was both the chauffeur and witness, he is in a position to confirm publicly what he stated to me on two occasions before the telephone conversation of 1 October. Tony Garry is a proud Clareman, I have no doubt that GAA people everywhere are entitled to know the truth on this issue from Tony. Tony should now confirm what he knows to help us to understand the events that transpired.

Perhaps the GAA can now clarify why a rule applied one way in relation to myself was applied differently to Paidí Ó Sé.

In September 1997, I was voted Manager of the Month, in October 1997, Paidí was voted Manager of the Month. A joint presentation sponsored by Phillips was held in a Killarney hotel. I was sitting beside Paidí at one stage during this function and I said to him 'Paidí, I know how you escaped'. Paidí looked at me with surprise and said 'Well Ger, I sold you down the drain anyway.' I took this to mean that he told the meeting he wasn't going to act like Ger Loughnane. I then pointed to a prominent Kerry official in the Munster Council and asked Paidí if he had defended him, knowing full well that he was not involved. Paidí Ó Sé answered – 'No, that b*****x did nothing at all for me.' His subsequent comments implying that it was friends from another county that helped him only confirmed what I already knew. I said 'Paidí, I know what happened and how you escaped.' Paidí then looked at me in a shocked state and shut up.

It became clear to me that there was one rule for Clare and a different rule when it suited for the rest. Here was a situation where a well-known person (Mr X) had orchestrated a strategy for someone appearing before the GAC on a disciplinary matter, with the intention of improving Paidí's chances of a 'get off free' punishment. This shook me to the bone in the light of my own experience.

REVENGE IS SWEET

Loughnane's reading material stretched into dense business manuals. He was very taken by an idea in the *Sloan Management Review* which stated that, 'By breaking the rules of the game and thinking of new ways to compete, a company can strategically redefine its business and catch its bigger competitors off guard. The trick is not to play the game better than the competition but to develop and play an altogether different game.' From the time he took over as Clare manager, he sought to put that philosophy into practice.

Photo: Courtesy of Bernard O'Dowd

'Genie in the bottle.' Loughnane prepares for the Championship clash with Cork.

Clare's preparations for the 1998 Munster Championship appeared to get off to a bad start when Cork handed them out an eleven-point drubbing in the National League semi-final on 3 May in Thurles. Seven weeks later the two teams would meet again in the same venue in the Munster semi final. Michael O'Halloran and Conor Clancy were both named in the original selection, but instead Brian Quinn and Alan Markham took the field against Cork.

In '98, the Munster semi-final against Cork was always going to be a crunch game for us. We drove home the message to the players beforehand that we couldn't let Cork beat us. That was the game we played our first real dummy team. I can still see Tom Cashman and Jimmy Barry Murphy looking out at the field, looking at their programme, looking at the numbers on the players' backs and trying to figure who exactly was playing and who wasn't. They were totally confused!

We wore Cork down physically and in the last 20 minutes we completely outhurled them with speed and skill and everything you'd want to see in your team. At one stage, Brian Corcoran got the ball. He turned to his right and PJ O'Connell was there. He turned to his left and Jamesie was there. Jamesie took it off him and put it over the bar. Corcoran looked over at Jimmy Barry Murphy and threw his arms up in the air. It was like he was asking: what can we do?

From a Clare perspective, the ends justified the means with an eight points victory.

CONTROVERSY

Like a wasp's nest, Loughnane is glued by something so powerful that it withstands the storms that whirl outside. But like the nest, if anybody probes too closely about the events of 1998, the memories fly out and sting: disappointment, sadness and above all a sense of injustice. The Colin Lynch saga and the controversy about the Munster final replay have been the source of much speculation. On this subject, he is so keenly alert that you worry about your next remark. He believes it is time that the truth, as he sees it, is finally brought into the public domain.

There was a brilliant article in The Clare Champion *by Joe Keane in which he spoke about Ernest Hemingway. After the publication of his book about bull-fighting,* Death in the Afternoon, *he was asked by an interviewer what he thought about bull fighting as a sport. He replied, 'One has to be in with the bulls to know.' It is amazing so many people spoke with such certainty about the Colin Lynch affair without knowing all of the facts and circumstances.*

There's a story told about the two grasshoppers who came onto the field before the Munster final replay in 1998. As the pulling started between the players, one said to the other, 'We're going to be killed here today. Do you feel the tension?'

The other replied, 'I do. Hop up here on the sliotar. It's the only place we'll be safe!'

How did such an atmosphere build up? Time won't stand still for reflections when the clash of the ash is at its fiercest but the seeds for the extraordinary scenes that day had been sown the previous week. There are major hazards in deciding to ration commitment according to assessments of the opposition. Clare paid the price for that lapse in the first game.

> We had made a savage effort against Cork in the previous game and we always found it very difficult to raise our game the next day after a heroic effort. Every team does. It was the second year of the back door system, so there was always a safety net there. There was no real rivalry between Clare and Waterford. There was nothing there to give us the edge against them. All of us went down there with the nearest thing to a casual attitude in my time as Clare manager. The same drive wasn't there.

From the beginning, it was clear that Waterford's attitude was anything but casual.

> Whenever we played in Thurles, the Clare supporters were always given tickets for one part of the ground and we sat in the dugout in front of them. If we had sat in front of the rival supporters, that could have been the recipe for all kinds of nastiness. When we went out against Waterford, the first thing we noticed was that all the Waterford subs and officials were in our dugout. We said nothing and went into the other dugout.

> Even though we were leading all through the game, Paul Flynn got a late goal and then he had a chance to win the game from a long way out but he put the ball wide. A few incidents had happened. PJ O'Connell was sent off but there was a photo published the following day which showed Fergal Hartley giving him a ferocious tackle just before. Yet it was O'Connell alone who was sent to the line.

> Gerald McCarthy had verbally abused not alone the umpires but he grabbed Pat O'Connor, the linesman, by the shoulder. I said, 'Jaysus Gerald, take it easy.' He was annoyed by some decision or other. He'd also gone on to the pitch on three separate occasions and verbally abused a different Clare player each time.

Writing in *The Sunday Independent* the following Sunday, Dermot Crowe observed:

> 'The unruliness on the pitch was often emulated beyond its borders, most notably by Waterford manager Gerald McCarthy, who was rightly booked by [referee] Barrett for berating an umpire after he made an error of judgement in waving Browne's crucial point wide. McCarthy is a passionate man, there was a huge amount at stake, and he is entitled to expect a more reliable method of calculating scores. But the point had been awarded when he shamefully launched a tirade against his unfortunate target. McCarthy shouldn't have been anywhere near O'Connell at the time of his sending off either.'

Fame can be a mixed blessing. One of the inevitable products of success is that there is increased interest in a new celebrity's private live. GAA players are not insulated from this trend and from time to time suffer the grinding of the rumour mill. Generally, the bigger the name the more outrageous the rumour. After their second All-Ireland in '97, a few of the Clare players became the subject of salacious gossip. They were by no means the first GAA players to suffer in this way.

> When the players came back into the dressing-room I had never seen them so agitated and I asked what was wrong. They were fuming.
>
> One of the rumours doing the rounds at the time was that one of our players was beating his wife. Anyone who knows anything about his character would have known immediately how scurrilous and far off the mark it was and wouldn't have entertained it for a second. One of the Waterford players had shouted at the player in question, across the pitch, that he was a wife-beater. A lot of our players heard it. The player himself said nothing but it was the other players who were incensed. If anything triggered our players huge response the following day, it was that.

If the entire Clare squad were galvanised by the wife-beating comments, Loughnane was livid with the poor showing of his team. Understanding the ambushes of the mind his team had capitulated to, he was determined to reverse the pattern in the replay. His eyes drove through his players like two steel nails.

> On the bus back, all I was thinking of was our performance which was brutal. At training on Tuesday night, the riot act was read! Mike O'Halloran was missing that night and when he came back the next night he said, 'I hear the paint was falling off the goalposts!'
>
> In retrospect there was no need for me to have said anything. The players were so pumped up about what had been said to one of their own. I was

angry with myself as much as with the players that none of us had picked up what was happening on the pitch and taken steps to correct it.

The first step was to get all the players together the following night. I didn't go into the dressing-room. I stood out on the field. They knew that there was something up. I think Mike Mac did a lap or two with them and then I called them in to the midfield and I laid into them about backing down. I said Munster Championships and All-Irelands weren't worth a damn. I didn't care about anything the following Sunday except we weren't going to be intimidated. Then I moved on about ten yards and laid into them about the next point. That was the pattern. I moved forward ten yards for every point 'til they all ended up in the net with me standing outside looking in at them, delivering a lecture about what was going to happen the following Sunday.

I picked on every player who had backed down. Seánie, Brian Lohan and Colin Lynch got special attention first. Whenever I wanted to attack, I started with the strongest players. Seánie got a ferocious lecture, Lohan 40 times worse, and Lynch as bad as the two of them put together for having backed down. I told them they could dump their medals because anyone who backed down from a challenge didn't deserve any respect. The next day we were not going to back down.

We then adjourned to the Sherwood. Our planning committee, Tony, Mike and I went through where we had gone wrong the first day. Tony pointed out to me about the dugout. Mike said that there were too many people in the dressing-room before the game with subs and officials. I said we'll get them out but we have to do it in a way that they would still feel involved. So we decided we would get them to secure the dugout. It was like a military operation!

In the meantime, Tony was to fire a few broadsides in The Examiner *about Gerald McCarthy's behaviour on the field so that everyone, especially the referee, was aware of it for the following Sunday.*

The players weren't allowed to train. They would be about to go training when I'd deliver another lecture about the way we were going to play and then take them back into the dressing-room so that by the Sunday they were itching to play. The only training was psychological.

99 out of 100 people will argue it was over the top. I didn't care whether it cost us the All-Ireland. We weren't going to be a team that backed down. I did emphasise that I didn't want any wildness but everyone was prepared to give their life for Clare to win.

On the day of the replay, we went to Cashel for a puckout before the game as usual. The players were unusually quiet. I was as sour as I could be with them. The message was being delivered loud and clear. This was the day to deliver.

Loughnane was fingered as a catalyst for the undeniable drama that unfolded in the replay.

We went out on to the field and there was a photo published in The Clare Champion of me really putting it up to Colin Lynch before the game. All I was saying to him was that he had really let himself down the first day with the way he hurled, that he was a much better player than Tony Browne and lucky enough he had one more chance to prove it. There were other players I had also singled out to deliver a similar message to, like Alan Markham, who had allowed themselves to be pushed around by Waterford the first day and that was never, ever going to happen again.

When Jamesie came out with a broken hurl after a clash between himself and Brian Greene, you could really sense the tension. There was a warning for all the officials to stay in the dugout but Tony Considine wasn't in the dugout. Just as he was about to throw in the ball, the referee spotted that Tony wasn't in the dugout and walked over to put him back. In the meantime, the four players in the centre-field were jostling and waiting for the ball to be thrown in. By the time the ball was thrown in, Lynch had let fly three or four times but the only one he actually hit was Ollie Baker! He hit him on the heel.

The first ball that went down was between Alan Markham and Stephen Frampton and both of them pulled a mile above the ball. I thought, 'Oh, f**k.'

I said to Tony Considine, 'It's lucky we're up for that one, otherwise they'd devour us.' The first day, Waterford caught Clare totally by surprise. Collectively our players weren't able to react to it. They were ready for anything the second day.

*Evasive Action. Colin Lynch sidesteps Tony Browne in the
Munster final (replay) in 1998. Liam Doyle looks on.*

Sport is agony and ecstasy. It does not lend itself to grey areas. The next
development would spiral crazily out of control.

> *For the first five minutes the pulling was absolutely ferocious. Then we
> had the Lohan and White incident. Out of the corner of my eye, I saw
> Colin Lynch and Browne flaking each other. Who started it? That's a
> different story. I honestly don't know.*

> *A hurley is a dangerous weapon. If a player wants to use a hurley to
> inflict damage he can do so. To the onlooker, pulling seems vicious but in
> reality it's just like sword-fighting. If you strike somebody, it's always on
> a part of the body that's least vulnerable. If Lynch wanted to injure
> Browne, he could have done so easily.*

> *Pat O'Connor, the well known referee, was a linesman on the day. He
> saw what happened and put up the flag. Lohan and White were sent off.
> The noise from the crowd was deafening. There was total chaos in front of
> the Clare goal. My immediate concern was to sort out the defence now*

that Lohan was gone. I wanted Brian Quinn to stay on Paul Flynn and let Frank cover behind him.

Meanwhile Pat O'Connor had gone to the referee, Willie Barrett, and reported the incident between Lynch and Tony Browne. Willie Barrett booked both of them. Gerald McCarthy went absolutely ape when Browne was booked and launched into a tirade against the referee.

After that the whole thing settled down and Clare completely outhurled them and demolished Waterford. About five minutes before the end of the game, I said to Gerald McCarthy, 'Sure the game is over now.' We chatted away for three or four minutes. He said, 'Oh ye're by far the better team.' There was no anger at all.

Dalo got the cup and we went into the dressing-room. Pat Joe Ryan, the chairman of Waterford county board, came in and said, 'Ye're the best team I ever saw in my life. Ye're hurling is way better than anybody else's. I hope ye go on now and win the All-Ireland.' There was no more about it.

I do admit it was a warlike atmosphere against Waterford. It was the same on both sides. Clare went into the game like never before. It was a day to kill or be killed. The players weren't thinking about winning an All-Ireland. It was about putting Waterford down. If we had won an All-Ireland by coming in the back-door, after allowing Waterford to intimidate us in the Munster final replay, it would have been useless. I freely admit putting down Waterford was absolutely vital. There were always hard physical exchanges in the Munster Championship but when it was over players shook hands and it was forgotten about. When Waterford were beaten, they should have just taken it. They weren't men enough to take it. That's the way it looked to me.

Whenever Waterford seem to come near the big prize, they always seem to lose their discipline completely. In the 1989 Munster final, the first one to be televised live by RTE, they were so aggressive and over the top. It was one of the most filthy Munster finals you could see. All of the incidents were shown again and again. It was the worst sort of ad for the game you could wish for. In '95 in the Munster Championship they gave another outrageous display. Waterford had all the players from their All-Ireland under-21 winning team come through and were rumoured to be about to make a big breakthrough but again they lost their discipline. Three years later the same thing again, but Clare got the blame even though in the first game Waterford were involved in tactics that were ignored. In the replay we could not ignore them.

In normal circumstances, we'd have loved to have seen Waterford winning the All-Ireland. Nobody remembers Daly's speech afterwards nor the cup coming into the dressing-room. Always when we meet since, we remember the glow of satisfaction we got from having downed Waterford.

THE LYNCH MOB

The following day there was a bit of a ripple about the physical exchanges in the papers but nothing extraordinary. The temperature rose dramatically on Monday evening after the 'Sportscall' programme on RTE radio. It was clear from very early that one Clare player was being singled out for special attention with comments like, 'the Vinnie Jones of hurling' and 'I'd love to see him tested for steroids.' It was not long before Loughnane was brought centre stage.

Caller A

'The Munster Council had people on the sideline yesterday to watch Clare and their tactics, Considine's and Loughnane's tactics. It was orchestrated violence for the first three minutes. They did it against Cork and it didn't work. They didn't do it against us last week because they didn't think they had to ... Willie Barrett has had Clare for three championship matches this year, he's had them against Cork, he's had them against Waterford, and he's had them against Waterford again, and with the luck of God maybe Loughnane will bullshit and talk enough to bring him all the way to Croke Park and then he'll definitely have his All-Ireland ... what you saw for the first three minutes was like what you'd see on the Ormeau Road. It was orchestrated violence .... You saw the lunatic attitude of Colin Lynch in the middle of the midfield ... and Loughnane must take full responsibility. He's the boss. There was a deliberate take-out-Tony-Browne policy within the first three minutes of the match yesterday .... We're not bitter about losing a Munster final. We are bitter about the treatment that was dished out and if it was the other way round we'd be lambasted by Loughnane and if he's in charge of schoolchildren in Clare ... if he drilled a man to be that kind ...'

Caller B

'I sat ... right beside the Clare dugout ... Willie Barrett came over to speak to Considine and as he did Anthony Daly passed Dan Shanahan they shook hands which is the usual thing to do. Ger Loughnane walked up to Anthony Daly and with his right hand clenched in the fist in his left hand and he roared into Daly. Daly hit Shanahan and Shanahan went down

Shanahan got up and he hit Daly back with his shoulder and Daly went down on his arse. It got a bit out of hand after that.'

Caller C

'Clare disgraced themselves ...'

Caller D

'It was like Drumcree for the spectators ...'

Caller E

'I'm a national school teacher of a long, long standing and I've been dealing with children for a large number of years on the sportsfield and off. I would be ashamed of my life if I prepared a team and they went out like the Clare people did yesterday. It was organised thuggery and there can be no apologies for it ... stands accused and I presume Loughnane if he was responsible for sending them out like that ... if Ger Loughnane had his players motivated the way they were yesterday ... with their eyes jumping out of their head, I'd say it's time we pulled back from all of this.'

Loughnane was well used to, and more than able for, comments about his tactics but the repeated implication that he was unfit to be a teacher or in charge of children crossed a new line.

The 'Sportscall' programme after the Munster final was totally scandalous, totally one-sided. Two solicitors approached me with the tape of the programme and said they'd take on the case for nothing to sue RTE but I said I didn't want it to go that route. They kept saying, 'but you'll win hands down.' After that programme, the media focus on us became crazy.

Gerald McCarthy went on local radio in Waterford and said he was just praying for the day that they could meet Clare again and set the record straight. He was playing for the sympathy vote but this was after he had admitted to me that Waterford were beaten by a better team!

The following Sunday, Tony Browne played the match of his life in the All-Ireland quarter final against Galway. This was the man who had been nearly killed by Clare seven days before!

As the week went on, the controversy developed a momentum of its own. Amid the hysteria, there were the occasional dissenting voices including those who pointed out that Clare had a very good disciplinary record under Loughnane's stewardship. In his 22 championship matches in charge of the Clare team, only two players were sent off, both against

Waterford in 1998. In an article in *Ireland on Sunday*, entitled 'Welcome to the Land of the Hypocrite', Martin Breheny situated the breaches of discipline in the game in a wider context.

> 'In fairness to Clare, it has to be said that their disciplinary record over four seasons at the top has been excellent. Unfair attempts are now being made to portray them as arrogant hatchet men, who would stop at nothing to win. Is there a touch of jealousy in the air? Clare have been the best side in the country over the past four seasons and four minutes last Sunday, unpalatable as they were, should not be allowed to undermine the team's status as great champions. The bigger issue is the question of the GAA's response to the latest discipline fracture. It has got to be dealt with firmly and honestly without taking the easy way out and scapegoating some players, whether they be from Clare or Waterford. That would be akin to blaming an errant pupil for a faulty education system. The discipline system stinks – clean it out and the rest will follow quickly and easily.'

However, behind the scenes judgement was being passed. The bigger issues were apparently ignored.

> I didn't realise there had been anything afoot. We went back training on the Thursday night. I'd been at the Galway races on the Wednesday and, looking back, there were rumblings that there was trouble ahead but I didn't pick up on them. It had been non-stop in the papers. One headline posed the question: Is this space age hurling? Were Clare trying to take hurling on to a new plane? It was total rubbish.

Loughnane's gut instinct was telling him to brace himself for trouble.

> The first inkling I got was after the All-Ireland quarter-final when Robert Frost, chairman of the Clare county board, had overheard a conversation that Lynch would get a three-month suspension. I dismissed it at first, but with all the clamour that was going on I began to wonder. The next thing we got the letter that Lynch was to appear before the Munster Council.

THE BOOK OF EVIDENCE

We prefer to play hopscotch in a familiar minefield. Loughnane was used to investing all his energies into battles on the field. Now he was finding himself concentrating most of his energies on an off-the-field battle. From the Clare perspective, there were a number of curious features about the actions of the Munster Council. The referee's report into the Munster final states:

'I sent off PJ O'Connell an Clár for dangerous play. After I had consulted with my umpire in which he had given an incorrect decision and I had altered his decision and gave a point to Port Lairge, Gerald McCarthy Waterford came onto field and abused the umpire, and myself when I booked him.'

Imreoirí chuireadh chuig an Líne
Players Ordered To The Line

(State Offence/s for which player/s were sent to the line. Be Specific and concise. Use guidelines on P.5.)

I sent off P J O Connell an Clár for Dangerous Play.

After I had consulted with my umpire in which he had given an incorrect decision and I had altered his decision and gave a point to Port Lairge Gerald McCarthy Waterford came onto field and abused the umpire, and myself when I booked him.

Under the G.A.A. rules, the referee's report is final and conclusive as to the fact and Gerald McCarthy would have to get a minimum of two month's suspension. It is noteworthy that the Munster Council acted immediately on the referee's report so far as PJ O'Connell was concerned and he was given a one-month suspension. Clare have no problem with this decision. However, what the Banner contingent found problematic was that the Munster Council did not deal with McCarthy at the same meeting. If they had, and the Waterford manager got the expected suspension, he would have to be absent for the replay game between Clare and Waterford on 19 July and the following game, the All-Ireland

quarter-final between Waterford and Galway on 26 July. In fact, he di‹
not come before the disciplinary committee of Munster Council unt
Friday, 7 August.

However, the major issues of this case arose in the replayed game o
19 July. To understate the case, tension was high between the players i
the opening minutes. As the referee's report on that game makes clea
Colin Lynch is named jointly with Tony Browne of Waterford for havin
engaged in rough play and was booked. It is clear that Lynch could n‹
be suspended under any part of this report.

Referee's Report

An interesting feature is that the referee booked S. Fitzpatrick and S. Ahern of Waterford team management for intrusions on the field of play. Significantly, the referee did not adversely comment on Loughnane in that context.

As the letter dated 30 July reveals, Loughnane was excluded from the pitch enclosure for the next senior hurling championship fixture arising from a decision made at that meeting on 28 July. Loughnane received no notice of any issue arising in connection with him for that meeting and was given no opportunity to deal with it.

COMHAIRLE NA MUMHAN
C.L.G.

Seán Ó Ceallaigh, Cathaoirleach
Criostóir Ó Cuana, Leas-Cathaoirleach
Déaglán Ó Maoláin, Cisteoir
Dónal Ó Nialláin, Rúnai
An tAth. S. Gáirnéar, Oif. Chaid. Poiblí

Árd Aoíbhinn,
Baile Nua, Aonach Urún,
Co. Thiobraid Arann
Fax/Guthán 067/31594
30/7/1998
. . . . 199 . . . . . .

Gearoid Uas. O Lachtuain,
Bainisteoir Foireann Iomana Sinsir An Chlair,
Fe/ch. Padraig Uas. Mac Gearailt,
Runai C.L.G.,
Dr. Abh. Uí gCearnaigh,
Co. An Chlair.

Re: Decision of Coiste Gniomhaiochtai na Mumhan Meeting for your exclusion from the Pitch Enclosure for next S.H.C. Game

A Ghearoid, A Chara,

Arising from the decision of the Coiste Gniomhaiochtai na Mumhan C.L.G. meeting held in The Limerick Inn Hotel on Tuesday 28/7/98, I have been instructed to inform you that **you are excluded from the Pitch Enclosure for the next S.H.C. game** i.e. An Clar .v. Uibh Fhaili at Pairc An Chrocaigh on 9/8/98 for reported repeated contravention of Regulation 7 of the "Regulations Governing the Organisation and Presentation of Championship Games" i.e. unauthorised incursions on to the field of play during recent Munster Championship Games in Thurles on 21/6/98, 12/7/98 and 19/7/98.

Mise le meas,

Donal O Niallain (Runai)

Coip: Padraig Uas. Mac Gearailt,
Runai C.L.G.,
Dr. Abh. Uí gCearnaigh,
Co. An Chlair.

CUMANN LÚTHCHLEAS GAEL
COMHAIRLE NA MUMHAN

1471198
Baile Nua,
Aonach,
Co. Thiobraid Árann

Foirm Oifigiúil Tuarascála an Réiteora
Referee's Official Report Form

Liam Mac D Baroid

Réiteoir C. L. G. Fíl. Thomhan

A Chara,
Your are hereby notified that you have been appointed by Comhairle na Mumhan to referee:

Comórtas .... M. H. Final Replay ....

Club .... Durlus .... v .... Portlaoige ....

Ionad .... Durlus ....

Dáta: ...... Aoine 19 Geabhar .... 3.30 ..... p.m.

Extra Time if necessary

You are requested:
(a) Be on the pitch ten minutes before starting time.
(b) Arrange for Match Umpires and Linesmen.
(c) Complete this form and return to me (together with Team Lists) within 3 days of match

In the event of being unable to act please notify me immediately,
(067-31594)
Sínithe:

Rúnaí, Do Niallain
Dónal Ó Nialláin.

Maybe Linesmen as
is it Sunday.

Imreoirí a fuair rabhadh.
Details of players cautioned.

Player	Contae	Offence
C. Lynch	An Clár	Rough Play
Tom Browne	Port Laoige	"
L. Doyle	An Clár	"
S. Smith	Portlaoige	"
F. Martin	Port Laoige	Personal Foul
S. Mc Mahon	An Clár	Rough Play

Injured Players - Nature of Injury

None reported to me

6

still did not deal with Gerald McCarthy on a more serious issue, which had been specified in a referee's report from a Sunday earlier.

Indeed the Council's treatment of Gerald McCarthy is particularly interesting on a number of levels. McCarthy did not comply with the request to attend the Munster Council meeting of 28 July. The minutes of that meeting disclose, 'Gearailt MacCarthaigh wrote stating that he could not attend the meeting because of his commitment to training on that night. He expressed a wish to be given the opportunity to attend the next GAC meeting as he was most anxious to be given a personal hearing.' The Council acceded to his request thus ensuring that he would not be suspended for the Munster final reply. From a Clare perspective, a training session seemed to be inadequate grounds for someone not to face a serious charge of abusing a referee and an umpire.

However, when the council got the opportunity to act decisively on 'such appalling conduct' at its meeting on 7 August a very different strategy was pursued, as is starkly highlighted in the enclosed minutes of the meeting as outlined on the following page.

As the minutes make clear, under Rule 136 (B1) 'abusive or threatening language by a player or official towards a referee or an umpire carries a two-month suspension. As is also clear, both the referee and the umpire had provided clarification of McCarthy's abuse of both of them, 'that he used foul language to the ref and even more foul language to the umpire.' The Council did not apparently take Frank Murphy's previous exhortation to heart. Instead they favoured the proposals from Sean Kelly (none of which are included in Rule 136 (B) and decided that Gerald McCarthy should only be severely warned, that he should furnish a written apology to the umpire and be excluded from the pitch enclosure for the All-Ireland senior hurling semi-final between Waterford and Kilkenny on 16 August.

It is very significant that when this course of action was initially proposed, the secretary of the Munster Council, Donie Neylon, felt compelled to say that they 'would need to be conscious of the rules and not to be setting a precedent for future cases of a similar nature.' His advice on the danger of an *a la carte* approach to the rules appeared to fall on deaf ears. I really admired Donie Neylon for highlighting the importance of sticking strictly to the rules on this and all cases.

It is also noteworthy that at the end of the meeting the delegates were instructed by the chairman of the Council, Sean Kelly, 'not to reveal the nature of the discussions that had taken place at that night's meeting to outside interests and bodies.'

The following is just the section of the minutes of the Munster Council meeting of 7 August which dealt with the Gerald McCarthy incident.

Extract from Munster Council minutes

Gearailt MacCarthaigh, Bainisteoir Foirne Sinsir Phortlairge attended and was, also, represented by Padraig S. O Riain, (Cathaoirleach Coiste Cho. Phortlairge).

An Cathaoirleach, Sean O Ceallaigh, apologised to G. Mac Carthaigh for the delay of one hour in dealing with his case because of unforeseen problems with C. O Loinsigh's hearing.

The above two ref's reports were read to G. Mac Carthaigh by the Cathaoirleach, who also informed G MacCarthaigh of the clarification received from the referee and the umpire re his abuse of both of them, i.e. that he (G. Mac Carthaigh) used foul language to the ref and even more foul language to the umpire who had made the incorrect decision.

Gearailt Mac Carthaigh thanked the Council for the opportunity to attend and regretted that he couldn't attend the last meeting because he had a business commitment that day in Dublin and only got late back to Waterford for a training session. He said that at the outset he wanted to state that he trusted in the Council's sense of fairness in dealing with his case. As regards his encroachment at P. Ui Chaoimh on 7/6 he only went on to the field to draw the ref's attention to the fact that a player was down injured at the lower end of the field and the umpire had been trying unsuccessfully to call the ref's attention to the matter. He said that he didn't say anything to the ref. and went off the field immediately. He never came on to the field in the first round v Kerry in Tralee.

With regard to the incident with the umpire, who had very obviously given a wrong decision on 12/7 at Thurles, he went on in fairness to his players to try and right a wrong that was being done to Waterford, i.e. a legitimate point had been waved wide and he said to the umpire, 'are you effing well blind?'. The referee in fairness to him then dealt with the matter and awarded the point to Waterford and he went back to the umpire and said, 'Thank God someone has decent eyesight and will give us fair play'. In response to a query from G. Mac Carthaigh, the Chairman read out and clarified Rule 136 (B1) i.e. that abusive or threatening language by a player or official towards a referee or an umpire carried a two months suspension.

Gearailt Mac Carthaigh then cited an number of occasions when Clare officials and players had misbehaved in various ways and abused him or interfered with the referee in performing his duties and the ref had not reported them at all.

So, he felt quite hard done by in the circumstances when others had transgressed much worse than he had and they were not reported.

He said that he had been honest and was telling the truth, had never been put off in his life, took great pride in Waterford's achievements this year and he appealed to the Council for leniency because of his excellent record over the years.

Padraig S. O Riain said that he concurred with G. Mac Carthaigh's evidence. Gerald had done wonders for Waterford hurling, had instilled great discipline into the team and would never dream of promoting any kind of rough play. He had never been sent off the field and a suspension on him now would do untold damage to the great progress that Waterford hurlers had made this year. Waterford Co. Board had great respect for the Munster Council and always found its officers to be most honourable and fair in their decisions. In conclusion, P. S. O Riain said that it would be very unfair to suspend G. McCarthy because it wasn't Waterford who went on with all the argy-bargy on radio and the media.

Gearoid O hIci said that it was unsporting of G. McCarthy to be blaming Clare mentors and players in support of his own case.

Gerald McCarthy in reply said that he was only telling the truth but he didn't want anyone else suspended.

G. MacCarthaigh and P. S. O Riain then left the meeting.

Seamus O Gormain (Portlairge) said that it was not acceptable for an umpire to make such a bad decision and it was understandable that G. Mc Carthy would re-act in the circumstances. Gerald honestly admitted abusing the umpire but didn't say very much to the referee.

Proinsias O Murchu said that there had been too many bad decisions by umpires in this year's championship and this was unacceptable but Gerald McCarthy should not be going on to the field like he had been in recent games.

Gearoid O hIci said that the Committee should be consistent in its decisions because G. McCarthy had been reported for abusing both the referee and the umpire.

An Cathaoirlech said that the Committee could either suspend G. McCarthy for abuse or

(a) severely warn him as to his future conduct

(b) request him to forward a written apology to the umpire and

(c) exclude him from the pitch enclosure for the All-Ireland S.H. Semi-Final at Croke Park on 16/8/98.

An Runai said that the Committee would need to be conscious of the rules and not to be setting a precedent for future cases of a similar nature.

Decision: Seamus O Gormain proposed that as there were mitigating circumstances for G. McCarthy's misbehaviour he would propose that he be (a) severely warned (b) furnish a written apology to the umpire and (c) be excluded from the pitch enclosure on the 16/8/98 in Croke Park, seconded by L. O Duibhir.

Gearoid O hIci. proposed that G. McCarthy be suspended for two months for abuse of the ref and his umpire but as his proposal got no seconder, S. O Gormain proposal was passed. G. Mac Carthaigh was recalled and informed of the decision.

G. Mac Carthaigh and P. S. O Riain thanked the meeting for the fair hearing received.

What a load of rubbish! smash rules when it suits you and let the culprit go completely free.

However, what really annoyed the Clare camp was that Colin Lynch was sent a letter on 29 July from Donie Neylon, secretary on the Munster Council which stated: 'I have been instructed as per decision of a meeting of Coiste Gniomhaiochtai na Mumhan C.L.G. held in The Limerick Inn Hotel on Tuesday 28/7/98 to inform you that you are **hereby charged with repeated striking with the hurley** (his bold print) on opponents in the early stages of the above game on 19/7/98.' The letter went on to state that 'the matter will be finalised at the meeting' on 7/8/1998.

With the finality of a door being slammed, the referee's report appeared to be totally ignored. First, as we have seen, the referee does not allege that Colin Lynch struck an opponent with the hurley or repeatedly struck an opponent with the hurley, but merely engaged with Tony Browne in 'rough play'. Second, as we have also seen, Tony Browne was equally blamed in the referee's report but he was not called before the Munster Council for any disciplinary matter.

A further grievance in Clare was that before the disciplinary meeting on 28 July, members of the Munster Council Disciplinary Committee apparently met with the referee and his umpires and linesmen and discussed the case without informing Noel Walsh, one of their committee from Clare, about that meeting. This caused the Clare camp to believe that the meeting was invalidly constituted.

As if the Clare camp did not have enough reason to feel sore, the temperature really rose on Sunday, 26 July. The chairman of the Clare county board, Robert Frost, attended the Waterford versus Galway All-Ireland quarter-final at Croke Park. He was in the V.I.P. section of the Hogan Stand. There were three clergymen, including two Father Kitts, seated immediately behind him. He overheard their conversation. It was impossible not to hear it. The Munster final replay of the previous Sunday was the main topic of conversation between them. The immediate response to this conversation was to the depiction of Loughnane and his players, the famous line that, 'the Clare team were tinkers, Loughnane was a tramp and the Clare team must be on drugs.'

The really significant part of the discussion on Sunday, 26 July, was that it took place two days before the meeting (scheduled for Tuesday, 28 July) of the Munster Council to make a decision on the referee's report and one of the priest stated:

> *A reliable source has told me that the Munster Council may suspend Colin Lynch for three months. By coincidence this is exactly what happened.'*

On hearing this, Robert Frost stood up and challenged the three priests about what they had been saying, and being embarrassed about having to do so in public, he then left. Of course, questions were immediately raised: how could three outsiders know Lynch's fate two days before the meeting to adjudicate on his 'crime'? How could this possibly reflect proper procedures? Could justice be served in this way?

Loughnane believes that Clare made a fundamental tactical error in this controversy.

> *At a meeting of the Munster Council, Waterford proposed having an investigation into the events of the match. Their proposal got no seconder. Clare should have seconded it to ensure there was a full, fair and open investigation.*

Instead the Clare county board went down the legal avenue, seeking a pre-emptive strike against the Munster Council taking disciplinary action.

Pat Fitzgerald said the only way was to get a court injunction against the Munster Council. If Colin Lynch was brought before them, the only question they'd ask him was: Did you strike Tony Browne? The context or the question of provocation wouldn't be considered.

The Council's verdict still wasn't announced, but essentially Clare's case was that Colin Lynch shouldn't be called in front of them in the first place. It all became very technical then. The court case was on the Friday before the All-Ireland semi-final against Offaly. I didn't think it had much chance of succeeding because the courts were not going to get involved in the rules of the GAA. I wasn't a bit surprised when it was thrown out.

FAMILY TIES

The previous year, a string of top-class performances had provided a convincing assertion of Colin Lynch's right to be considered as one of the radiant stars in the hurling firmament. His loss to the team in '98 cannot be overestimated. The media attention on Lynch came at an extremely inappropriate and unfortunate time for all his family. They had suffered two serious bereavements over two months when his uncle's wife and his grandmother passed away. He was unable to attend the meeting of the Munster Council on 7 August because that evening his grandmother suffered a serious setback and was dying.

The Lynches are a very close family. Colin was very close to his grandmother. We had been waiting all day for the verdict from the courts. That night when we got to the Limerick Inn, there was an incredible atmosphere. There were 120 Clare people there to show their support. There were camera crews and media. I was interviewed and Marty Morrissey misunderstood a comment I made about Colin's grandmother's condition. He thought that she was dead when she was very, very close to death.

We were in the back-room waiting all night. At one stage I got a call. It was Colin Lynch's aunt. She said, 'Do you know that Marty Morrissey has just announced on the television that Colin's grandmother is dead?' I apologised profusely to her for the distress the inaccuracy had caused the family. I tore out and saw Maurice Reidy, a senior producer in RTE, was there. I said, 'Where's Marty Morrissey?' Lucky for him, he was gone. I'd have nearly killed him. When he discovered his mistake, he went to the hospital to apologise to the Lynch family.

We sat there until twelve o'clock, but there was no way we were going to be let in to speak on Colin's behalf. The Munster Council knew from previous experience that if I was let in, there would be a serious confrontation. We decided to go home. We heard on the way out that Colin had indeed got a three-month suspension. There were still Clare people in the foyer. The rumour was that the Munster Council went out through the window to escape them.

Alex Ferguson will always defend his players regardless. Loughnane was cast in the same mould. The solidarity that had been so assiduously nurtured in the team over four years could evaporate in a flash by a moment's carelessness.

Everybody on the team appreciated that no matter whether Lynch was wrong or right, he was going to be defended and that was important.

Colin Lynch was a very good under-age hurler and footballer. I regarded him as a great hurler at under-21 level. When Len Gaynor took charge, he didn't seem to take to him and he never featured while Len was here. When we took over, we brought him on to the panel straight away. He then got glandular fever which took a lot out of him and he missed over a year's hurling.

He's as professional as Jamesie in his preparation. He never said a huge amount but was a strong character in the dressing-room. He had great leadership qualities. He was outstanding in '97 and against Cork in '98. Although he had a bad game in the Munster final that year, he completely outhurled Tony Browne in the replay. He was outstanding the second day against Tipperary in 1999. I was going to be loyal to him because he had given so much for Clare.

I have no regrets because the players knew that I would go to any lengths to defend any player on the panel – until they were proven guilty. If he was seen by the referee or the linesman or if there was video evidence, that was fine. They would deserve to be suspended but I think that nobody deserves to be suspended unless there's evidence. You can't suspend someone on the basis that somebody in the crowd saw something. That was the basis on which I fought the case. The only reaction that mattered to me was that of the players. Anybody else was only an outsider.

We had a policy in the Clare team that we would never complain after what happened in a game. We never made an issue out of it at the time, but the most serious injury inflicted on a Clare player came in the Munster Championship against Limerick in 1996. Ollie Baker's eye socket was smashed very, very seriously with about five minutes to go in the match. We lost our way after Ollie went off. It showed how crucial he was to the team. He was able to make the difference at vital times. Likewise in 1999, we lost the Munster final when he went off injured.

It was the sort of injury that could end a career. It could also have been very damaging for him professionally because it could have stopped Ollie from getting a position in the guards. Yet nothing was said about that. Action should have been taken against the player involved. This is not sour grapes about losing that match. I never said anything about it afterwards. I don't have a problem with justice, but I do have a problem with selective justice.

It was fair game for the media to lacerate me. I give it and I take it, but what I objected to was that Colin Lynch, who had no contact with the media whatsoever, did not get the opportunity for a fair trial, with the verdict apparently decided before the meeting to discuss it.

Loughnane's summation of the Colin Lynch saga is said with a sideways grimace. What is certain is that he feels his team were wronged.

The problem was that there was no evidence either from the video or from the referee's report.

DESTINY'S CHILD

Having such an unseemly public squabble leaves a legacy of bitterness which will take a long time to heal. The resilience Loughnane showed through that episode is a positive theme in a career that has interspersed highs with sickening lows. It is adversity which proves the true testing ground of heroic status. The human spirit is an extraordinary thing, but Loughnane was to face a further test. Fate was destined to booby-trap Clare once again that summer.

8

Who Fears to Speak of '98?

When we learned there had to be a second replay after the Jimmy Cooney saga, I thought to myself: Jesus, that's the last thing we want. We were beaten by Offaly in a terrific game. If ever the mental toughness of Clare was tested, it was against Offaly in that third game.

Offaly had the hangman's noose around their neck – the next thing they found they were free. They woke up in the next world and they were alive. Clare had won and were in the All-Ireland but now not in the All-Ireland. Offaly had a massive psychological advantage.

We were devastated by injuries. PJ O'Connell was injured. Ollie Baker was injured. Liam Doyle was injured. Brian Quinn had suffered a blackout the previous Tuesday, which I didn't know about. Barry Murphy was injured. I thought we'd be trounced by Offaly. What Clare produced in the second half that day was really out of the top drawer. They did everything you could do when your last ounce of energy is drained out and your back is to the wall. They fought like lions and only for three great saves by the Offaly goalie we'd have been in the All-Ireland. Lucky enough we weren't, because Kilkenny would have beaten us in the final, no question about it.

It was the day I was most proud of them in every way – with all the odds stacked against them and all the media stacked against them. Their manliness and courage against tiredness and injury was something to be cherished.

I n 1998, the whole Irish sporting world seemed to be swept up in the myth of Ger Loughnane. Having travelled the stoniest road to stardom, it seemed that the outrageous vicissitudes of his career came to a climax that summer. As the Colin Lynch controversy grew out of control, Loughnane's role in helping to lift hurling to unprecedented heights was seldom mentioned. Such was the media frenzy that when Clare faced Offaly in the All-Ireland semi-final, the fact that his team were just 70 minutes shy of a third All-Ireland final appearance in four years seemed almost secondary. Hurling's capacity to outreach the wildest imaginings of fiction was shown that year.

Robert Greene and Joost Elffers in their book *The 48 Laws of Power* articulate ingenious guidelines for dealing with your superiors, your colleagues and, most critically of all, your enemies. Enemies are unexpectedly vital stepping stones on your route to success and, the authors go so far as to exhort, 'if you have no enemies, find a way to make them'. Friends betray you more quickly, and they are easily made envious, but employ a former enemy and he will be more loyal than a friend. They quote the seventeenth century political philosopher Baltasar Gracian, 'You must learn to grab a sword not by a blade, which would cut you, but by the handle, which allows you to defend yourself. The wise men profits more from his enemies, than a fool from his friends.' Friendship blinds you to your best interests, while 'an enemy sharpens your wits.' Loughnane courted enemies with a passion. Of course many people believed his rhetoric in 1998 was ultimately counter-productive.

> *If something wrong happens, you have to speak out about it, whether it costs you an All-Ireland or not. As Anthony Daly said to me afterwards, in October of that year, we wouldn't change a thing about it and make no apologies for anything we did or said.*

Loughnane's primary purpose, to which he returned again and again, during his infamous Clare FM interview with Colm O'Connor, was to encourage the Clare fans to lift the team especially the new players that would have to come on the team on Sunday. The interview achieved its objective.

> *There was so much unfavourable comment in the media that the Clare players were starting to wonder when I was going to reply to it. I wanted to leave it as close as possible to the Offaly match to lance the boil. When I came into training that night, all the players were looking at me! Although they said nothing, I knew they were relieved I had taken on the criticism. In all of the controversy, I never spoke to any of them about anything that was going on off the field. I wanted them to concentrate just on the hurling.*

> *In my experience of Gaelic games, I've never seen a team as united with its supporters as that first day against Offaly. When we came on to the pitch, there was just an electric feeling and a great ovation. It was an*

incredible feeling of oneness with the crowd and considering that at stage we had already won two All-Irelands it was just incredible.

After player power had led to Babs Keating's departure as Offaly manager, the Offaly players had a major point to prove.

Offaly were going to be out for revenge for '95 and had such outstanding players and leaders on the pitch like Brian Whelahan, Martin Hanamy, Hubert Rigney, Johnny Pilkington, the Dooleys and Michael Duignan. Lohan's loss through suspension was incalculable that day. We had Richard Woods at full-back and he played well, but obviously he didn't have the experience for such a match and was caught out badly for the Offaly goal.

DOYLER

One player typified the Clare squad's steely response to adversity. Loughnane was forced to ask him to make a supreme effort against Offaly, above and beyond the call of duty. News of his injury cut a swathe of desolation among Clare hurling fans. All they could do was pray in the hope God would make time run backwards and everything could be as it was before. But Loughnane, to nobody's surprise, was undaunted by such loading of the dice and spoke to his players in a quiet voice that rang out like cold surgical steel.

Both Brian Lohan and Colin Lynch were suspended. I said to Liam Doyle, 'Doyler, you have to play. We can't play without three All-Stars.' He went out and used his head and hurled away and made nothing of it. That's the men they were. You wouldn't find that in any professional sport. There's something about the GAA that lends itself to that. They had such a bond between them that allowed them to do that. Nobody wanted to let the other person down. You're lucky if once in a lifetime you meet men like that.

On the Wednesday before the Offaly game, Doyler could barely walk, but by the Saturday he had recovered some mobility. I didn't like to have to ask him to play with such an injury but with a rookie full-back we couldn't have a novice in at wing-back as well. He survived by using his brain. It took a supreme person to go out on one leg in the three games against Offaly, but in the third game it caught up with him. He had the most brilliant competitive streak.

Whenever you mention Doyler's name among the players, there's usually a laugh. Any time there was a booze-up, he was in the middle. He had been around the scene for a good few years before I came. Most people would have regarded him as having great hands but no legs,

145

because they thought he wasn't fast enough. People had him playing corner-back, but I didn't think it suited him because the quality of his play was too good for it. He's one of the players who looks as if the hurley is part of his hand. Instead of saying Doyler cleared the ball, I would say Doyle wove his magic wand and the ball was gone.

The contradictory thing about him was that you felt that with his temperament off the field, he could never be an inter-county hurler. To an outsider he could appear nervous, even to the point of being timid but perception and reality can differ. I always gave him a sleeping tablet the night before big matches and really encouraged him to take it. It was an absolute release for him to get out on the pitch because once there, he was calm and ruthless. The field was the stage where he could express himself much better than anywhere else. The faster the opponent, the better he was.

Initially, he was very careless off the field. He liked the easy life. After the '95 All-Ireland, he came back to training for the '96 campaign two stone heavier. He was massive! The Limerick match went badly for him that year. He was determined that would never happen again. He loved the hurling but the physical training killed him. He was a dream person to have on the team. You could drive the living daylights out of him and he still responded. He could mark any type of player.

Doyler was one of the backs that could do something without you noticing him. There was a famous incident with John Leahy in '99. Leahy had been 'putting himself about'. Jamesie's hand was broken in a controversial incident during the match. Leahy made a few comments to Clare players, including Doyler. Liam hit him with the side of his hurley right in through his helmet and on to the side of his jaw. He'd push to the point of danger now and then but that was the roughest thing I saw him do at inter-county level. You could argue that he was our most skilful striker of the ball. He always relied on his anticipation and his reading of the game which, meant that he could mark somebody who was three times faster than him.

Clare led Offaly by four points with ten minutes to go but it required a late free from Jamesie O'Connor to tie first the match at 1–13 each after Offaly scored 1–2 without reply. In the circumstances, Loughnane was delighted.

I was relieved we had survived and I knew we would play much better in the replay.

Much of Clare's performance in the replay was a monument to patience, nerve, courage and technical brilliance, the mature masterwork of a great team. As normal, Clare concentrated on setting a dominating, draining pace. This was essential for a team in which goals had to be mined like nuggets.

What I always felt about our team was that, for us to be effective we had to play the whole game with the pedal to the floor. It had to be constant, constant going, constant closing in on the opposition. When you faced into draws and replays, it just sapped your energy. No matter what you did, you didn't have the same zip as if you had a break between games.

After the three games with Offaly in '98, everybody felt that the end was nigh. In particular, we felt the second Offaly match was like the end of the road. The hurling we produced that day was absolutely out of this world. For the first 40 minutes of that game, the Clare hurling was exceptional. The speed of the game, the quality of the scores were excellent and then, like Kilkenny had done against us the previous year, Offaly came back. We let them back in but were still winning by three points with two minutes to go and Barry Murphy was goalbound on the 21-yard line.

Houdini could not have escaped from the pit the Offaly team were in and Mr Micawber would have been hard pressed to find any reason for optimism. Clare's calculated challenge was intensifying towards its thrilling crescendo when suddenly the fickle hand of fate interfered. Nobody knows. That's the mystery, the fun, the drama of hurling. Referee Jimmy Cooney intervened and blew full-time two minutes prematurely. There is a very thin line between laughter and loss.

When the game was over, there was no sense of elation, but a feeling of anger. The question in my mind was: Why the hell did the ref blow as Barry was going through? I said to Colm [Flynn], 'What he's doing?' Colm said, 'It's over'. He started jumping up and down. I felt no sense of exhilaration. I was preparing to give the team the most ferocious bollicking in the dressing-room for taking the foot off the pedal and allowing Offaly back into the game. Jimmy Cooney didn't deprive us of the All-Ireland that year but he did deprive of us of getting there.

A new hurling soap opera was about to unfold.

*'Time gentlemen please!' Loughnane in happier times
with Jimmy Cooney and Eamon Cregan.*

THE MORNING-AFTER OPTIMISM

*After that match, I was sitting down in the Burlington Hotel when
someone came in around seven o'clock and said there was a call for me. It
was Marty Morrissey telling me that RTE had been put on standby for 3
p.m. the following Saturday in Thurles. I had just been talking to Phelim
Murphy, who is on the Games Administration Committee, about the
rumours that had been circulating about a replay and he said it was pure
rubbish. There was a massive confusion that night, but I said if we were
going to have a replay, we had to have Colin Lynch back.*

*I knew Joe McDonagh was supposed to be in the hotel, so I asked John
Glenn, then manager of the Burlington Hotel, to arrange a meeting with
him for me. He told me that McDonagh was gone down to Galway to
present medals that night, but he would be having breakfast in the
Berkeley Court in the morning and I might be able to meet him. I had the
very distinct impression that the president of the GAA did not want to
meet me then with the controversy about Colin Lynch at its height. So I
rang Pat Fitzgerald. He was half-way home at this stage. He rang me
back and told me there was a GAC meeting set for 10 o'clock the next
morning. Then I knew something was definitely up. All the players were
in the pub drinking, so I went in and said, 'Take it easy lads. There's
going to be a replay on Saturday.' Anthony Daly summed up the
attitude of the players when he said, 'Ah, f**k it. We'll take them on
again. If they bate us, what about it. If we're going to lose it, let's lose it
on the field.'*

For Hamlet, the 'play was the thing' but in 1998 the replay was the thing. As the spectre of another replay floated into view, Loughnane summoned all the officers of the Clare county board for a council of war at 8 a.m. the next morning in his room in the Burlington. Meanwhile, he had instructed Pat Fitzgerald to arrange a meeting with Liam Mulvihill, the GAA's Director General, with a view to getting Colin Lynch back into the fold.

> I drove Pat Fitz's car into the back of Croke Park. This man in a black suit and dark glasses opened the gate and waved us through. He told Pat to get out and ordered me to drive over to the Hogan Stand side. Pat went into the labyrinth of the Cusack Stand and we waited and waited for him to come back. About five minutes before the GAC meeting was due to start, Pat returned and said, 'There's going to be a Management meeting on Wednesday night. We can't say for definite, but there is a good chance that Colin Lynch will be back.'

> The Offaly delegation, Christy Todd and Brendan Ward, were waiting in the corridors and looked really uptight. I said to them, 'What's to worry about? There's definitely going to be a replay.'

> They asked, 'How do you know?'

> I replied, 'Sure what are we here for? There's going to be another game. It's going to be on next Saturday in Thurles at 3 p.m.'

> Both of them were looking at me, 'But there's going to be an investigation.'

> 'There's going to be no investigation. It's already sorted.'

> They lightened up then. We went in first and Pat Fitz presented our case as to why there shouldn't be a replay. There was very little argument on either side. Offaly went in, presented their case and came out. Then we were both brought in together and given the verdict.

To nobody's surprise in the Clare camp, they were told that there would be a replay in Thurles on the following Saturday. Additional features were that the money generated would be given to the Omagh fund, and that there would be a 'big' donation to the holiday fund to both counties. The only shock was the news that Dickie Murphy would be refereeing it, as the practice at the time was that the same referee who officiated at the original game refereed the replay. At this juncture, Loughnane intervened to ask why Jimmy Cooney would not be in charge. He was told that the Galway man had asked not to be considered. Loughnane stated, 'I want to make it quite clear that we have no objection to Jimmy Cooney refereeing it.'

I said, 'We have no problem taking on our great friends here from Offaly next Saturday.' They were all aghast because they were expecting a massive row over it. My attitude was that once you win anything on the field, if there's any question mark over it: what good is winning it? I also believe that no matter what else happens, the All-Ireland is sacrosanct. We would do nothing that would jeopardise or compromise its status in any way. Mind you, many people in Clare did not agree with me.

The following Wednesday, Colin Lynch's appeal was heard by the Management Committee in Croke Park. Lynch travelled up for the meeting with Pat Fitzgerald but was not asked any question or afforded the opportunity to speak.

The Munster Council produced a witness from Tipperary, a Mr McDonnell the primary school representative on the Munster Council, who claimed to have seen Lynch striking Tony Browne.

The popular perception is that the Munster Council had an investigation into the Lynch affair, but that is not the case. The reasons for this omission were three-fold. First, they wanted to take quick action. Second, an investigation like that is governed by strict procedures which have to be observed by the letter of the law, otherwise there would be an appeal and the case would be lost on a technicality. Such an investigation, like a court case, goes on and on which was the last thing the Munster Council wanted. Third, they were badly hampered by a lack of evidence.

That meeting of the Management Committee was designed to investigate the procedures that the Munster Council used in the Colin Lynch case. By introducing Mr McDonnell's evidence, the Munster Council were seeking a partial re-trial of the Lynch case instead of investigating the way it had been conducted. Significantly, Mr McDonnell was never questioned as to whether he saw the start of the incident.

At the meeting, the chairman of the Munster Council, Sean Kelly, claimed that he received a call from Joe McDonagh, then president of the GAA, urging them to take action following an incident in the Munster hurling final replay.

Sean Kelly opened the Munster Council's case with a bombshell that astounded everybody by saying, 'When the Uachtarán got in touch with me and told me I had to take action ...' A clear message was being sent out. How could any member of the Management Committee go against the Munster Council after that, even though it is not the role of the president of the GAA to interfere with, or seek to influence, the disciplinary functions of a Provincial Council? As soon as they left the *meeting, Colin Lynch turned around to Pat Fitzgerald and said, 'When I heard about McDonagh, I knew I was f**ked.'*

This intervention raised questions in the Clare camp. Did any members of the GAC or management committee receive similar calls from Joe McDonagh following an incident in the All-Ireland semi-final replay?

Resentment over the episode in Clare was compounded by the failure to take comparable action against an Offaly player. As there was no similar disciplinary measures taken against Michael Duignan, even though his blow had been captured live on television and reproduced in a photograph in the national newspapers, the feeling in Clare was that Joe McDonagh had left himself open to very serious questions of partisan behaviour.

Out of the whole episode, the person who is held in the most disdain in Clare is Joe McDonagh.

Following his retirement in March 2001, in an interview with Brian Carthy, Michael Duignan admitted that he was very lucky not to have been sent off for what he described as a 'desperate' challenge on David Forde. He generously conceded that Clare fans must have felt a great sense of injustice with the way he got off without any sanction whereas Colin Lynch received such a severe punishment. Like Lynch, Duignan too had been booked for his 'indiscretion'.

At the meeting, Lynch was told that the GAC could not grant him clemency. As it was the Munster Council who had suspended him, only they could shorten his sentence.

Lynch wrote to the Munster Council and delivered it personally to Donie Neylon's house, but Donie didn't recognise him. He asked him who he was and then took the letter from him.

The Clare camp were understandably keen to have Lynch's appeal heard before the second replay.

That night I went to Pat Fitzgerald's house to see if we could get the Munster Council to meet before the game to discuss Colin's case. Pat knew that the chairman of the Munster Council, Sean Kelly, was on holidays in Wexford so he rang the vice-chairman, Christy Cooney. Christy was very sympathetic but then said that the only way they could contact Sean Kelly was from a pay-phone half a mile from where he was staying.

As the enclosed minutes of the Munster Council meeting of 10 September reveal, quite apart from any logistical difficulties of organising such a meeting Sean Kelly was concerned that it 'would have been fraught with danger and would have led to unprecedented media hype.'

Only the relevant section of the minutes of the Munster Council meeting of 10 September which deals with the decision on Colin Lynch's appeal is reproduced here.

Decision by An Coiste Bainisti on C. O Loinsigh's Appeal

At the request of the delegates An Runai read out the decision of An Coiste Bainisti on C. O Loingsigh's appeal as received from Ard-Stiurthoir C.L.G. i.e. "It was decided that the appeal of C. O Loingsigh failed in accordance with Riail 150 (d) in that it was not proven that Comhairle na Mumhan had infringed or mispplied any rule. It was pointed out that C. O Loingsigh had a right to make application to Comhairle na Mumhan for a reconsideration of the charge and penalty imposed by them."

An Cathaoirleach explained that the letter had been received by the Runai in the afternoon of Thursday 27th of August, but he (the Chairman) was away in Wexford on holidays. He had contacted the Runai and Leas-Chathaoirleach on Friday 28th and it was decided that to try and convene a meeting for late on that night or in Thurles on Saturday morning, the 29th of August, prior to the re-fixture v. Offaly, would have been fraught with danger and would have led to unprecedented media hype.

Criostoir O Cuana, informed the meeting that he had spoken to Padraig Mac Gearailt, Runai An Chlair, on Friday morning the 28th of August re. C. O Loingsigh's letter and had explained to him that it would not be feasible in the circumstances and in the absence of the Chairman to hold a meeting to consider the matter prior to the match on the following day in Thurles.

Conchur O Murchu and a number of other delegates expressed disbelief and annoyance at the rider added on to An Coiste Bainisti's decision on the appeal, as Management should know that a minimum suspension cannot be reduced and, therefore, adding such a rider was ridiculous.

Gearoid O hIci said that Colin Lynch's letter set out the trauma he had suffered in recent weeks. He though he would win his appeal in Croke Park and was very disappointed when he didn't. It would be a nice gesture if something could be done so that he could now play with his club and Management must have had a reason for having added on a rider to their decision.

Decision

After lengthy consideration of the request the meeting decided <u>that it was not possible, within the rules of the association, to reduce a minimum suspension</u>, therefore, the suspension of 12 weeks, which was imposed for repeated striking with the hurley in the S.H. Final Replay on 19/7/98, still stood.

A few months after the controversy had died down, Seán Kelly contacted me and asked if he could meet me for dinner. Of course I agreed. We met in the Greenhills Hotel in Limerick at 6.20 p.m. and he had a room booked upstairs and we went there for a meal and had a chat 'til 11.30 p.m. He gave me to understand that none of the other officers of the Munster Council knew our meeting was taking place and declared his intention to build bridges between myself and the Munster Council in general and Donie Neylon in particular. At the end I asked him if the only way the Munster Council could have contacted him when he was on holidays in Wexford was from a pay-phone up the road. He said that in this day and age that was nonsense. Enough said!

Ironically, the meeting designed to build bridges in fact built a new wall and was to spawn a fresh controversy between Clare and the Munster Council.

During our meeting, Seán asked if I had any suggestion as to how I could bury the hatchet with Donie Neylon. I replied that they should make me manager of the Munster team for the Railway Cup because Donie always acted as a selector of the team. When Seán announced at a Munster Council meeting that I was to be Munster manager, there were big objections but the protocol was that the team who were Munster champions supplied the manager of the Munster team and we were the Munster champions so my appointment was ratified.

After that, Donie resigned as Munster selector. When I was informed of this, I resigned too because the whole thing had been designed to heal the wounds between Donie and myself. Mike Mac acted as manager of the Munster team but no Clare player lined out for Munster. It was never discussed between myself and the players nor did I ever encourage any of them not to play for Munster. There was controversy afterwards about the Clare players showing disrespect for the Munster team but the first man to pull out was Donie Neylon and his resignation created a domino effect.

RULES ARE MADE TO BE BROKEN

After the storm of controversy had abated, Colin Lynch could not but feel that he received rough justice particularly when he checked what happened, in point of fact what did not happen, to Michael Duignan after All-Ireland semi-final replay.

To some Clare fans, this raised questions about whether an organisation like the GAA with such a democratic intent has elitist tendencies.

Like every player, Colin Lynch was entitled to the protection of the rules of the GAA. However, the Clare camp are adamant that Lynch was not allowed to do so on a number of counts.

1. The Provincial Activities Committee of the Munster Council carried out a de-facto investigation prior to his suspension. This investigation did not comply with the provisions of rule 152 of the GAA. In this case, the Provincial Activities Committee actually decided at a meeting on 28 July not to carry out an investigation into the replayed Munster hurling final.
2. The Lynch case was considered by the Activities Committee and not the Munster Council. It is clear that only the Council itself is empowered under Rule 138 to investigate irregularities and to suspend members.
3. The referee did subsequently provide clarification of his report of the Munster final replay. Under Rule 1.5, a referee cannot un-decide on any issue once his report is submitted irrespective of any prompting from any source for whatever reason.
4. Under Rule 138, the Council could deal with the facts of the match or the basis of evidence available from members at the match, but only where the referee fails to submit a report within 14 days – this did not arise.
5. Every member of the Association has an absolute right under Rule 139 to an oral hearing in relation to an 'alleged offence'. That right was denied to Colin Lynch on 7 August. As his grandmother was so close to death, he was unable to attend the Munster Council meeting. His chosen representatives were not allowed to speak on his behalf.

THE MIGHTY QUINN

With the toll of replays, the Clare team could no longer rely solely on talent to carry them through. They would have to use their minds more effectively to offset their loss of flexibility and speed.

Nobody ever wanted to shirk anything. Brian Quinn is one of those people who never says a thing. If you tell him, 'Jump over a wall', he'll say, 'Which wall?' He just smiles. Whether he's on or off the team, he smiles. If you put him on, then he'll do anything he can to win, but if he's dropped he'll say nothing. He's not a huge name but he's a player for whom I've the greatest regard.

One of the reasons why I admired him so much was that in the Munster final replay in '98 when Brian Lohan was sent off, he was absolutely superb. In my marking that day, he got nine out of ten. He was brilliant. Put him in a gap in the most tense situation and nothing will get to him. He's ice cool. He has lovely skill though he lacked a bit of pace.

154

He had played in both semi-finals against Offaly. During the second day, the officials in Croke Park, with their green jackets, were stopping the young lads from giving water to the players. We had a constant running battle with those people in Croke Park (shades of Jack Charlton in USA '94), and Brian got totally dehydrated in that game but he said nothing as usual.

In fact, my son Conor was booked that day for trying to give water to one of the players. My sons were just at the right age for acting as water carriers. Mike Mac's two sons, Conor and Kenneth, were the exact same age. The four of them carried the spare hurleys and looked after the water bottles. They travelled with us, the players knew them and at the slightest sign from the players that they wanted water, they were in. They shared in all of Clare's great days. It is an experience they'll only treasure when they are much older. I think their involvement helped in a huge way when all the controversy erupted. Regardless of what was written in the papers, they always knew what was going on, so whatever was written had no effect on them.

Young Conor Loughnane is booked by a Croke Park official for bringing water on to Clare players.

The problem with the lack of water on the day would later come back to haunt Clare.

After the match, Brian had a few pints that night with the rest of the lads. He's a farmer and on the Tuesday he got some sort of blackout and was found lying down in a field. The dehydration he experienced during the match had taken its toll. Again, he never said anything.

In the third game, he was totally out of sorts. Joe Dooley scored five points on him, though Brian held the fort well enough. It was one of those days that if Dooley had hit the ball from the stands it would have gone over the bar. At the same time, I have to say that nothing should take away from the achievement of Joe Dooley, that day. Joe was an excellent player and when things were going his way he could beat a team on his own.

It was only after that we found that Brian had a blackout the Tuesday before. It wasn't a question of Brian hiding it. He just didn't admit that he was injured. They were all like that. Seánie was like that with his shoulder. Lohan was like that. You'd never have anyone saying, 'I can't play today'. They would say, 'I'm going to play and that's that and if something is broken so be it.' They wouldn't admit any weakness to each other.

WHEN HOPE AND REASON DO NOT RHYME

Ger Loughnane, like all great leaders, is a dealer in hope. Yet it was a real struggle to generate any optimism going into the third Offaly match.

On our way to Thurles, we stopped at the usual hotel in Cashel. We were walking up the steps when Tony Considine said to me, 'I feel awful tired.' This really surprised me because Tony is never tired. Trying to cheer him up, I replied, 'I don't feel a bit tired.' For once, there was a total atmosphere of deadness on the bus from Cashel to Thurles.

Loughnane's problems combating the fatigue factor were compounded by the ever-increasing toll of injuries. In the dressing-room, the players looked exhausted. Now more than ever, Loughnane needed one of his famous motivational ploys.

I had to do something to try and lift them. Just before they went out onto the field, I put up the picture of Michael Duignan striking David Forde on the door and said: are we going to let that beat us? Give them their due, they all woke up and went out fighting.

'Are you wrong there, Michael?' Michael Duignan leaves his mark on David Forde in 1998.

The hallmark of the Clare team in the Loughnane era was their ability to build up a momentum which no rival could live with. In '98, they had gone to the well once too often. The laws of attrition reaped their vengeance.

> *We were in trouble all over the field. Doyler and Brian Quinn were really struggling. At half-time, I was late getting back into the dressing-room. They were all exhausted. We were facing demolition. I had to do something dramatic to get them going again.*
>
> *Baker was lying on the treatment table. Colm Flynn said to me, 'He's f**ked. He'll have to come off.' I said, 'Baker, get off that f**king table. Do you realise what state we're in? There is a war on here. We're going down the Swanee. Get out there. I don't care if you are on one leg. Doyler's done it already. Now it's your turn.' He jumped off the table and went out and had a brilliant second half. He almost single-handedly brought us back into the game.*

157

There are lies, damned lies and statistics but it was significant that Clare's tally of 13 points, in the final twist in this tale of the unexpected, was the lowest recorded by them in the Championship since the 1993 Munster semi-final against Cork when they managed just 2-7. And yet, were it not for the brilliance of Stephen Byrne in the Offaly goal ....

If Clare were to triumph, the team had to be driven not by the thought of medals or fame, but by their love for the game. They lived for those moments when they could lose themselves completely in the action and experience, the pure joy of competition. The emotional intensity of an unforgettable contest could not dilute the pleasure Loughnane took in the quality of Clare's performance.

Losing was as integral a part of the Clare glory years as winning. It has been said that the best part of winning is that it's not losing, but losing was a lens through which Loughnane could see himself and his team more clearly. From time to time, a keenly-contested defeat made him feel better than a victory in which the team didn't perform to its optimum.

I went into the dressing-room and sincerely congratulated the Offaly players. It was bedlam inside. All the journalists were there. The previous Saturday evening, we had been drinking with the Offaly lads and they were slagging us about giving them a replay. When I walked in after we lost, Joe Dooley said to me, 'A week is a long time in hurling, Ger.' On the day, Offaly were the better team and deserved to win.

When I got back into our dressing-room, Michael Bond, who is really sound, said a few words. I shut the door after he left and said, 'In years to come, you'll look back on this as a brilliant year. There are a lot of lessons that can be learned about life, about trust, and the way people behave. I'm prouder of you today than on the day you won your first All-Ireland.'

As we walked out to the bus, the place was thronged with Clare people and they gave us a fantastic reception. It was so emotional that some of the players were in tears. It was the first time I'd ever seen any of them crying.

When we got to the hotel, I met Kilkenny selector, Dick O'Neill. He said, 'It's a pity ye didn't win.' I replied, 'Ye were waiting for us. Now ye're in right trouble.' I knew that with this kind of momentum Offaly would be unstoppable.

It was nearly a relief that it was over. I was exhausted.

Although Clare had many strong, resilient, abundantly skilled players, their performance was probably even more a definition of courage than of talent. Loughnane never believed that the only goal worth striving for was winning. Hurling was not primarily about beating someone else, but to search out the best in yourself. Of course winning medals and media adulation provide a big morale boost but working for merely external rewards only exposes you to the mercy of the fickle hand of fate. Unity is absolutely critical. There are so many factors outside your control that can decide the outcome. An unlucky bounce of the ball or a bad referee's decision might snatch the prize from your grasp and leave you disappointed. If you enjoy the performance for its own sake, experiencing involvement each moment of the way, then hurling is worth the energy expended regardless of what happens in the end. It is the journey that counts, not the destination.

> *Everybody wants to win and we were obsessed with it, but it's not the end in itself. When you win an All-Ireland, the first thing people ask you is, 'how do you think you'll do next year?' I often compare it to someone coming home from America for the first time in ten years and the first question they're asked, 'When are you going back again?'*

> *The enjoyment of sport is from game to game. People say, 'Ye won nothing in '98.' We won the Munster Championship. People said in '99, 'Ye won nothing.' We had six brilliant days. A year is never wasted once you have matches.*

> *'98 was one of the best years we ever had. Even though we didn't win the ultimate prize, we gave it everything to win again. It tested our mettle, mental reserve, hurling, resolve, the unity of the team like never before. There are more fundamental things than winning like standing up for your principles. You've got to stand up for what you really believe in. If you don't, you're nothing.*

It is difficult to speak about '98 from a detached perspective, particularly if you have had a direct involvement. After the defeat by Offaly, Peter Finnerty attempted a dispassionate analysis and wrote an article in *The Sunday Independent* about the apparent hate some people felt for Clare.

> 'I hear you say it was Loughnane who was hated. But why? Just because he stoutly defended a player and tried every trick in the trade to get him free for a vital game. Should he be condemned for that? My opinion is that this was not hate, it was sheer envy.

> 'Envy of a side that looked so powerful they seemed unbeatable. Envy of discipline that saw players accept any treatment. And then there was a jealously of one man's achievement. Like men who drive black Mercedes

accompanied by leggy blondes, Clare were branded out of envy, spinelessly disguised as hate.

'For 21 hours, Clare thought they were in the 1998 All-Ireland final and it is difficult to determine what effect this had on the team. It must have been shell-shocking when they discovered that Jimmy Cooney's final tune on the whistle wasn't the end of their clash with Offaly. Perhaps he [Loughnane] thought that by accepting the decision in a quiet and dignified manner, Colin Lynch might receive clemency .... But Croke Park showed no mercy or gratitude for Loughnane's willingness. And worse still – neither did they punish the blatant Offaly offenders .... What will Loughnane do now? He must be disillusioned by the whole system.'

In fact, Loughnane's faith in the system was restored by a meeting on 11 November that year with the Games Administration Committee.

The Munster Council had made a complaint about us to the GAC about my Clare FM interview. There were rumours that the Munster Council were going to take Clare FM and I to court.

Robert Frost, Pat Fitzgerald and I had no inhibitions about travelling up. Unlike any of the meetings from earlier that year, we made no serious preparation for it. Luckily, in their wisdom the GAC excluded the Munster Council representatives. The chairman was John Greene from Longford and the others included Brian McEniff, the former Donegal manager and Seamus Howlin, now chairman of the Wexford county board. Basically, they were people we never met before.

At the start of the meeting, things were very tense. Initially, they were unusually aggressive. They tried to deal with the interview in an overall context but we said no and insisted they take it step by step. After we eyed each other up, gradually the meeting settled down and the level of confrontation decreased. We began to realise that this was not like a Munster Council meeting.

I knew they were hearing our side of the story for the first time and they were taken aback with some of the detail we presented. From time to time, there were long pauses as they absorbed what we said. We spent three hours in discussion until they were left with nothing to say. They could see that we had a grievance. Coming out, I wasn't thinking about their verdict. I was just happy that at last we had met with people who were prepared to listen to what we had to say.

We had to wait until 22 December to hear the GAC's verdict. The Munster Council got the same letter. People with a suspicious mind might think that the reason that they left it 'til three days before Christmas was that they didn't want their decision to get any publicity!

*They did express their disappointment that we hadn't pursued our grievance through the proper GAA channels. I completely understand that. However, the really significant part of their letter was their admission that, 'We **acknowledge that there have been some inconsistencies in the manner in which disciplinary matters have been dealt with by the Munster Council and that Clare may have perceived grievances.'***

I don't want to be like Albert Reynolds after the beef tribunal and talk about, 'a total vindication' but here was a top-level committee of the GAA investigating another powerful organ of the GAA and rapping the Munster Council on the knuckles in relation to inconsistency in applying discipline over the course of the Munster Championship. To my knowledge, this is the first time something like that happened.

The letter is couched in the most diplomatic language but there is no ambiguity about the meaning. Whatever about the means we used, there is no doubt they were saying that we had a legitimate reason to believe that proper procedures were not deployed in the case of Clare that summer. We weren't looking for publicity about the verdict. We were satisfied that at last we had got a fair hearing and had got fair play.

I'm convinced that the Colin Lynch debacle was the catalyst for the change that took place in the GAA's disciplinary procedures when disciplinary measure were taken out of the hands of the Provincial Councils and put in the hands of the GAC. The Munster Council were hoist by their own petard. They had made the complaint about us, but the result was that their powers were curtailed.

The intensity of feeling surrounding the series of controversies in 1998 does not alter the reality. Clare were widely considered to be the best team in the country but they were not All-Ireland champions. That year, Loughnane could have been forgiven if he looked about as cheerful as a man trying to get a cyanide capsule out from behind his teeth, particularly as the rumble of disapproval that greeted his tactics was not softened by his graciousness in defeat. It was his self-possession that saved him from being overwhelmed by the celebrity and notoriety that engulfed him.

The great thing in life is not to ensure that we never fall but to ensure that we never fail to get up when we have fallen. When all the vitriol had been finished, Loughnane had survived the sort of sequence of events that could have broken him but whose main effect had been to increase his self-sufficiency, strengthen his capacity to live with the fickleness of other people's reactions to his forceful personality.

Mighty Munster. Loughnane flanked by his selectors on the 1996
Munster Railway Cup team. Rory Kiely (left) and Donie Neylon (right).

It was unpleasant at the time but retrospectively worth the endurance. Loughnane's muted tone is not long sustained. Although the firm planes of his face melt readily into smiles, the eyes are alive with a challenging directness. Strength grows on difficulty. Given the emotional rollercoaster that was '98, Loughnane might be expected to be bitter but surprisingly this is the chapter of his life that furnishes his most nostalgic reminiscences.

> *1998 was a never-to-be-forgotten year. I wouldn't swap it for anything. It was the experience of a lifetime. It was a test of yourself. Could you not alone survive but triumph over all adversity? I wouldn't change anything about 1998, despite all its controversies, with the games against Waterford and against Offaly. A year like that, strangely, was as enjoyable as the previous year when we won the All-Ireland. I know a lot of people who didn't go through such an experience would find that strange, but there is a certain satisfaction from having survived it.*

TRAGEDY

Yet the most significant event in Loughnane's life did not come on the hurling field. His perspective on the proper place of hurling was radically altered by an incident which cast a long shadow on his professional life.

It was the 18th of September 1998, a beautiful, fine day. I can remember it as if it happened a few minutes ago. For some reason we had run out of oil in the school. The secretary rang the oil delivery man, a lovely decent man. He arrived with the oil to the school. It was about ten to two and he came in with the docket to sign. I said, 'You better wait now 'til all the parents are gone' because the parents came in for the young kids at two o'clock. He was sitting down in the office and one of the teachers came in and asked if he would move the truck because it was in the way.

I went out with him just to keep the traffic back as he was backing out the truck. He reversed and drove out of the school at snail's pace. I still waited on just to direct the traffic because there were other parents passing and I didn't want anybody backing in to someone else.

Then it was like everything slowed down. I heard a scream about 50 yards out on the road. It was Marion, the school secretary, who was driving home behind the truck and she ran back in to the schoolyard and said, 'There's a child injured. Call the ambulance.' I answered, 'You call the ambulance. I'll go out to the accident.'

Pain smoulders in Loughnane's eyes like fever. His restless mind scurries frantically through the corridors of his nightmares as he recalls the incident.

I saw a young pupil, Jack Myers, just five years old, lying on the ground. A local nurse, Mary Fitzgibbon, a wonderful woman, was busily attending to him. She was kneeling down over him and trying to give him first aid. I could see almost immediately her efforts were in vain.

When she saw me beside her, she looked up and said, 'I can't get any pulse.'

I replied, 'Mary. He's dead.' I knew from his eyes.

Christ. This is your worst nightmare. To see a five-year-old lying on the ground like that. Dead.

What happened was, he was going home along the path beside the road. He was used to going home on his own. His friends had run on up ahead and he was trying to catch up with them. There was a ladder on the side of the oil lorry and Jack jumped up on it to get a lift. Unfortunately, the lorry hit a kind of a ramp on the road and Jack fell off and tragically the wheel ran over him. It killed him instantly.

Death always sends a chill through the bones. Each death is a painful reminder of the ultimate and unwelcome end for us all. It is all the more harrowing when a young child dies and all the promise of a young life is denied.

The doctor came and I said we'd have to tell the parents. Nobody else wanted to go, so I said I would. I knew his mother, Alice, very, very well. I went up to the house with the doctor, but he didn't know the family so it fell to me to break the news. Then I made a mistake. I didn't ask Alice if her husband, Denis, was home. He is in the army and I just presumed he wasn't there.

Alice said to me, laughing: 'What's he done now?'

I told her: 'It's much worse than that.'

'Is he injured?'

'It's worse. He's dead.'

You can imagine telling a mother that her five-year-old son has died. Then I asked her where Denis was and she said, 'He's out in the back.' So I had to go out and break the news to him.

I asked them to come down to see him before the ambulance took him away. It was only a journey of 200 metres. The people who were there already were in total hysterics. When Alice saw Jack on the ground, it was the most traumatic thing you could possibly imagine. Denis was totally stunned. I'd seen people dead and dying but I've never seen anything that would have such a lasting effect as Jack's death.

Shocked onlookers were taking a morsel of comfort from the fellowship of the besieged, but Alice's screams of pain cut like swords of sorrow into Loughnane's heart. Nobody could comprehend why Jack's radiant eyes had to surrender their very sight or why his sweet voice had to give away its speech. Justice should not allow the sacrifice of such innocent wealth. How could such a harmless young boy come to harm? Loughnane's mind, though flooded with shock, raised barriers against the unendurable.

Jack had two brothers in the school. Davy was in junior infants and had already gone home. Danny was in sixth class and had to be told. I brought Alice into the staff-room and I had to bring Danny out of class. He knew it was about Jack. I said, 'It is very, very bad news.' It was harrowing.

Then of course, all the parents and teachers were in a total shock. One of them asked me, 'What are you going to do now?' I told them, 'We're going to have to tell the children.' The last thing I wanted was everybody going home, full of rumours and all kinds of stories flying around. We called them into the hall and I told them what had happened to Jack. By that stage, Fr Harry Bohan had arrived and he came into the hall with me. Although he was only in high infants, Jack was a well known character in the school. Everyone was mad about him. In fact they all loved him.

Jesus, you should have seen the scene after I broke the news. I've never seen such mass devastation. Many of the children were hysterical. I held them there 'til the hysteria had calmed down. Then I made arrangements to make sure that nobody would go home on their own. After that I sent them home.

I'll tell you it was a very dark day. It was incredibly tough. I've never had such a difficult day in my life.

For the next few days, all of us were going around in a daze. The funeral Mass for Jack was really a celebration of his life. Alice was absolutely fantastic. It takes a long time to recover from something like that. You can see the pain in everyone all round you.

Although Jack's life was tragically short, his memory will linger forever on all who knew him. A few days after the All-Ireland final, Loughnane was left mulling over a might-have-been but not one that hurling fans across the country would ever have dreamed of.

The inspector, Michael Connolly, really brought it home to me when he came into the school and said, 'If ye had won the All-Ireland this year, Jack's death would have been the week after the game and you might be gone somewhere with the cup and you mightn't have been there.' If I wasn't there, I never would have forgiven myself.

I CAN SEE CLEARLY NOW

Unfortunately, Loughnane had a few days earlier another reason to contemplate the fragility of our mortal existence. It was another abrupt and brutal reality check for him. It does not take an archaeologist of the deepest regions of the heart to realise that for even the obsessive Loughnane, hurling seemed for once like an intrusive side-show.

The morning of the 1998 All-Ireland, Joe Buckley came to do some painting in our house. The first thing he said to me was, 'Christ wasn't it terrible what happened to Anthony Daly's brother, Paschal.'

I asked, 'What happened?'

'He died. He died last night.'

Paschal was somebody Dalo was really close to. The Dalys are a really close family. Paschal lived in England but he came home for every big game, so Anthony associated meeting him with the matches. So I said to myself, 'Christ, thank God we're not in the All-Ireland?' Even if we had won the All-Ireland, what good would that have been, when Dalo wasn't there? He was the man. He was the talisman. Everyone had such high regard for Dalo, knowing how close he is to his family, it would have knocked the heart out of everybody.

I don't even want to contemplate what it would have been like, what decision would have to be made if we had been in the final. There is no way I wouldn't have told Dalo what had happened. People often say, 'Say nothing' but you couldn't. Without Dalo, we would only be going through the motions. Winning the McCarthy Cup would have been meaningless.

Given those two incidents people may understand me when I say perhaps it was better that we didn't win it. I have absolutely no regret about not being in the All-Ireland in '98. In fact, I think fate was kind to us, not having us there that day. It wasn't meant to be.

9

The Game I Love So Well

The biggest problem with hurling is that it is in danger of being swamped by football. The GAA is a contradiction in that it is made up of two games that are in competition with each other. People say it is soccer and rugby that are the competition, but I was involved with a dual club for a while and I know that it is football.

About 26 of the 32 counties are dominated by football. In the hurling-dominated counties like Kilkenny, football suffers and in the football-dominated counties, hurling suffers. At the moment, you can forget about ever getting hurling strong in a county like Longford. All we can hope for is to keep hurling strong in the counties it is strong in now, and ideally even stronger. Hurling will get weaker in the weak counties because the county boards are not really interested in it.

This raises a crucial question: should hurling and football be treated within the umbrella of the GAA as two separate entities? I found it totally ridiculous that when we went to a meeting with the GAC that people from Tyrone or Derry were adjudicating on incidents that happened in the Munster Championship without knowing the minutiae of the topic under discussion.

Football is the dominant force, and hurling cannot thrive while it is under the shadow of its big brother. It would be better off as a separate entity where it could paddle its own canoe.

B ureaucracy has never been a contender for Loughnane's enthusiasm. Watching him as he talks about officialdom, one can sense the anger rise within him – anger at the inertia of those in the GAA seemingly too petrified to change the status quo, too scared to swim out of the safe, anonymous river of mediocrity. As a player, even on All-Star trips, he never ceased to be amazed by the heavy-handedness of officialdom.

I went on two All-Star tours. The first was in 1975. It was my first time in America. It was a dream come true. The Dublin footballers were on the tour with us. When we were staying in Los Angeles, we were having a party around a swimming-pool at one stage and one of the Dublin players was pushed into the pool. Within five minutes, all the players had been pushed into the pool fully clothed much to the consternation of the officials.

When we were in Boston, we were given a free day but we were told that we absolutely had to be back for a function at 7 p.m. As the day was very drizzly, there wasn't much we could do so a few of us spent most of the day in the pub. The main character in the group was PJ Molloy of Galway. We forgot about the time until we suddenly realised that we were going to be late for our function. We rushed off to the venue. When we got there, we went through what we thought was the main door, but in fact was the door to the stage and we found ourselves at the back of the stage as the president of the GAA was giving a speech. He was talking about how the GAA in Ireland would never forget the GAA in Boston.

At the time, Mike Murphy had a show on RTE radio every morning. One of the features of the programme was that he played what he called a 'rotten record' every day and when it was over he said, 'Yowsa, Yowsa, Yowsa.' The president was going on and on with a most boring speech when PJ Molloy shouted, 'Yowsa, Yowsa, Yowsa.' The whole place erupted with laughter! Afterwards PJ got the most ferocious bollicking from the officials and didn't play in any other match on tour.

GOING DUTCH

In 1981, the Clare team went to Holland to play in an exhibition game against Wexford. There was a hockey team there called 'The Hurling Club' even though they had nothing to do with hurling! They were celebrating their centenary. The organisers made a serious mistake at the start, because the first place they brought us to was the Heineken brewery in Amsterdam! We started lashing into the samples pretty fast. Next thing a sing-song started so the only way they could get us all out was by promising to take us to a barbecue. We were starving at this stage so we had everything devoured in a few minutes!

The Dutch tourist board had probably never targeted such clientele before. It is a reasonable assumption that they will not do so again.

Our hosts gave us a really great weekend. We were determined to enjoy every minute of it and we certainly did. The trip produced some bizarre moments such as the sight of a Clare selector urinating into a canal in Amsterdam at three in the morning!

Although they were in a different country, all Loughnane's old feelings about the Clare County Board surfaced again.

We played a match on the Sunday, on manicured lawns. We got on great with the Wexford lads, and 20 years on when we meet any of them that were on the trip we have a great laugh about it. We had arranged to swap jerseys with the Wexford team after the game, but the Clare county chairman said in the dressing-room afterwards that our Clare jerseys had to be handed back. He said, 'I'm going to give you five minutes to hand them back.' He went out and the quiet lads and the young players who we knew they were going to pick on gave their jerseys to the established players. I had three jerseys in my bag. When the officials came back all the jerseys had disappeared. They said, 'We're going to search the bags.' Predictably they searched the bags of the subs but the rest of us walked out past them.

Yet it is the good times he chooses to remember.

My abiding memory is of being in a pub in the seediest part of the red light district in Amsterdam on the Saturday night. We had a great character on the team and later that night I saw him walking out of the pub. I went out after him because I knew he didn't know where he was going. He was going into this dark street which was really dangerous. So I brought him back, and as we were walking into the pub he asked, 'Is this f**king O'Connell Street?' He thought he was in Ennis!

Loughnane is frustrated by the depth of factional acrimony bedevilling the games in recent years and does not want the association torn apart by internecine fighting. He would like to see GAA people talking more about the Irish weather than the Association's political storms. There is infinitely more fun in watching the clash of the ash in Semple Stadium rather than in monitoring the boardroom machinations of men in sober suits.

What is certain is that in the new hurling order, players will have to be looked after properly. This was one of the hallmarks of Loughnane's term as Clare manager. Not all of his attempts to reward his players met with universal acclaim.

WE'RE ALL GOING ON A WINTER HOLIDAY

There is no scandal like a sex scandal, and Loughnane provided plenty of ammunition for GAA gossips after Clare's historic All-Ireland triumph in 1995. His eyes shine mischievously as he recalls it.

We did something in Clare that was totally innovative. We had just won the All-Ireland for the first time in 81 years and something special had to be done to reward the players. Mike, Tony, Colm and I decided we would set up a Holiday Fund Committee that would be totally independent of the county board. I contacted Johnny Callinan, who had played with me for Clare, who is a brilliant guy and a solicitor in Ennis; Gerry Kelly, a great Clare supporter and one of the most popular publicans in Clare, and Seamus Hayes who writes for The Clare Champion and they raised the funds for the holiday. I went into the travel agent and was looking for something different, and I began to look at the east and stumbled on Thailand.

Back in '95, everyone associated going to Thailand with Bangkok with sex! Here you have a team full of bachelors going to Bangkok! When the news broke, all hell broke loose! We didn't mind. This was an exceptional achievement and we were going to do something exceptional to mark it. It was a holiday of a lifetime in a totally different culture. We had an absolutely fantastic time and the incidents that happened will be remembered forever. It was the making of the team. The holiday copperfastened the bond between us, and that intense bond kept us together over the following years when we faced many a battle on and off the field.

Loughnane's belief that players need to be looked after better stems from his conviction that top-class hurlers deserve proper treatment. He showers superlatives on many of the stars from his playing days, particularly on those who made his life on the pitch difficult. In the twilight of his inter-county career, the spirit was willing but the flesh was as usual.

All the most difficult opponents came in later years when I was slowing down – like Nicky English and Pat Fox. Eamon Grimes of Limerick was a terrific player. He had lightning speed, and given the slightest chance he was away and he'd score. He was a very difficult player to mark because he was constantly on the move and had great confidence and was a great leader of the Limerick team.

There were many days when I was cleaned out by my opponent, but the one that stands out was against Seánie O'Leary in a League match on a November day. I don't know how Seánie was playing wing-forward. He

scored two goals and two points and when you let a wing forward score
that on you, you've really been taken to the cleaners. Then I had to travel
back to Dublin that evening with that horrible feeling of having played a
stinker.

I think Seán O'Leary was the real powerhouse in Cork's All-Ireland
success in 1999. As a player, Jimmy Barry Murphy was a genius. He had
great skill, a great brain and got spectacular goals. Off the field, he's the
nicest person you could meet but he hadn't that steel in him. As a player
I was surprised to find that Jimmy was the greatest moaner I ever came
across. He was constantly complaining and moaning to referees, looking
for frees, complaining about decisions. He was the greatest moaner I ever
came across to referees! I don't think that he'd survive if he was playing
today with the type of physical exchanges there are now. His strength as
a manager was that every player would like and respect him and want to
do all the best they could for him. Seán O'Leary, though, had the
ruthlessness, toughness and cutting edge that really brought that Cork
team on in 1999. It is significant that as soon as he left they started to
slide.

Loughnane's success as a manager was prodigious but he is more
interested in looking to the future than living off the glories of the past.
One huge concern for him is how abysmally deprived of vibrant new
blood, hurling has been in recent years.

I had hoped that the arrival of Offaly, Clare and Wexford would
encourage other counties to do the same but I was wrong. Since I gave up
last year I've been invited to give talks in many counties. When people
ring up I always chat to them about the state of the game in their county.
What has really frightened me is the amount of dejection that's about,
even in what we could call the strong counties like Tipperary or Galway.
I was talking to one of the leading lights of the juvenile scene in Galway
and I was saying that if every county was doing what they were doing,
things would be great but he was most pessimistic about the situation. I
was talking to a man in Tipperary recently and he was very concerned
about what's happening there. There's a major worry there that from
minor down, in the younger age groups, there's a huge decline in
interest, a huge fall-off in participation, and a marked reduction of older
people willing to coach youngsters.

At the moment, there is still a high standard at inter-county level. I
thought the Kilkenny team that won the All-Ireland in 2000 were
excellent. They were streets ahead of anybody else. Nobody ever doubted
their skill, but they had a hunger last year that nobody else was going to

171

match. Recapturing the same hunger this year was always going to be very difficult.

The problem is that there are not enough counties to challenge counties like Kilkenny and other counties are not joining the inner circle. Waterford threatened to do it in 1998, but they seem to have faded. The big hope is that Limerick will come, but the problem is that the number of counties capable of winning an All-Ireland is shrinking and that's a serious concern for the future. Hurling needs a new team to come and light up the Championship.

The thought of new blood painting a canvas of pure, breathtaking delight on the hurling landscape, as his own team did, seems to excite him.

NEIGHBOURS

If there is a need for philosophical justification for the irrational enthusiasms that keep Loughnane in thrall to hurling, I must concede defeat from the outset. What is certain is that his appetite for the game was whetted by Clare's intense rivalry with Tipperary. Not everyone sees the rivalry as positively as he does, particularly after the Munster under-21 final in 1999 when a brawl broke out between the Tipperary and Clare camps. Neutrals reported that rivalry between the two counties had given away to hate.

In spring 2000, *The Clare Champion* attached such weight to the issue that they devoted an editorial to it. They referred to a Harty Cup match in 1999 where supporters of Nenagh CBS were alleged to have chanted, 'Go home, you Banner bastards' to their opponents, St Joseph's of Tulla. Their main focus, though, was on the booing of Jamesie O'Connor by a section of the Templemore CBS contingent at the 2000 Harty Cup final. They speculated that Jamesie was a talent 'far too rich' for their Tipp rivals. They went on to apportion blame:

> 'Up to three years ago, a healthy rivalry existed between the counties, but it was based on the premise that Tipperary were, and always would be, a vastly superior force while Clare, after their flash-in-the-pan win of 1995, would inevitably retreat to the land of no-hopers whence they came. Since that script changed, the bitterness has crept in.'

Loughnane's experiences lead him to view the rivalry in a more benign light.

A lot of people said the rivalry is too intense, but rivalry only lasts for a short time. Tipperary and Galway had a great rivalry on and off the field in the '80s, which boiled over a few times. Then in the '90s, we had the

Clare-Tipperary rivalry. The really die-hard Tipperary supporters are the most knowledgeable that you could meet and the most honest. They are more severe on their own team than everyone else. Rivalry between counties is great because it fires up everybody and gives terrific publicity and profile to the game.

After we beat Tipperary in the replay in '99, Tony Considine and I decided we'd walk into Cork city from Pairc Uí Chaoimh. It was about three quarters of an hour after the game. The crowd had dispersed. We were walking along and we saw this van up ahead of us with a Tipperary registration. When we were about 20 yards away from them, they spotted us and one of them jumped out of the van. I said to Tony, 'Here's trouble.'

The man said, 'Howya Ger? Any chance of the autograph?'

I was relieved that he wasn't going to attack me! I told him no problem and he handed me the programme to sign. He told me it was for his wife. I wrote, 'To Marion. Best wishes. Ger Loughnane.' He never looked up at me but turned to his friend and said, 'Jesus, Johnny, she'll get some surprise when she comes home this evening. Christ, wait 'til she sees this.'

Then he turned to me and said, 'You have no idea how much she hates you!'

There was no other word. He got back into his van as happy as he could be and off he went.

Another time, one of the women who teaches in the school with me was in hospital. She was beside a lady from Cavan who asked her where she was from. When my colleague told her she was from Tipperary, her new friend said, 'Ah sure you don't get on with your neighbours down there.'

'What do you mean?'

'Sure, with Clare. Do you hate Ger Loughnane as well?'

She associated being from Tipperary with hating Ger Loughnane! That's all part of the rivalry and most of it is comical. People who take it too seriously are looking at it from the wrong angle. Without it you have nothing. It shouldn't be regarded as something to be afraid of. It is something to be embraced.

What Loughnane knows about the game does not appear to have been softened or blurred by the years. Like everybody else, he is not keen to flaunt his neuroses in public but it is betraying no great secret to say that no issue caused him to agonize more than the choice of his own successor as Clare manager.

THE CHOSEN ONE

No hurling manager is an island. He needs a good team behind him on and off the field. Loughnane was not guilty of harbouring the presumptuous thought that the good times would continue in Clare regardless of the team's stewardship. He effectively anointed his heir to the throne, but the decision was to lead to disappointment for two people.

I thought after '98 we, as a management team, could go no further. I spoke to Tony Considine. He felt the thing was getting a bit flat and that a change was needed. I looked around the Clare scene to see who could come in and succeed me. People with the proper pedigree were very scarce. The only one I could think of was Seán Stack because he had success at club level with Toomevara in Tipperary. There were rumours that Galway were chasing him but it had nothing to do with that. I thought you could get somebody for a year and allow him get to know the players, build up a rapport with them and take the good things from our regime and bring new ideas of his own. I thought he was someone who could learn from what we had done over the years and then take over from me. I was wrong.

Loughnane's conviction that fresh blood was need in the management team was sharpened by events from within.

There were a few things that happened in '98. Mike McNamara owns a pub and he made a few comments about me there that got back to me, but I let them go. But it was his actions that forced a change.

On the morning after the Offaly replay when Jimmy Cooney blew up early, I had to go with Pat Fitz to Croke Park and get the replay sorted out and, I hoped, the Colin Lynch situation also. Before I went, I told Mike Mac to take the team down the road to Belfield and do a good warm-up, a few fast sprints and a good warm-down to liven things up before we made the journey home and to burn off the effects of any drinking the night before.

When I got back, I knew something had happened. There was an air of despondency among the players and I asked Tony Considine what was wrong, but he didn't want to talk to me in front of them so he said he'd tell me later. I asked my son, Conor, and he said, 'Mike is after running the shite out of them.'

Afterwards, when we got back to The Poteen Still, I asked Dalo what happened and, true to form, he answered, 'Ah stop'. He told me that, luckily enough, neither he nor Baker had trained because they would be wrecked for Saturday. Mike had played up to his tough man image and really gone to town on them and they were absolutely crippled. Worse still, Barry Murphy pulled his hamstring. I said nothing to Mike, but I said to myself, 'This is the beginning of the end for you.' I knew he could not be put in charge of the Clare team because otherwise the team would be running around the field all day and hurling would be forgotten. That's what Clare was about hurling, hurling, hurling and at pace.

I met Mike and Tony after the Championship was over and I told them about my plan to bring in Seán Stack. Mike said immediately, 'No, this won't work at all.' I replied, 'Mike, you can take a few days to think about it but Seán Stack is coming in. It's as simple as that.'

The next day he rang and asked if he could meet me. We did and I asked him what his big objection to Seán Stack was. He replied, 'I thought when you went, I would become manager. That was going to be the final chapter in my book.'

I said, 'That's a noble ambition but right now you're not the right man for the job. The last thing the players need is the sound of our voices for the next few years.' I told him it wasn't just his voice the players were tired off. It was all of us and I advised him that he should take a break from the Clare scene for a few years and then come back when there were a lot of new players in the squad. When I met him after Galway's great win over in Kilkenny in the 2001 All-Ireland semi-final, I told him that he still had a major contribution to make to Clare a few years down the road.

Anyway, the following day, he rang me again and asked me for another meeting. When we met, he asked, 'Is there any chance I could be manager for a year and then Stack could take over.'

I replied, 'No. Seán Stack is coming in. You have to decide whether you stay or go. You've given brilliant service and we've had great times. If you stay on, maybe Seán Stack would want you as his trainer.'

We left it at that. Mike didn't show up for the presentation of the Munster medals. That was another night to remember. Seán Kelly, the Chairman of the Munster Council, had insisted that all the members of the Munster Council attended the presentation. Of course when I got up, I let fly! I just pointed out that all we were looking for in the Colin Lynch affair was fair play.

We were going for a week's holiday to the Canaries after Christmas. Nobody knew if Mike was coming or not. On the day we were leaving, Mike turned up and came with us. We were staying in London first, but

Seán Stack wasn't going on to the Canaries, so I decided London would be the right time for us to have a meeting. After our meal in the hotel, the lads went off for a night on the town and the four of us met. I began by saying that this was a good time to look ahead to our plans for the Championship. Straight away, Mike said, 'I want to have a higher profile this year.' I looked at him and asked him what he meant. He said, 'I feel my profile isn't high enough. As far as I am concerned, I'm the best trainer in the world.' Seán Stack said immediately, 'As far as I am concerned, I'm the best trainer in the world.' I looked at Tony Considine and thought to myself, 'Sweet Jesus. Is this really happening?' I've often debated in my mind if I should have sacked both of them right away.

In booking the hotel, I had booked them into the same room but neither of them knew about it. After that meeting they spent the full night together in the same room! I don't think it was conversation that kept them awake but the following day, both of them said they hadn't slept a wink!

Mike was a very strong presence and was crucial to our success in the early years. When I think about Mike now, I have great affection for him. He brought great fun to training sessions. It was drudgery, but he gave us all a lot of laughs with his sayings like, 'The bollixing is over.' Another one when players were getting tired was, 'Ye'll be thrown down like an old CIE horse.' He's a great character and has the heart of gold. He would do anything for you and was a massive support when we were starting off, but as time went on he started to believe his own publicity. He once disappeared from training, expecting me to follow him, begging him to come back. I totally ignored the fact that he was gone and we carried on regardless. About ten days later, I met him by chance on the street in Ennis and asked him if he'd been sick. He said no, but he was very busy in the pub and would be back for training that night. He had broken the unwritten covenant between us, and after that the show was over.

Loughnane decided to give Stack the chance to learn the ropes away from the white heat of the Championship.

I said I'd take a break from training and leave both Seán Stack and Mike in charge of training for January and February. I stipulated that the weekends were for working on the skills, and the rest of the time the physical work had to be done.

They started off with a training session in Shannon. It was like something out of the 1940s. Seán turned up in a pair of wellingtons and carrying a bucket of sliotars. We were used to training with about seven dozen sliotars flying around at pace. They spent the two hours standing up and pucking balls to one another. There was no movement, no pace whatsoever. It was like what you'd do with a junior B team. After the session, Anthony Daly rang me and said, 'What have you landed us with?'

I replied, 'He'll learn.'

Tony and I had to come back before the two months was up, because the players were dropping off training big time. They were only five or six players at some sessions. Tony would just see what had to be done and he'd do it. That's the kind of person I wanted. Cyril Lyons did just that the following year.

I took the training solidly for four weeks. After that, I let Seán take training the odd evening. One night, a player asked me, 'Are you taking us tonight or will we be just wasting our time?' I still hoped Seán would learn and that he would gain the confidence of the players, but shortly after this my hopes were dashed.

The incident which led to a major breach in Loughnane's confidence in Stack came after one of Clare's most disappointing performances.

In 1999, in the Munster semi-final against Tipperary, we should have lost but we scrambled a draw, with a last-minute penalty from Fitzie. Nicky English's tactics that day were brilliant: draw Clare out and play the ball in fast behind them, and it almost worked. The replay was set for the following Saturday.

That night, Ollie Baker and Anthony Daly were staying in Jury's Hotel in Cork and were having a few pints. Seán Stack and his wife were staying on in the same hotel. The next day, Seán Stack told me that Baker and Dalo had been drinking heavily the previous night. This was to lead to a very embarrassing situation for me.

I called a meeting for Mike, Seán, Tony and I, before the training session on the Monday night. We were just in the gate and had discussed what had happened when who comes in, only Dalo. I called him over, and I said to him, 'I heard you were drinking last night.'

'What?'

'Seán here was in the hotel and told me you were drinking.'

'We only drank about three or four pints.'

Seán Stack said, 'Ye drank a lot more.'

Considering that he had been watching his two star players drinking six days before a huge match against Tipperary, I asked Seán, 'Did you talk to them last night?'

'No. No.'

I asked Dalo, 'What time did you go to bed?'

'About 11.30.'

'Tog in and forget about it.'

It was a real embarrassment for Seán. Here was a future manager of the Clare team in the same hotel as two of his leading players, and he didn't even speak to them. I dismissed him out of my mind and got swept up in our Championship run. After we lost to Kilkenny, I said to Seán in the Burlington, 'It will be over to you now.' There was no reaction whatsoever. I just knew he wasn't the right man for the job. I also knew that if he was appointed there would be a players' revolt, and the team would have broken up straight away.

An alternative heir to the crown had to be found and quickly. Mindful of the minefield that constitutes the politics of Clare hurling, Loughnane had to tread carefully.

As time went on, I became more and more convinced that my successor would be someone who had been with us, but would still be his own man. I knew that Dalo and other players had approached Cyril Lyons. I arranged to meet Cyril and I said, 'I'm getting out of it. The best thing is if there's a total change.'

He said, 'I'm not going to come in unless you stay on for another year. I need to get to know the new players and then, if things work out, I'm interested in taking over, but no way unless you stay on for a year.'

We thrashed it out for two hours 'til finally I agreed. I went to Tony Considine and explained there had to be a total change. He understood immediately. I had to be very careful that there wouldn't be a challenge to the changes at the county board. On the night that it was going to be announced, I rang Mike Mac and told him that it was over and there had to be a change. He agreed.

Seán Stack called in to see me at school. I told him, 'I'm going to stay on for another year. There's going to be a total clear-out.'

He replied, 'You're not going to get rid of everybody.'

'I am.'

'What about Tony Considine?'

'He's volunteered to go, but Sean, it just hasn't worked out with you.'

Loughnane is at pains to point out that his decision to drop Stack from the management team was not prompted by personality conflicts.

We should always be careful in evaluating people in differentiating between their professional ability and their personal characteristics. An individual can have outstanding personal qualities, but may not be able to translate them into a particular professional setting. In my opinion, that was the case with Seán Stack.

He is one of the most affable and likeable people you could meet. You could not find a more popular person with anyone who knows him. His priorities are absolutely right: his family, his love of the land and the simple things in life. As a person, there is none finer but at this particular time, with this particular set-up of players, he is not the right man to manage Clare.

Everything that has happened in the meantime has convinced Loughnane that he made the right choice.

Cyril Lyons came in with Louis Mulqueen. Some people are just respected. The players have such respect for Cyril. He is such a genuine person. He's religious, as straight as could be, trustworthy and truthful. People also know that anything he says is out of fairness and honesty. He also has a really steely streak in him that people completely underestimate, and a drive about him that most people outside the panel don't realise. He's absolutely brilliant.

I knew he wasn't going to be a Ger Loughnane II. He'd be a new voice, bring a new approach and would do things his own way. He's done a fantastic job. He was very unlucky in the Championship in 2001. Four of his forwards let him down against Tipperary, but they could still have won it were it not for a few referee's decisions that went against them. When a lot of people felt the team were finished, he got a great performance out of them. He's young and energetic and a totally different personality than me, and is the perfect person for the job right now.

10

The Hurlers on the Ditch

Following Clare's victory in the epic Munster final in 1997, Anthony Daly made a speech in which he articulated the feelings and motivations of all Clare players and supporters on that day. Daly had that uncanny knack of putting into words exactly what everybody was feeling and his comment, 'We're no longer the whipping boys of Munster' captured perfectly the mood of the day. A massive cheer went up from the Clare supporters when he uttered these words.

To the utter consternation of everyone in Clare, Liz Howard, the PRO of the Tipperary county board, wrote in a newspaper article that the statement was 'conduct unbecoming'. Liz, or Libby as she was then known, spent most of her youth living in Feakle, where her father was the local sergeant, so her comments hit a nerve, especially in her former home village.

However, when she repeated this 'conduct unbecoming' theme two weeks later, the whole thing spiralled out of control. Other newspapers picked it up and it became the topic of conversation. Dalo said to me, 'This whole thing has gone out of control.' So I said to Dalo to leave it to me. I wrote an open letter to Liz Howard and that's when the whole controversy really started.

It finally came to a head when Dalo called me and said that a man came to the door of his shop in Ennis and said, 'You shouldn't have said that.'

Dalo replied, 'What did I say?'

'Well, I don't know. But you shouldn't have said it.'

That is the perfect illustration of what people pick up from the paper. That's why I'm glad I always treated the press with the respect they deserved!

A s a farmer's son, Ger Loughnane ought to have a guilty conscience. He must have been responsible for the destruction of dozens of rainforests to provide the acres of column inches written about him. Much of it he generated himself by the way he played the media. Five major titles were not going to be won by a deluge of journalistic praise. Loughnane's perception of the media was shaped early in his playing career.

When the All-Stars nominations came out in '74 I was absolutely stunned that I was nominated. I was just 21 and it was even a bigger surprise that I got on the team. It was a bit of a fluke that I got on it. The Munster football final was on in Killarney on the same day as the Munster Under-21 hurling final between ourselves and Waterford, and on their way back from the football final all the journalists came to our match. We had beaten Tipperary in the senior Championship that year for the first time in years. I played really well. In the Munster under-21 final, everybody expected Clare to win. Even though we lost, I played well again. The All-Stars had been running for a few years but a Clare player had never won one. Clare had made something of a breakthrough that year and the selectors felt that if they didn't give one to Clare, it would be saying that Clare was a non-hurling county.

There was huge surprise when I got an All-Star. I didn't deserve an All-Star that year. There were other years that I did deserve to get one but didn't. Because there was such controversy about it, everybody was trying to disown responsibility for selecting me! That night, above at the presentation, Jim O'Sullivan was the only journalist who came over to congratulate me. The others were washing their hands of it!

WHAT IT SAYS IN THE PAPERS

In 1995, Loughnane could have been forgiven for getting a swelled head because of the elegiac tone of the reams of celebratory prose around his name. In the early days of his management, though, Loughnane was a bit naive in his dealings with the media as one incident memorably illustrated.

Immediately after the All-Ireland semi-final in '95 against Galway, there was the typical media scrum and I was asked the usual questions. The next thing this stocky man asked me, 'What did you say to the team at half-time?' In complete jest, I answered, 'I told them to take it easy because I didn't want us to win by too much because it would make us favourites for the All-Ireland.' I laughed a bit after saying it.

To my utter consternation I read The Irish Times *the next day with my very words quoted in full with no addendum or comment. The man that asked the question was Tom Humphries. I had never heard of him before, let alone recognise him. Cliona Foley wrote afterwards that I was giving guff. I can't remember her exact words but she was basically saying that I was only a few months in the job and already I was acting a bit like a bold child in school!*

The message I took from it was that you should never say anything serious to those people, if that's what they took from something said as a joke. It really brought home to me the insignificance of what they write and the significance they attach to something trivial.

As he grew into the job, probing the Clare manager was at times like trying to trespass behind forbidden gates. Loughnane retained the ability to retreat to some inner corner where nobody could penetrate. Answers were furnished, but laced with eloquent concealment. The mystery remained deep within the man. He will never be chosen as the subject for a 'how to win friends' manual. His epic self-containment, when it suited him, and the eloquence of his reticence was not going to endear him to the media. That left journalists with no option but to talk matter-of-factly about a career that testifies to something magical at the core of his gifts, a rapport with his team and its fans too profound to be rationally explained. His mystery resisted all attempts to unravel it. No one doubted that he was born with deep reserves of obsessive will but the most vital elements of his character seemed too enigmatic to be satisfactorily excavated.

Yet when he wanted to, Loughnane left no room for ambiguity. After the 1997 All-Ireland final, he clashed publicly with Eamonn Cregan on 'The Sunday Game'.

Following Cregan's analysis, Loughnane began his response with the comment, 'After that ten-minute whinge from Eamonn Cregan.' He then launched into an attack on Cregan. Given the intensity of Loughnane's comments, it seemed to outside observers that there must have been some history between them.

I played with and against him. I always thought he was a fantastic player. He was so competitive. He had a passionate will to win that so few players have, to go with the great skill he had.

That was why it was such a disappointment when he came to train the Clare team in 1983. He'd have known the top three or four players but he never made a great effort to get to know the rest. He had no plan in training or matches. There was nothing you could say he did that brought on Clare hurling. Worst of all was that, after a while, the players started to treat him as a joke. He had a rule whereby training started at seven and if you were one minute late you did one lap of the field, if you were two minutes late you did two laps and so on. There was one player in particular, Declan Coote, a very talented individual who could have been a really great player if he was handled properly but he never achieved his potential. He'd come to training at a quarter to seven and would stay deliberately in the dressing-room until a quarter past seven and then he'd come on the pitch and say, 'Eamonn 10, 15 or 20?' He'd start off his 15 laps of the pitch at near walking pace and by the time he was finished the training session was nearly over. Everybody saw that system was stupid, except Cregan.

There was one specific incident where I lost all respect for him as a coach. We got to a League final against Limerick and were getting hammered at half-time. Everybody was crying out for some instruction as to what was going wrong and what we could do to turn things around. All he did was to go ballistic and launch into a tirade which went way over everybody's head about how bad we were. There was no diagnosis of our problems, nor prescription to cure them, which is what I think good coaching is all about. You were just looking at him and thinking, 'Would you ever shut up?'

Never once during a game did he ever give a direction that would change the way a match was going. He never showed any of the characteristics of a good coach in Clare. Maybe he showed them somewhere else. I'd no regard for him as a coach. I'd have way more regard for Justin McCarthy. I'd have a thousand times more regard for Len Gaynor. He was exactly the wrong one to come on and criticise Clare, considering he had no success here. There is always a suspicion that if you don't have success somewhere, and somebody else comes on and has success there, you may have a chip on your shoulder.

I was inside in the hotel that night listening to Cregan and I was thinking back to that day in Thurles and those training sessions in Cusack Park and here was the same man criticising Clare after they beat Tipperary in an All-Ireland final. Who would ever have thought that possible when he was in charge? I was standing beside Ger Canning, who is a really smart guy, and he sensed that the crowd was aghast. He looked me straight in the eye and said, 'That's terrible isn't it.' I replied, 'Pay no heed. That's only Cregan.' I knew we were going live on air in a few minutes and I waited 'til we did and then I let fly!

To some people without the same emotional entanglement in the issue, Loughnane ought not have launched such an attack in such a forum. Does he have any regrets about it?

If I have a regret, it is that I didn't go further. I think it was totally small-minded of him. What he said didn't seem to me to be a fair judgement of the game. It was never going to be a 2-24 to 1-25 game. Given the two teams involved, you were always going to get a tense, bruising encounter. If you want an open match, go to a League game.

We had a function at the end of the year. As part of the ceremony, they showed five minutes of highlights of the final. At the end, when the speeches were over, they left on the last 20 minutes. I was talking to Marty Morrissey and after a while I noticed there was nobody else talking. Everyone was sitting down, glued to their seats, watching the end of the match. It just showed how tense the game was. Yet Cregan could find nothing good about it. A few years on, I really feel I should have tore into him much more strongly that night.

BANNER HEADLINES

Earlier in 1997, Loughnane unwittingly found himself in the centre of another media storm.

Jim O'Sullivan did a lengthy interview with me in shorthand after we won the semi-final against Kilkenny. At one stage he asked me who did I think would win the second semi-final between Tipperary and Wexford. I answered, 'I'm certain that Tipperary are going to win it.'

He replied, 'Surely Wexford will be way too tough or too rough for them?'

I tapped him on the elbow and said, 'The biggest mistake you could make is think that roughhouse tactics could work against Tipperary.' I went on to say that if you look back at the history of Tipperary hurling, you will not beat them by roughing them up. We had played them earlier that year in Cusack Park and tried that with them but they beat us. The only way you could beat them was by outhurling them.

Some days later, I was over in London with my wife, Mary. I rang my two sons at home and they told me that a big headline had appeared in The Examiner to the effect that I had said Wexford were hatchet men. I didn't know the exact wording at that stage.

On the Monday morning, I was walking down a street off Oxford street in London and I saw a shop with the Irish Independent. I was shocked to discover that Rory Kinsella had been asked in his post-match interview what he was going to do about Ger Loughnane's comment that Wexford were guilty of 'roughhouse tactics'. What struck me immediately was that if Wexford had qualified for the All-Ireland, there would be no denying that I had said it and it would really have polluted the atmosphere coming up to the final.

I was debating in my own mind whether I should let it go because Wexford were out, but I decided it was too serious to leave it. When we got home, I rang The Examiner and asked for Jim O'Sullivan. Most people don't realise that the person who writes the article does not write the headline. The problem was not Jim's article but the headline which accompanied it, 'Loughnane accuses Wexford of roughhouse tactics'. The headline writer obviously wanted it to be as sensational as possible. The then editor, Brian Looney, came on the line. I explained how damaging the headline would have been if Wexford had qualified for the All-Ireland. He said, 'I admit we made a high tackle. What are you looking for?' I explained that all I was looking for was an apology. They published it later down the page, but who reads an apology at the bottom of the page?

The Sunday Independent had reproduced the article. I then contacted their sports editor, Adhamhnan O'Sullivan. They also printed an apology but few people saw it. Even this year, many of the Wexford players referred to this in the build up to the semi-final against Tipperary. To this day, most people in Wexford think I said something I never did. Ever since, I've always insisted that if somebody was coming to interview me, they had to have a recorder, because denying something after it's printed is a waste of energy. No one wants to know.

I would say though that in '98 the one paper who did not jump on to the Clare bandwagon was The Examiner. We have to hand it to them for that, even though I was the one with the biggest gripe against them the previous year. To give credit where credit is due, their coverage was well balanced. They criticised the events that took place, and rightly so. They said there should be an investigation into it, and rightly so. They said the punishment should be dished out equally, and rightly so. That, of course, didn't happen but The Examiner is one paper we cannot have any gripe with after what happened.

Cumann Lúthchleas Gael

ARD STIÚRTHÓIR: LIAM Ó MAOLMHICHÍL

Páirc an Chrócaigh, Áth Cliath 3
Guthán: 8363222
Fax: 8366420

SÓL/TNíR

24 Lúnasa 1997

Gearóid Ó Lacthnáin, Uasal
Bainisteoir Foireann An Chláir
F/Ch Pádraig Mac Gearailt Uasal
Runaí Coiste Contae An Chláir
Baile Caisleán Crainn
Sixmilebridge
Co An Chláir

Maidir Le: **Guinness All Ireland Senior Hurling Championship Semi-Final
An Clár v Cill Chainnigh (Páirc An Chrócaigh) 10.08.97**

A Chara

You are hereby notified that having been reported for "unauthorised entry on a number of
occassions" during the above game, you are confined to the dug-out for the next Senior
Championship game i.e., the upcoming All Ireland Senior Hurling Final for contravention
of Regulation 8 of Regulations Governing the Organisation and Presentation of
Championship and National League Games..

This decision has been taken by Coiste Riarcháin na gCluichí.

Mise le fíor mheas

Seán Ó Laoire
Bainisteoir na gCluichí

cc: Runai Contae

THE TIMES THEY ARE A CHANGING

The same critics who were throwing bouquets at Loughnane in 1995
were swinging cleavers in 1998. As the summer unfolded, barbed
murmurs gave way to clamorous denunciation. Some of the criticism
was of such persistence and hostility, it might have made Nixon wince.
The unspoken laws of hurling are complex and mysterious. When you
violate them, as Loughnane appeared to have done the previous year,
you pay a price, though seldom in a predictable way. What caused the
media backlash?

Initially, naturally enough, everyone was in favour of Clare. We were a new team that hadn't won an All-Ireland in 81 years or a Munster final in over 60 years and we were enthusiastically welcomed at first. Then, when you win a second time people may start to think that it's somebody else's turn.

A lot of the controversy I'd say we brought on ourselves. Some of it was on purpose. Naturally enough, there is no better way of firing up your own team, especially if they are beginning to lag, or get smug or become over-confident on themselves, than to have a bit of controversy or to create a situation where people think everybody is against them. There's nothing wrong with that.

After the Waterford replay in '98, we did get a lot of bad press but it would be a serious mistake to think it was that game that caused the tide to turn. It was what lanced the boil, but the controversy had been festering for a long time. The previous year, for instance, we had fielded teams that weren't on the programme. Journalists were banned from our dressing-rooms before matches and it had been a tradition of some journalists, notably Micheál O Muircheartaigh, to come into dressing rooms before games, but I had locked the door on those.

From Clare to here. Loughnane with Maureen Potter collecting their People of the Year awards in 1995.

The dressing room was their sanctuary, the focal point where players and mentors came together to prepare their hearts and minds for battle, cocooned from the probing eyes and ears of the media.

1998 was the first time I started locking doors on journalists. We had been beaten badly by Cork in the League semi-final. It was a huge wake-up call. What we saw for the first time was that the media had turned against Clare. Depending on what rumour you heard, Clare had trained for one hour, two hours and three hours beforehand. While the game was on, Clare were being trounced and things were going so badly that Mike Mac said that we had better do something. I admit I said to Mike, 'Leave it alone. The more they beat us by the better.' I said that because things were going so badly that you're better off to let them go to the absolute bottom completely – once it's a League match.

I was absolutely disgusted with the way we played against Cork and there wasn't a sound on the bus on the way back. We stopped off in Nenagh and Mike Mac said, 'The funny thing about this, if there is a funny side, is that they'll all think this is part of a plan.' I replied, 'You must be f**king joking'. He was dead right though, because the media went to town on us. Liam Horan apparently rang up the garda sergeant who had let us into the field where we had gone for a puckout before the match and was told that we'd only been there for 20 minutes or half an hour and that we had done nothing only puck the ball around. It showed the suspicion about us that was building up in the media. They were going to be waiting in the long grass for us.

In '98, the Munster semi-final against Cork was the day that we began our new media policy. As soon as we got into the dressing-room, I told Pat Fitzgerald to lock the door and keep those journalists out. There had been a barrage against us.

It was a fantastic match. The last 20 minutes of the game was the stuff you dream of from your team: we were driving at savage pace, getting great scores, everything you'd want your team to do and totally in charge. By pure chance, I was going along the sideline and the Clare crowd were over at that part of the stand, and they started cheering as I was passing. Without thinking, I raised my two hands to them. That gesture seemed to drive every journalist there totally mad!

The Liz Howard and Examiner controversies fuelled the flames, but what really turned the tide was that defeat of Cork when we totally pulverised them in the last 20 minutes. The reaction of the crowd and I really got up their noses, as did the realisation that these guys weren't going away.

With the benefit of hindsight, Loughnane might have pondered the wisdom of the old adage more profoundly: kindle not a fire you cannot extinguish.

There's a lot of give and take in the whole thing. What goes around comes around. I knew very well that when something went wrong for Clare that we were going to get a backlash. A well known journalist had rung me to warn me. He said, 'They're out to get you.' I replied, 'I know'. I thought it would be after we lost rather than after we won the Munster final but it was coming. Some people probably feel we deserved it and maybe we did.

There were some who felt that Loughnane was the architect of Clare's own destruction in '98 because he became bigger than his team. Is there any truth in that argument?

I never made a list of mistakes. I never look at anything in my mind as mistakes. If I had kept my mouth shut and taken it, would we have won the All-Ireland? No.

THE HOGAN STAND

Clare felt they had been unfairly treated by the media in 1998. 1999 would be a year for retribution.

I admired the writing of a lot of journalists. To take one example, I appreciated the writing of Vincent Hogan, even though he gave Clare a hard time now and again. He thought he was right, and fair enough. I respect that. He is a quality writer and has great insights into the game. I've always enjoyed reading his stuff and he's one of the first guys I would read before or after a game. The best Irish sports book I've ever read was his book Beyond the Tunnel, *the biography of Nicky English. It was terrifically written and a very honest book. I wrote to him after I read it to tell him how much I enjoyed it. I do think, like many others, he went way over the top on the Colin Lynch controversy. He was part of the clique.*

He asked if he could come down to interview me in '99. I agreed and told him to come down to training one particular night and that I would meet him in Cusack Park, knowing that we weren't training there. When he arrived, he was told we were training in Crusheen. When he got there, he discovered we were actually training in Flannans. When he got to Flannans, I stopped the training exercise we were doing and told Mike Mac to take over. Every time I saw a journalist attending one of our training sessions, I handed over to Mike because I wanted to reinforce the view that all the Clare team did in training was run around the field. The more they believed that, the better I liked it. Hogan started talking to someone on the sideline so that I went over and told Mike Mac to take the players away, away over to the far end so that he would see as little as possible.

The rest of the training session went on for about an hour on a wet, miserable evening. As we finished, he asked where he could talk to me. I told him to meet me in the Sherwood because all the players would be going in afterwards. When he heard this, Tony Considine asked me privately, 'Are you going to talk to that c**t after what he wrote about Clare?' I replied, 'No danger. I won't be in the Sherwood.' I went straight home and he was hanging around all night in the Sherwood. No one he asked had a clue where I was. He drove back to Dublin without getting his interview. You could say it was very petty on my part. I just wanted to give him something of what he gave us.

Retirement has done nothing to diminish Loughnane's capacity to surprise and the old bloody-mindedness surfaces occasionally. Asked if he has any regrets about the way he played the media, a look of granite hardness appears and his answer is typically forthright.

Yes. My slight regret is that I didn't really go to town on them and that I ever let them into the dressing-room.

SINS OF OMISSION

Loughnane did not pay much attention to the news unless a problem cropped up that he had to address. He tried to downplay stories in front of the players to show that he did not deem it very important. Nonetheless, he knew that while the players were not playing for the media, their unity and sense of purpose could be deflected by the media. Any threat to the harmony of his team had to be taken seriously.

Nothing that was ever written about me got to me. I was so hell bent on making sure that we won the next game that the distractions didn't deflect me.

Martin Luther King once said, 'At the end of the day it is not the words of your enemies you remember but the silence of your friends.' This is a sentiment Loughnane would readily agree with.

The one person I will never forgive is Pat Hartigan. We were on the All-Stars tour to America together and we had great craic. I really looked up to Pat. He won an All-Ireland hurling medal in '73. I was there that day, wearing a Limerick hat, and got drenched to the skin. The dye even ran down my clothes. I really liked him. I thought he was a top class sort of man.

The facts were as I stated on the famous Clare FM radio interview. Mary and I were invited to the Galway races for the day by the Lynches, who own a lot of hotels in the locality. We were heading down from the

*hospitality tent towards the betting ring and who comes along but Pat
Hartigan who grabbed me and said, 'Don't let the bastards break you'. I
replied, 'What Pat?' He reiterated his comment, 'Don't let the bastards
break you.' I replied, 'There's no danger of that Pat.' Apart from my wife,
Mary, there were other witnesses to this conversation including a very
prominent figure in business circles in Clare. What Pat was referring to
was the media, because at that stage the Munster Council hadn't come in
to the equation at all. There was no big controversy about Colin Lynch at
that stage. It was the following Sunday that the incident with the priests
in Croke Park happened and the following week that the controversy
with the Munster Council erupted. So he couldn't have possibly been
referring to the Munster Council.*

*Pat went on holidays and came back in the middle of all the controversy
about the Munster Council. Impulsively, he issued a statement that he
had never said what I had quoted him as saying, which of course became
a banner headline that 'Limerick hero lashes Loughnane'. He went on to
say that he had the greatest respect for the Munster Council and its
officers. It was a classic case of remarks being taken out of context. There
was no excuse for Pat's reaction despite his closeness to one of the
Munster Council's officers.*

As was often the case, Loughnane first got a hint that the story had
moved on to a new level from the media.

*During my time as Clare manager, the biggest distraction was the
telephone. Journalists seemed to feel that they could ring at any time:
morning, noon or night. They didn't seem to have any thought for your
family life.*

*I first got an inkling that something was breaking when Liam Horan
rang my home. My son, Conor, was the only one at home at the time, but
Horan told him everything that Pat Hartigan had said. Conor had no
idea what he was talking about. He was only ten at the time. How was he
supposed to answer a senior journalist from a national newspaper at that
age?*

Away from the glare of media publicity, Loughnane did make an attempt
to heal the rift with Hartigan.

*I wrote to Pat and told him that I was very disappointed that he had
denied saying what he had, but I wouldn't be contradicting him in the
newspapers because I didn't want to add yet more petrol to the flames. I
fully explained to him the error he had made and encouraged him to
listen to a recording of the interview. If he had even written back to me*

191

and explained himself, and asked me to keep quiet about it, that would have been fine.

Few media appearances ever stirred a more emotional response than Loughnane's infamous Clare FM interview. It was broadcast to people to whom Bill Shankly's infamous 'life or death' quote doesn't even begin to describe their bond to the Banner county. Afterwards, he was 'invited' to attend a meeting of the Games Administration Committee to explain himself, because of the critical comments he made about the Munster Council.

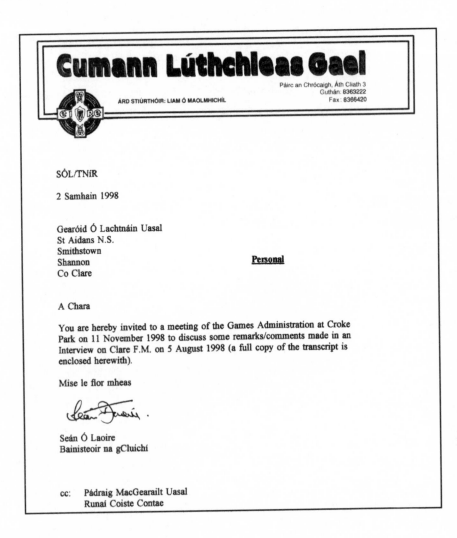

Cumann Lúthchleas Gael

Páirc an Chrócaigh, Áth Cliath 3
Guthán: 8363222
Fax: 8366420

ÁRD STIÚRThÓIR: LIAM Ó MAOLMHICHÍL

SÓL/TNíR

2 Samhain 1998

Gearóid Ó Lachtnáin Uasal
St Aidans N.S.
Smithstown
Shannon   **Personal**
Co Clare

A Chara

You are hereby invited to a meeting of the Games Administration at Croke Park on 11 November 1998 to discuss some remarks/comments made in an Interview on Clare F.M. on 5 August 1998 (a full copy of the transcript is enclosed herewith).

Mise le fíor mheas

Seán Ó Laoire
Bainisteoir na gCluichí

cc: Pádraig MacGearailt Uasal
       Runaí Coiste Contae

The Hartigan controversy was raised in that forum.

The GAC, without the Munster Council representatives, were brilliant. When we went in, they thought that we were a desperate shower of scoundrels but when we explained our case in minute detail, they saw the other side of the story. One of them said to me, 'Jesus, why didn't you contradict Hartigan?' I replied, 'There was so much sh*t flying, I wasn't going to add to it. What was another piece on top of me the way things were going?' They all laughed.

I ended up with the greatest respect for the GAC. They handled that situation with the greatest integrity. It was something I never expected from the GAA.

SINS OF COMMISSION

Sometimes criticism cuts deeply, but only one article about one of his players outraged Loughnane. A cloud of searing indignation is stamped on his face as he recalls the incident which maligned the player who in full flight gives the hurling addict the ultimate fix. To watch him in full gallop is one of the wonders of the hurling world: power without weight, force without strain and speed without fuss. He is a perfect example of genius.

Jamesie O'Connor is a professional player in terms of his diet, training and attention to detail. His way of focusing before big matches is to listen to tapes. He learned to become a great free taker. His speed of foot, of thought and wrist were his hallmark and his winning point in the '97 All-Ireland final epitomised this. He was always extremely popular and well liked by fellow players. He has strong opinions and is serious but can easily be snapped out of it and has learned to relax more.

When Jamesie plays at his best, he is poetry in motion. There is something about his movement that no other player that I ever saw has. I cannot understand journalists who fail to appreciate how people react when Clare are on the field. That's what I've been doing since I retired – going to watch Clare play. It is a joy to watch the reaction when Jamesie is on the ball. They are just awestruck. Not just Clare people, everyone is 'looking out of their mouths', as we'd say at home, with the runs he makes and the way he moves. He sends a kind of current through everybody watching. His movement is absolutely marvellous and even DJ Carey hasn't that. DJ is a brilliant goalscorer but the movement of Jamesie is out of this world. He has deficiencies in his play. People say he doesn't score goals but what he brings to Clare is enormous.

The only article that really hurt me appeared after the '98 Munster final replay and characterised Jamesie as a thug. You might as well have said Mother Teresa was a woman of easy virtue. On the field, off the field, the way he carries himself, the image he projects is everything you'd want to see in a player. He's fantastic.

Loughnane sees that incident as symptomatic of the underlying malaise in journalism.

What struck me is the way journalists behave with a herd mentality. Individually they are fine but they come on something and they all seem to get the same opinion of it. Nobody wants to questions the other's opinion. There are a few that lead the pack. No one is prepared to stand back and really consider the case and say, 'Maybe there's another angle to the thing completely'. There were a few honourable exceptions. Take a journalist like Diarmuid O'Flynn in The Examiner, *you couldn't bracket him with them, because he has his own mind. He'd go against you six times out of ten, but he always stood on his own two feet.*

In the case of the Colin Lynch saga, I could never understand that none of them ever said: 'let's take it that Loughnane is completely wrong, but let's look at the Munster Council's role. Did they follow proper procedures? Did they have video evidence? Did the referee's report support their actions?'

I read a great book once by Frank Kilfeather. He basically said that a lot of reporters think that the public are hanging on to their every golden word. They over-rate their own importance. His key point was that whatever they write, people will make up their own minds. As I said to a journalist once: 'who ever remembers an article that is written in the paper?' You remember the general theme but not the specifics. Very few in the GAA have got as much negative publicity as I have, but very few get as many invitations to give talks as I do.

Even though the many controversies of '98 brought their own pressures, Loughnane's zest for the dramas of the hurling field was undiminished. The media vicissitudes were never likely to grind down someone whose long playing career had been overloaded with disappointments.

I don't think you should ever get a persecution complex and think all journalism is bad. There are always journalists like Martin Breheny who try to look at both sides of the story objectively. I think the standard of sports journalism, especially in relation to hurling, has really improved. The coverage has increased enormously. The problem is that some of them have not the real expertise that you need to write about hurling and this adds to the problem of the herd mentality when the opinions of one or two journalists prevail. To be a good journalist, you must put your own prejudice or allegiances aside and report the facts. Anyone who does not do that is failing as a journalist. Journalism is too much dominated by opinions.

Loughnane felt that the media did not give him sufficient credit for the way he reacted to defeat.

Whenever we lost a big match, I always went into the opponent's dressing-room and congratulated them on their victory. When we lost to Offaly in '98, I went into their dressing-room I told them that they had been the better team on the day and deserved to win and that whatever had happened before was all forgotten. The media would say that was no more than my duty, but when we beat Offaly, Eamonn Cregan didn't come into our dressing-room; when we beat Cork, Jimmy Barry Murphy didn't come into our dressing-room, and when we beat Limerick, Tom Ryan didn't come into our dressing-room.

I didn't go into the opposition's dressing-room after we won, in case it would be seen as provocative, except when we beat Tipperary. I started this policy out of respect for Len Gaynor because of all he had done for Clare hurling. I always said that after the game was over, all the hype was to be forgotten and told them that in spite of what I might have said before games, nobody had more respect for Tipperary's hurling record and traditions than Clare people.

That policy continued when Nicky English took over because of all the paraphernalia that went with Clare-Tipp matches – some of it created by my comments! Nicky always got a great reception when he came into our dressing-room after a game. He is a hurling man through and through and hurling men can relate to each other. He cuts to the core and knows that all the bullshit before the game is just mind games. All those skirmishes beforehand are part of the battle and without them you'd have nothing.

Loughnane becomes uncharacteristically reticent when asked about the reception he got when he went into the Tipperary dressing-room after the 1997 All-Ireland final.

My comments were listened to in silence.

FROM THE INSIDE LOOKING OUT

Loughnane is now the classic poacher turned gamekeeper as a weekly columnist with *The Star* newspaper and as a perceptive and articulate interpreter for 'The Sunday Game'. As a disciple of the John Giles, rather than the Trevor Brooking, school of analysis, he pulls no punches –

animated, intense at times, he maintains a flow of relevant information and interpretation.

For media bosses, the temptations to plunder the thoughts of former star players and successful managers and benefit from their judgements are overwhelming, particularly when, like Loughnane, their name has become the touchstone for controversy. For those personalities who have retired, media involvement affords them the platform to continue their happy addiction. As a television pundit, Loughnane goes much further, never ceasing to inform, enthuse and to entertain, drawing on the depth and authenticity of his experience. It does mean that he has to comment on the players he once managed, for example after the 2001 League final, he was critical of Ollie Baker and Colin Lynch. How difficult is it for him to criticise the players he was once so close to?

> *It is very easy for me. When I was manager of the Clare team, I did everything I could for them to win. Now though, as analyst and columnist, I'm there to comment on what happens as it happens. I'm not there to sit on the fence. Whatever has to be said, I'll say it. I'd be selling myself, those players, or those reading or watching short if I wasn't fully honest. It doesn't mean I respect any Clare player any less. Anyone who was ever involved with me would say that I always gave an honest assessment of what happened in a match whether it be victory or defeat. I'm continuing in that vein now.*

When stimulated, he still displays the old ebullience, he is still full of ideas and opinions; the eyes are no less challenging. His new role affords him the platform to continue to be a thorn in the side of those in authority.

> *I was a player and manager for a long number of years. I see where the deficiencies are. I see where the cracks are now. Unless they are faced up to, hurling will be in big danger. I have no hesitation in pointing them out. Officials are there to serve the game so that it can be handed on to future generations. If I think they're not doing their job, I'm going to point it out.*

Memory is softened by time. Hurling needs every nostalgic prop it can muster and when the controversies are forgotten, the powerful grip the Clare team exerted on the popular imagination in the Loughnane years will be their legacy. Perhaps the verdict of history will share that of Tom Humphries. In an article in *The Irish Times*, on 23 August 1999 entitled, 'Why I'm missing Clare already', he wrote:

'In becoming wrapped up in the exasperating personality wars, we in the media missed the point and failed entirely to place Clare in their proper perspective. We got the critical balance wrong. People enjoyed Clare and what they brought to hurling, the good they did far outweighed the bruising left by any wild pulls across the shins of the media.

'Clare drew criticism, not of all it related to how they played games or spurred by the purest of journalistic motives. Meanwhile other counties were indulged and cajoled.

'In terms of the things we are supposed to be looking out for on our media precinct, Clare had a clean bill of health. They were the best thing to happen to hurling in a long, long time.'

11

One Man and His Dog

Clare people were used to seeing me on the sideline and they had a certain confidence in me on big days. But that couldn't last forever. For the last couple of years, I was looking around to see who might come in. Clare hurling is not dependent on me or any other person. What it needs is to be constantly renewing itself by bringing in new people. I feel I was the luckiest person ever to manage Clare at the time I did. But it's over. To come back? Well, what are you saying there? You're saying no one else here can do the job. That would be a ridiculous thing to do. There are plenty of others to do the job.

Ger Loughnane is confirmation of WB Yeats's assertion that each of us is, 'rooted in one dear perpetual place'. He was born in a dazzingly beautiful spot in Feakle. In many ways, he has never left it. He talks about Feakle with such a passionate feeling that one could almost see where the half-light mist silently settles on green fields and hear the winds whistling on purple marshes. His mind is a theatre of happy childhood memories, particularly of his father, who had a decisive influence on his life and he is deeply appreciative of the self-sacrificing efforts which his parents made for their children.

Loughnane deploys his sharp observation and keen sense of humour to provide perceptive and intriguing snapshots of Clare life – particularly the comings and goings of everyday rural living. The absence of troublesome experiences from his upbringing confirm the view that the Feakle of his memory is more Alice Taylor than Frank McCourt. He may have been voted the manager of the millennium but in the Feakle roll of honour, he trails in a distant third.

Not alone am I not Feakle's most famous person, I am at best only the townland of Kilbarron's third most famous person. Its most famous resident was Biddy Early, and its second most famous person was Johnny Patterson, who lived down the road. He wrote a lot of famous songs like 'The Stone Outside Dan Murphy's Door' and 'Goodbye Johnny Dear'. He was also a world famous circus performer who performed political sketches on stage. He made it really big in America in the nineteenth century before he came back to Ireland. He was killed after a performance in Tralee where he did a sketch in which he brought an orange and green flag together on stage and put them together to signify the unification of the two traditions on the island. This caused uproar in the audience. A massive row took place and he was hit on the head with a hammer and died as a result of his injuries. It seems that people from my townland just cannot avoid controversy.

A Davy Fitzgerald puckout away from the family home is Kilbarron Lake, where Biddy Early's famous blue bottle now resides. The 'witch of Feakle' put a curse on the hurlers of Clare. Over a hundred years later, the wizard from Feakle would undo her curse. Nice story but it might be more plausible if Biddy Early hadn't died well before the GAA was founded.

Loughnane's late father, John James, won four national cross-country titles. Although Ger is most likely to be found listening to the dulcet tones of Eva Cassidy, his father's fiddle has pride of place in the Feakle family home. Every morning, Ger handmilked four cows before going to school. The farm was divided in two parts. The smaller part, around the house, and the other a mile and a half away.

I had the luckiest childhood of all time. I came at a bridge between the old and the new. Having experienced the old but having lived with the comforts of the new, I've had the best of both worlds. It was a great grounding for life, and the value system that was passed on was wonderful. It's great to have the memories of the old times, but you wouldn't like to live in them.

The back-breaking work farmers did then was unbelievable. There were no tractors nor machinery, so everything had to be done by hand. People had such a great work ethic back then. There were so many skills a farmer had to have. He had to be a butcher to kill his own pigs, a carpenter, a vet and a weather forecaster. People never spoke of stress but my father had seven children and the guillotine was always just over his head. It was hardest of all on the farmer's wife. My mother had to look after seven children as well as the geese, chickens and the calves. She also cycled for Mass at 8.30 every morning, winter and summer.

Family man. Ger, with Mary and sons Barry (left) and Conor.

FOR LOVE OF THE PARISH

In his later years, Feakle offered Loughnane a fixed beam he could hone in upon when he needed to escape from the pressures of life in the media spotlight. One of the proudest moments of his life came in the Feakle colours in 1988.

Having being born and reared in Feakle, and having started hurling with Feakle and above all having listened for years to all the stories about hurling in Feakle, I wanted to play my part in bringing glory to the parish on the hurling field. Feakle had a great team in the 1930s and won four county titles, but there was a massive gap until we won the next one. We had a great team that won the Clare Cup, a League competition, in the '60s. They got to the county final but lost. They were just not able to get over the final hurdle. It was a replica of the Clare team.

We won an Intermediate Championship when I was 20. When you are an inter-county player, you feel a huge sense of responsibility of delivering a

ONE MAN AND HIS DOG

county title to your club, especially when they haven't won for a long time. Coming to the end of my inter-county career, I was living in Shannon so I played for Wolfe Tones in Shannon for two years. Feakle won four under-21 Championships in a row. Those players were coming on to the senior team, and although they potentially had a great team, there was something missing. One night in the West County hotel, Fr Harry asked me if I'd go back to Feakle. I said I'd go back for a year because I was thinking about retiring at that stage. When I went back, there was a new spirit and a new set-up. A new man, Tony Hayes, was in charge. He was the parish equivalent of an excellent county manager. He was so well organised and such a sound man. He had no insecurity about taking advice from outside. We had great inter-county players like Michael and Tommy Guilfoyle and Val Donnellan. We won the Clare Cup and got to the county final. We had a puckout before the match and afterwards I said to the team, 'I've been gone from Feakle for a few years, but I'm going to have the game of my life to make sure that Feakle wins today.' We were playing Clarecastle but something punctured the whole team. It was like one of the Munster finals I played with Clare. They just couldn't get going and do themselves justice. It so happened that I did play the game of my life but we lost by a few points.

It had everything a good county final should have, including a massive row in the tunnel at half-time! I was in the dressing-room when it happened but I knew the row would cause our young players to lose their concentration. Clarecastle were like the Meath footballers! They are a brilliant club but a row suited them down to the ground!

Afterwards, everyone said we'd give it one more go for the following year. That year we won the Clare Cup again and had a fantastic game to beat Eire Óg in the semi-final. The young players were playing with great confidence. I played corner-back. Our full-back was Seamus McGrath who was an outstanding player. He had a brilliant brain and we had a telepathic understanding. We beat Ruan easily in the county final, but like the Munster final in '95, we didn't believe we had won until the final whistle went. It was on a par with winning the Munster final. It was just a wonderful feeling to deliver for your parish. If we hadn't won, there would have been a massive gap in my career. It was so near the endline for me that if we didn't deliver that day, there was going to be no other opportunity.

I'll never forget that night in Feakle. It was almost like when we came home with the Munster cup in '95. It was a special thrill to see people who had been around in the 1930s and had lived through 50 barren years but at last they had seen the gap bridged. I had worked with some of these people saving hay and in the bog and eighty per cent of our time was spent talking about hurling.

Most of Loughnane's daydreams on those days had Croke Park as their setting. Then in 1972 came news of his first step on that journey.

CUMANN LUITH-CHLEAS GAEDHEAL

TIR MHIC CHOILEAIN, INIS

at wing back 30/10/42

You have been selected to play for Clare v.

Tipperary (National Hurling League)

at *Tipperary* on *next Sunday*

Let me know by return if you will be home for the break. Vincent Loftus will take you back on Sunday evening

If unable to attend please notify the undersigned immediately.

MICHAEL MAC TAIDHG

By this time, his career path had been mapped out. He trained as a teacher in St Patrick's College Drumcondra.

I drifted into teaching. When I came to my Leaving Cert, I still hadn't figured out what I'd like to do. I got a scholarship to St Pats and a scholarship to anywhere was a big thing in those days. Being a boarder in St Flannans was like being in prison. My two years in Pats were like a two-year holiday! It wasn't a degree course back then, so there was no academic pressure. You don't need to be a rocket scientist to know the primary school curriculum. The skill is to be able to communicate it and motivate children and give them the confidence to learn. Pats opened up a whole new world to me. The authorities were so enlightened. They knew that our social development was as important as our academic development.

In St Pats, he won the Dublin under-21 hurling championship and the Dublin Advanced Colleges competition. He regretted that they were not allowed to play in the Fitzgibbon Cup, as he felt that they would have had a good chance with the team they had in those years. One of his teammates was destined for greatness.

Brian Cody was a year behind me in St Pat's and lived in the room opposite me. We got on really well, and when we played together in college, he could do things with the ball that'd make you look completely stupid. His level of skill was a delight. He wouldn't say much but when he spoke everybody listened. After he retired from playing, I thought he'd be managing Kilkenny minors or under-21s, because I remember that when he came on the field at Pats, he had a very strong presence. I really admire him as a man and as a manager, but when he was appointed manager of the Kilkenny team I said, 'Everybody's in trouble now.'

Fr Harry Bohan, who would have a huge impact on Loughnane's playing career, also had a major influence on his professional career. After he qualified as a primary teacher, Loughnane was employed for a year in Chapelizod in Dublin. This brought huge pressures in terms of attending training sessions in Clare. Fr Harry arranged a job for him in Shannon. The interview consisted of a brief discussion with the local PP after Mass, in which the cleric coolly informed Loughnane that he would start the following Monday. Things are different now. With the sort of forceful personality that would fill every corner of a classroom, Loughnane was a natural for teaching.

Once I started teaching, I really loved it. I took to it like a duck to water. After the success of the Clare team in the '90s, I got two lucrative offers to get involved in Human Resource Management but I wouldn't swap teaching for anything.

Photo: Courtesy of Billy Stickland/Inpho

Mr Nice Guy. Loughnane and some of his students.

THE ROAD NOT TAKEN

After he stepped down as manager of the Clare team, there were rumours that Loughnane would be interested in getting involved in politics. His mischievous streak may have been a contributory factory to this round of speculation.

> *In 1999, Matt Purcell, who works on Clare FM, rang me up to see if I would be willing to take part in an April Fool's Day joke. The local elections were coming up at the time, so I announced on Clare FM that I was resigning from the Clare team and was going to stand for the county council. I stated that there were some things more important than hurling and that I was going to stand as an independent, and that a lot of the Clare team were going to campaign for me. I launched into a passionate tirade about the need to improve the roads in east Clare! I think the presenter, Cormac MacCormack, was a bit shocked at how far I pushed it. The phone calls started coming in to beat the band and they had to issue a statement that evening to admit that it was all a joke!*

> *Politics is a different game altogether – it's even worse than managing a county team. You have to be a bigger rogue to be involved. Anyway, I wouldn't agree with anybody in politics because I would probably say what I thought and when you say what you think in politics, you're finished.*

THE SECOND COMING?

Loughnane is not contemplating a return to inter-county-management.

> *Well the first thing I should do is purchase a gun and leave it to my wife at home. Because if I ever even insinuate that I'm returning to county management, then I will tell her to have me shot straight away! It's something you should do once and once only.*

Loughnane feels it would be a step backwards for Clare if he were to take the reins back again. There is a view that he never really retired from the Clare job but has simply taken a rest.

> *I know that the possibility is there but for me, it doesn't really apply. The way I train a team and approach it, you give so much of yourself that after a while, you just wear yourself out. Motivation goes and when it goes, I don't get it back.*

Loughnane has learned the lesson from the experience of other managers.

Cyril Farrell had two comings as Galway manager. The first was in the '80s. I think that Galway team were the best team of the last 30 years. They had great players all over the field. Cyril was the best manager of that era. He brought drive, intelligence and ruthlessness to the job. I think he was right to back Tony all the way in the Keady affair. They had the Indian sign over a great Tipperary team when they had a full team.

He made a big mistake coming back in the mid '90s. The lesson for all of us is that you don't come back, certainly not in your native county. The other lesson is that you can't run with the hare and hunt with the hounds. Cyril was writing in the newspapers at the time and working as an analyst for RTE. You can't manage a team and be writing about them in the newspapers. Galway gave a spectacular performance against Kilkenny in the All-Ireland quarter-final in 1997, but Nicky Brennan and DJ Carey outfoxed them and they lost. It would have been touch and go if we could beat them if they had qualified to play us in the All-Ireland semi-final that year.

THE LAST WORD

A woman was having her 104th birthday. The intrepid reporter from the local newspaper came and asked, 'What's the best thing about being 104?' The woman paused theatrically before replying in a strong voice, 'No peer pressure!'

Ger Loughnane is a man with no peers. He occupies a unique place in the annals of the GAA – as a player, a manager and as the subject of the most intense public and media interest. There is no fan of Gaelic games who does not have a strong opinion of him. Despite his happy capacity for weathering hostility, the strains that had been mounting mercilessly over the years as manager, strains whose ravages the obsessive in him deflected, were taking their toll. The biggest casualty was his hairline.

At the height of our success, there was a table quiz in Shannon. For one of the rounds, they showed pictures of well known people when they were young. A photo of me was included from back in the days when I had really long hair. When one of the teams were asked to identity my photo they answered, 'Princess Diana'!

Despite his near iconic status in Clare, Loughnane's ambition is not to join the ranks of the self-advertising celebrities. Hurling-wise, he has just one remaining aspiration.

I would love to be in the stand and watch Clare win an All-Ireland. You'd see it from a different perspective. In the All-Ireland semi-final against Galway in '95, I was the last out of the dressing-room and I'll never forget the shock I got when I came onto the pitch and saw this sea of colour and heard this incredible noise. It was such an emotional occasion for Clare people, but I looked down at the ground immediately because I couldn't allow myself to get distracted. You're surrounded by 70,000 people and yet you're distant from them. Unfortunately that kind of detachment does take away from the enjoyment of a game.

Now I can go to Croke Park without dreaming what it would be like for Clare to win an All-Ireland. Before Clare won in '95, every time I went to Croke Park I was always trying to visualise what it would be like to see Clare winning there. In 1984, Neil Diamond came to do a concert in Croke Park and Mary was very keen to go. I liked his music too. We were sitting in the Hogan Stand and all around us were people from Clarecastle. This was obviously the Clare section. Although I liked the music, all I could think of throughout the concert was, 'Jesus what would it be like to be in a place like this and see Clare winning an All-Ireland.' I can still see where I was sitting in the stands that night. When the 90s came and we had success, it was like a dream. You wonder at times did it really happen. It is such a monkey off our back.

How would he like to be remembered?

As somebody who once he got involved in something gave it his absolute best whether it was cutting a field of hay, playing on a team, managing a team or in my job.

When looked back upon from the vantage point of years, all his trials and tribulations have been put in the proper perspective.

The great American swimmer Matt Biondi failed to win a gold medal in the Olympics against all expectations. After the final, journalists queried him on his disappointment at 'only' winning the silver medal. Biondi's reply sums up my philosophy of life, 'When all is said and done, when I go home my dog will still lick my face.'

INDEX